Spirits of Just Men

SPIRITS OF JUST MEN

Mountaineers, Liquor Bosses, and Lawmen in the Moonshine Capital of the World

CHARLES D. THOMPSON JR.

UNIVERSITY OF ILLINOIS PRESS
URBANA, CHICAGO, AND SPRINGFIELD

305033002594399

© 2011 by the Board of Trustees
of the University of Illinois
All rights reserved
Manufactured in the United States of America
C 5 4 3 2 1
∞ This book is printed on acid-free paper.

Library of Congress Cataloging-in-Publication Data
Thompson, Charles Dillard, 1956–
Spirits of just men : mountaineers, liquor bosses, and lawmen
in the moonshine capital of the world / Charles D. Thompson Jr.
p.   cm.
ISBN 978-0-252-03512-8 (hardback)
ISBN 978-0-252-07808-8 (paper)
1. Franklin County (Va.)—History—20th century.
2. Distilling, Illicit—Virginia—Franklin County—History.
3. Lee, Charles Carter, d. 1958—Trials, litigation, etc.
4. Mountain life—Virginia—Franklin County.
5. Mountain people—Virginia—Franklin County.
6. Franklin County (Va.)—Religious life and customs.
7. Franklin County (Va.)—Social life and customs.
I. Title.
F232.F7 T494   2011
975.5'68—dc22   2011006822

For those who lived it
and those who have lived because of it,
including my family.

To the general assembly and church of the firstborn,
which are written in heaven, and to God the Judge of all,
and to the spirits of just men made perfect. —HEBREWS 12:2

Contents

Acknowledgments

AS I RESEARCHED and wrote this book, I met scores of people who experienced what I have tried to represent here, and I am indebted to all for entrusting me with their memories and photographs of their ancestors they shared with me. My heartfelt thanks go to all of you. I also want to thank the staff of the Blue Ridge Institute of Ferrum College, the Franklin County Historical Society, and the Bassett Historical Society, all of whom stand out as true experts on the Blue Ridge region. The Franklin County Historical Society and the Blue Ridge Institute have put together archives, exhibits, and publications about Franklin County moonshine from which I've drawn extensively. I also thank the Special Collections librarians at Virginia Tech; the Newberry Library; the Virginia Room at the Roanoke Public Library; the Centre for Migration Studies in Omagh in County Tyrone; the Bushmills Distillery in County Antrim, Northern Ireland; as well as the Appalachian Studies Association for their contributions to this project. This book would not have been finished without my fellowship at the Virginia Foundation for the Humanities; I thank especially its president, Rob Vaughan, and his colleagues at VFH, particularly William Freehling, Roberta Culbertson, Hilary Holiday, Jon Loman, Nancy Damon, Susan Coleman, Jesse Dukes, and Camille Wells, for their help and encouragement while I was there.

Many others helped me finish this project: my mother and father and our extended family—both sides, my wife, Hope Shand, our son Marshall, our ancestors, my friends, and my colleagues at the Center for Documentary Studies all stand out. Ruel Tyson and Duncan Murrell read the manuscript at key times and helped form it. Lisa Addams gave me invaluable pointers in its early stages. Kendra Boileau painstakingly read every word more than once and made countless improvements. Rob Amberg cheered me on, as did Bruce Martin, Lee Smith, Ron Rash, Will Campbell, Bonnie Campbell, Steve Fisher, Pat Beaver, Tim Tyson, Tom Rankin, Linda Stanley, Vaughan Webb, Roddy Moore, T. Keister and Ibby Greer, Lane and Diamond Boyd,

Danny Nasset, Sam Stephenson, Jesse Andrews, Mike Wiley, Steve Kruger, Lynn McKnight, Greg Britz, Nancy Kalow, Cece Conway, David Cecelski, Randall Kenan, Roger Lucey, Joe Mosnier, Kathy Rudy, Ruth Jones, Orin Starn, Bill Peck, Jim Peacock, Sally Gray, George Loveland, Carol Burwash, and the Gentleman's Book and Bottle Club. Lissa Gotwals, Harlan Campbell, and Jackie Woolsey helped make the photographs come alive. Also, a certain cabin in the Blue Ridge features prominently in the formation of this book, and I pause to appreciate those who built and preserved it. I am indebted to all the people of Franklin County and Floyd County and to the Floyd General Store for keeping music and other traditions alive for my grandpa and the rest of us. Finally, my heartfelt thanks go to all at the University of Illinois Press for believing in and making this book a reality. Thank you all.

Prologue

I STEERED THE PICKUP TO A STOP on a gravel road alongside a thicket of dried honeysuckle and blackberry canes near Shively Branch in Endicott, Virginia. "It's right over yonder," said my grandfather pointing through the brush. I got out in the crisp October air to search while he and my mother waited in the truck. I had to fight through yards of dry briars higher than my head before I found, nearly rotted through, a wooden floor perched on top of stacked rock corners. The roof and the walls had fallen in, leaving a heap of rubble that people afraid of snakes—including the two in the truck—wouldn't dare go near. I stepped carefully onto the cluttered old floor and overturned some of the loose boards. I found the front door with a porcelain knob and under some old boards a rusted Drink Nehi sign. This was the store I had asked about.

I felt grateful to have made the pilgrimage when we did because Grandpa was in declining health and cold weather was already coming on. I knew he wouldn't have gone outside to explore in the dead of winter, and I was afraid there might not be another chance. Sadly, I was right. Grandpa died just weeks later, in the early part of December.

I had never met or even seen a picture of my great-grandfather Pete Thompson, the man who had owned that store, and hadn't exactly wished to, as Grandpa had told me enough about his childhood with this man—of the snow falling on blankets on the boys' beds upstairs while the old man slept with heat near the kitchen downstairs, of the old man's drunken rages and the beatings and the verbal abuse, of having to work on the farm for a pittance, and of my grandfather's pledge to get away as soon as he was able. Grandpa's own mother had died in childbirth, and the new Thompson wife and stepmother had no time for the older children. Too many of her own were being born. But Pete Thompson was my ancestor, my own loving grandfather's father, and I wanted to see this store—and to go there with Grandpa to hear him talk about it.

FIGURE 1. Shooting Creek mountain farm near Endicott, Virginia, in the early twentieth century. Photograph courtesy of the Blue Ridge Institute of Ferrum College.

"What did he sell there?" I asked. He had a little bit of everything, he told me: some dry goods and a few hardware items, some drinks and a few food items. He sold a lot of sweet feed: molasses-soaked grains for cattle and hogs. But most of his profits came from his sales of five-gallon metal cans and fifty-pound bags of sugar, malt, and yeast. He didn't have to tell me these items were for the bootlegging trade, the business that people back in the store's heyday in the 1920s and through the Great Depression of the 1930s sometimes called blockading. But I pressed for a few more details. "Liquor was the only way people had to make a dollar," was about all he said that day. Maybe it was because my mother was along. Maybe it was because the memories were of a hard, hard time. No chuckles or jokes—just a look of pity on his face about his people who had lived in poverty. He had a way of choking up when he talked about people and hard living. "They had it rough," he said.

Moonshine is what we call it today, and you see references to it everywhere in Franklin County, Virginia. T-shirts and ball caps emblazoned with the slogan Moonshine Capital of the World are for sale in all the convenience stores. The local historical society in Rocky Mount promotes moonshine lore and history today as a central part of the county's heritage, with tours and reenactments. Also, Ferrum College's Blue Ridge Institute and Museum has long collected and displayed stills and other liquor paraphernalia as part of their folklore collection. Their exhibition White Liquor—Blue Ridge Style was their most popular ever. You don't grow up with connections to Franklin County and fail to know something about the clear whiskey produced there. Though my family had been deeply involved back in Pete Thompson's day, there was still so much I needed to learn.

My grandfather could look through patches of weeds and even into seventy-five-year-old forests and see things that used to exist in them—houses and farms owned by people he knew when he was growing up. A network of stores, gristmills, and a post office tied people together in Endicott then and continued to exist in his memory. Three main hollows named for the creeks that formed them composed the community: Long Branch, Runnett Bag Creek, and Shooting Creek, made famous by Charlie Poole's song by the same name. "Going up Shooting Creek, going on a run; going up Shooting Creek, have a lot of fun." A subsequent verse turned less friendly: "Going up Shooting Creek, gonna take my razor and my Gatling gun." The place that inspired North Carolinian Charlie Poole, Grandpa could still see it in his mind's eye.

Today the shady state road that winds along Shooting Creek is part of the increasingly popular Crooked Road Music Trail, a driving tour celebrating

FIGURE 2. National recording stars Charlie Poole and the North Carolina Ramblers (Poole, banjo; Posey Rorrer, fiddle; and Roy Harvey, guitar) frequented the Endicott community, playing for dances and learning the local fiddle tunes. Shooting Creek was one of their favorite places to play, so much so they named a song after the community, changing the words of "Cripple Creek" to "Shooting Creek." Photograph courtesy of Kinney Rorrer.

mountain music from the area; but during my grandfather's childhood more than forty families lived on farms there, along with equal numbers up the other creeks—on land that today seems to be pristine forest and on terrain seemingly so steep and forbidding it could never be cleared and farmed. But it was, and the people who farmed there survived. Driving through those places brought Grandpa a flood of stories of people and their history that I loved to listen to. I drove with him as much as I could, and slowly the stories began to connect.

Only a few weeks before Grandpa went into the hospital for the last time, I took him to the Friday night Jamboree at the Floyd General Store about ten miles from Endicott, where he still loved to get out on the dance floor to flatfoot, just as he had done as a young man to bands like the North Carolina Ramblers. He didn't dance but a song or two that night, and that fact above all said he was truly ailing; maybe that reality setting in is why he told me more that night than he ever had. As we drove up to Floyd County from his farm through Shooting Creek and Endicott and back, I asked him questions about his father, his leaving home, and his own start in farming. Dropping his usual reticence, he answered in detail. Though I tried not to show it then, I was stunned by what he said.

"I left home when I was fifteen," he told me. "I only went to the seventh grade in school. That was all they had back then. I knew I couldn't make no money working on my daddy's farm. I used to work for him and he'd give me a few cents. I even washed the dishes after dinner [midday] while the other ones rested. I'd earn money that way, enough to buy a drink down at the store and save up some. When I got old enough and had enough money saved to buy me a car, and I started hauling liquor to West Virginia." "To the coalfields?" I asked. "Yeah," he replied, "I had the car loaded down with liquor, driving as fast as that car would go, trying to make it through Roanoke and over the mountain into West Virginia. I was shot at several times by deputies. I had a few bullet holes in the car, but they never hit me, or my tires. Used to have several cars running together, and one would stay behind and try to cut off the deputies so the others could get through." All this told by my gentle grandfather who never took even a swig of alcohol as far as I knew.

I wish the road had been longer. But in the next few miles on the way to the farm I found out as much as I could. He told me that he had also sold whiskey cans, sugar, malt, and yeast from an old store building that had set out behind his house. He had bought the farm complete with the old store and house and then built a two-story brick home where my father and his siblings were born and where all the grandchildren went to visit as often as we could—all with seed money he had made from liquor hauling and ingredients sales. He had always been a farmer and a logger as far back as I could remember. I had never known until then how he had made the leap from Endicott, where land was steep and poor, to the rolling farm he ended up with five miles from Endicott. There was more to this on my grandmother's side as well. Her father, Luther Smith, had been a revenue officer for the county and he, too, had sold liquor-making supplies on the side. Having some extra cash, Luther Smith purchased my grandparents' farm first and in turn sold it to them. So in my family, the sales of ingredients and hauling the finished product led to some savings and to a down payment and beyond. That, along

FIGURE 3. "Mother and Dad are sweet." William Clifford and Cloey Smith Thompson, the author's paternal grandparents, were born in Endicott, Virginia. They lived their entire married life on a farm in Ferrum, Virginia. Photograph circa 1940. Author's personal collection.

with a lot of hard work on the land, is how my grandparents came to own the family farm I grew up with—though it all was so hidden that the fact came to me as a revelation long into my adulthood.

That same night on the road, Grandpa also told me that one of my grandmother's brothers—a character deeply enmeshed in a liquor conspiracy in the county—had put a gun in my grandfather's face and threatened to kill him, saying something about suspecting him of informing on their liquor ring. That accusation goes against common sense, since informing would have hurt my grandfather's own income, and it contradicted pretty much everything I know of my grandfather's ability to keep secrets. But arguing the truth can only go so far when staring down the barrel of a gun. Grandpa, though small, was stout enough then to win a bet that he could carry a hundred-pound sack of corn on his back two miles from a store to his home. He knocked his brother-in-law flat with his fist and got away. But from then on until the brother-in-law died, Grandpa never went anywhere without carrying his pistol to protect himself. All those times we were together throughout my childhood, he never let on. He was that discreet. Thankfully, he never had to use it. All that we children knew from our grandfather was his love for his family, his way with cattle, his soft heart, and that he would do pretty much anything we'd ask of him. Indeed, he kept his knowledge of the past to himself for us. So, with these revelations driving down a road that night, my innocence ended, and my questions about my family's past got all the more serious.

On Sunday two days later, I stopped by to see Grandpa one last time before heading back to my home in Chapel Hill, North Carolina. My aunt was there, so I refrained from asking more questions about what we had been talking about. But he did show me a book he had been poring over—the only one I'd ever seen him read. "Here's a good book and you ought to read it," he said, "I'm halfway through." The book was a local memoir published by a daughter of Endicott named Gladys Edwards Willis, someone Grandpa knew growing up. The book is entitled *Goin' Up Shootin' Creek*. The exchange we had about it was our last.

A few weeks after Grandpa's funeral, I stopped by the family farm, where my Aunt Lucille was staying. After visiting for a while, I asked her about the book Grandpa had been reading. He said I should take a look at it, I told her.

She scanned the small bookshelf in the den and found it. I held it reverently. There halfway through the book was Grandpa's bookmark. She let me borrow the book, so I took it and, as if I was poring over my grandfather's own memories, read it all that night in a log cabin a few miles from his birthplace. Mrs. Willis, like Grandpa, was keenly aware of how moonshine supported the families she knew as she grew up.

While she searched on the shelf, Lucille also had shown me another book she had just purchased entitled *Calendar Record of James Goode Lane Hash*. She said, "If you're interested in this history, you ought to look at this, too." The book is a large hardbound volume, transcribed by Hash's son, Vanderbilt Professor Emeritus John Hash, and John Hash's wife, Mary Hash, consisting of all of Primitive Baptist Elder Goode Hash's notes he had kept on large wall calendar for fifty years. The family found the preacher's calendars neatly rolled and stored in a trunk. The calendars had waited decades for discovery. When the family did find them, they realized the calendar contained the story not only of their own family but of an entire community, with memorable notes of births, deaths, and even the weather on nearly every date. The Hashes printed up the transcriptions for family and friends, had them printed and bound, and promptly sold all of them. Everyone with any connection to Endicott wanted one, as Hash was a beloved pillar of the community and his notes recalled many forgotten facts about their own families and gave them actual dates. Fortunately I was able to borrow a copy from my uncle right away, photocopied it, and began sifting through the years with Elder Goode, as most people knew him. This fascinating collection of notes, a testament to people's desire to preserve their histories however they can, helped inspire this book. I couldn't have written about Endicott without Elder Goode's help, or his family's.

Also, a few years after my grandfather's death, the Virginia Foundation for the Humanities graciously awarded me a two-year field research grant to conduct oral histories with those who remembered early life in Endicott, including Hash's children and many others. The grant also allowed me to plunge further into archival research about the community my grandfather and grandmother grew up in. The Center for Documentary Studies at Duke University, where I am employed, provided the means for me to get away to do the work. In my fieldwork within the community, I heard numerous stories about Goode Hash, whom everyone remembered fondly. Also, two women missionaries emerged as central characters in Endicott's story. Miss Ora Harrison and Miss Maude Beheler started and ran for nearly five decades the mission known to most as the Rock Church, but officially named St. John's-in-the-Mountains Episcopal Mission. Much of their story and writings are preserved in the Special Collections archives at Virginia Tech. This collection, along with Goode Hash's calendars and photographs of the family lovingly preserved at the Blue Ridge Institute, became the lodestones of my research. Fortunately these leaders left me many clues, and their work prompted yet more interviews and archival searches.

As most people know, official records regularly leave out the poor and the unsung. From the ship records of travelers from Ireland and Scotland to Philadelphia and on to the Blue Ridge to the agricultural census in Virginia, clues are often sketchy and fit together at best like a patchwork quilt—which in my grandparents' day was a covering made from the frayed scraps of old garments that were never complete as single parts. Memories of neighbors and kin, as anyone who's tried to do oral histories knows, are like that. Indeed, when I found the one man people in the community considered most knowledgeable about the liquor trade sitting in a Franklin County nursing home, he was unable to tell me anything more than a few words. "I sold liquor for a living," he said with a smile. I sat with him trying different routes to get a story to emerge. It never emerged. The gravestones in Endicott are often only flat rocks stood on end with no dates or inscriptions there to help. The homes are but a pile of foundation stones buried under leaves. Old store signs like the one I found with my grandfather, or the still boxes—usually riddled with axe holes—I have found while walking along creeks, or old stoves rusting at old home sites show how people made a living and that they bought and sold things in those hills. Rusted iron and old crockery lie silent. These artifacts, while hard evidence of lives lived in what now seems to be forests, are a good start, but they call out for more explanation. Yet even with many people willing to tell me their memories and letting me use many of their photographs and written documents, I still had to piece together this story out of remnants. Is history ever otherwise? Certainly not, but those with education and wealth have more written documents to begin with, and that fact often skews history.

Fortunately there were others who came before me who have kept remnants from old cloths and connected them before I arrived. Many have worked hard at this task, including Endicott's own, as mentioned previously. In addition, a Franklin County native researcher and lawyer, the late T. Keister Greer, self-published an extraordinarily helpful resource entitled *The Great Moonshine Conspiracy of 1935*. His work contains the official court transcripts and details gleaned from newspaper stories of the countywide conspiracy and federal trial and provides much-needed facts regarding the moonshine business and its investigation by federal officers. Like many other readers, after buying the book I went straight to the index of the nine-hundred-page tome to see whether my family members' names were in the book. They were, particularly my great-grandfather Luther Smith's name, who Mr. Greer, in an interview I conducted with him, was gracious enough to call one of the "heroes of the story" because Smith quit his job as deputy rather than join the pay-to-play scheme. My grandfather Thompson is in the index, too, as are others of my relatives. My grandmother's brother, Roosevelt Smith, is mentioned eighty-six times. He was one of the convicted conspirators.

This is not a fact to celebrate exactly, but a reality that I must claim. In pursuing this project, I wanted to understand why people—especially ones I knew to be gentle and honest—got involved in whiskey making to begin with. Of course, some of the characters that emerged from my search turned out to be greedy and some were up to pure meanness, but many were simply trying to live. At the same time, people weren't naive. They knew they were producing an illegal substance. That fact made them both wary of those in power and vulnerable to exploitation. Their secrecy and vulnerability in turn gave an opportunity to certain unscrupulous county leaders, including those elected to enforce the law, to create a huge liquor ring employing hundreds of men and women who produced, hauled, and sold liquor for the profit of a few. So the drink that started out as a way for poor farmers to make a few dollars to keep their farms and families solvent later turned into a racket that netted countless thousands of dollars each for a small cadre of power brokers—at least until they were caught and brought to justice, though some say afterward as well.

All this corruption led to three interrelated trials that started with a grand jury hearing in 1934 and ended in 1937—all of them stemming from the same conspiracy. The first of the three is known as the conspiracy trial per se, and was held in Roanoke, Virginia. In that trial thirty-four of Franklin County's most powerful were indicted for conspiring against the federal government. Fifty-five others were charged with aiding the ringleaders. The second trial was also a federal trial in Roanoke and directly related to the first in that it charged some of the defendants and their collaborators with bribing jurors to sway the outcome of the conspiracy trial. The third, held in Franklin County, was a closely related murder trial, though the government didn't prosecute it that way. In that trial, Hubbard and Paul Duling, two brothers out of West Virginia, were charged with killing one of the deputies involved in the conspiracy and leaving his body riddled with shotgun and pistol wounds on a

FIGURE 4. Luther Smith, born in Endicott, was a farmer, storekeeper, and onetime deputy sheriff. Author's personal collection.

Franklin County back road. The murder trial was prosecuted in the Frank-lin County courthouse by the state of Virginia using only Franklin County prosecutors, which became the source of much controversy.

These three trials, likely the most sensational events ever to take place in Franklin County, are only part of the story to be told. To understand the broader realities of moonshine in the Blue Ridge, we must begin with acknowledging that moonshine was first an agricultural commodity produced on farms and, like other commodities, one that was affected by federal and state policies from Prohibition to the Agricultural Adjustment Act. To know that moonshine was a way to buy and save mountain farms is to begin to understand why people living in Endicott and the thousands of places like it turned to an illegal sub-stance. The conspiracy trial was only an outcome of this reality.

To further understand moonshine's full story, we need to find out why people settled in Endicott to begin with, where those settlers came from, and why they felt compelled to leave their places of origin. It's important to know what religious and cultural beliefs and practices they brought with them to the Blue Ridge; how missionaries tried to bring religion and change to people living in the mountains even though they already had their own faith; what changes and new influences people living in the mountains experienced over time; and how, through all these changes, they made a living and fed their families in a seemingly impossible place to live in a time we call the Great Depression. All this sacrifice and risk eventually resulted in my life in a place where I sit in a temperature-controlled office and write undisturbed. My life would not be possible without that moonshine past. Thanks to my grandfather's willingness to tell me, I understand better how I got here.

As I walked away from the old heap of rubble bearing with me the Nehi sign, a doorknob, and a few pieces of hardware, my head began to fill with questions about what I could not see about Endicott, particularly what hap-pened in the 1920s and '30s when my great-grandfather's store was in its heyday. I started with the fact that my ancestors had made their living from moonshine and its products, but every other family surrounding the store, even the ones who didn't drink, even the preachers, even the missionaries, got by because of it. I knew that fact more than any other needed saying here.

Stating that truth isn't easy for everyone who came from this background. Some who grew up knowing that life personally have been embarrassed to admit their family's prior association with making the strong drink. Gradually, however, my people, and I mean "my people" broadly here, are speaking more about their pasts and, through the process of telling, are embracing the pride associated with having and then overcoming a hardscrabble background. No one is proud that their family members broke the law of course, but those who have searched for answers know that the reasons people made liquor are more complex and nuanced than many first realize. Many descendants of old moonshiners are starting to disabuse themselves of the simple stereotypes still prevalent in too many media sources. They have claimed their moonshining ancestors as strong people who struggled against and overcame poverty. Through historical exhibits and cultural promotion, any guilt that people have harbored about moonshine—at least the variety made in the past when there were few alternatives—is fading away. Those who lived during moonshine's heyday during Prohibition and the Great Depression also knew that moonshine was no local commodity when it came to sales. Alcohol had to be sold broadly in order to bring in money to the community, and consumption in cities and towns far away, where mobsters made a killing off speakeasies and where people converted denatured alcohol in their bathtubs into a form of gin, was all part of the same industry. Blame can't be placed on the shoulders of mountain producers. In fact, no community in America was immune from buying and selling hooch.

Far from being just about what went on in hollows in the Virginia mountains, moonshine is an American story. Moonshine may conjure in some minds stereotypes of lazy, drunken people sitting at home who could do nothing else, as the cartoons and movies often depict them. In fact, moonshining starting with local ingredients grown in the mountains was hard work and required complex strategies for sales networking and clever means of transport. And through transport, moonshine tied Endicott together with the drama of the American haves and have-nots of the 1920s and '30s. My grandfather, like countless others, hauled moonshine to hubs like Roanoke, where other distributors made sure it got into big cities. Others hauled it to mill workers and coal miners who were usually displaced people, some of them sharecroppers and children of slaves, or refugees from failing economies elsewhere, often the very mountains where these families made their liquor and their living. Moonshine was the mental and physical salve used to soften their farms' losses. It was also one way of remembering the tastes of home and of forgetting at the same time. Moonshine was also entangled with the greater American story because the labor of the Blue Ridge refugees was being used to sell coal to the steel mills in the Northeast, which built the rails that tied America together. Franklin County moonshine also likely made it to the back doors of bankers and politicians in big cities, even some politicians whose constituents insisted they vote for Prohibition to begin with. And this network tied directly to my grandfather's quest to buy his farm just a few miles from where he grew up.

So to understand moonshine and even my grandfather's farm, I had to look into such broad topics as national politics, industrial development, agricultural policy, and trade, both national and international. I had to connect the fact that during the Great Depression, government officials, the G-men and their local compatriots associated with liquor taxation, were going after whiskey producers in order to raise national revenue, with the very local scene of deputies shooting at my grandfather, who was trying to escape poverty and to be a taxpayer in the first place. This led me eventually to the conspiracy trial and the crimes associated with it, but it also led me to broaden my search into the

FIGURE 5. Hosea Thomas's still workers: (left to right) Arthur Martin with banjo, Sparrell C. Rakes, T. P. "Press" Martin, and Wiley Thomas used a turnip-style boiler near Shooting Creek. Note the mash barrels to the right and the copper worm on the left. Endicott, Virginia, 1915. Photograph courtesy of the Blue Ridge Institute of Ferrum College.

structure of agriculture and the story of small farms. I had to ask why national inequalities needed to be played out violently in a place so small.

I found that government decisions, seemingly for the good of the people, bore down on Blue Ridge communities and to some extent gave people little choice but to break the law. The feds sometimes saw it in their best interest to pursue not only the ringleaders, but also the poor families who were making liquor in a time hardest for rural people, yet they did nothing to build schools or roads and railroads to their sections of the mountains. Most officials neglected to think about agricultural development projects to replace the distilling they were trying to eradicate. Moonshiner farmers were left on their own even while others in other regions were getting government help, in the form of road and railroad transportation tax subsidies and commodity price supports, in order to expand farm production in the Midwest while leaving the Appalachian farmers on their own. Choices people made when turning to liquor production have to be judged in the context of opportunities people had. What farmers chose to produce in their world had a lot to do with broad national policies and economics.

Just as artifacts around the ruins of Pete Thompson's store help reconstruct a larger story of the whole, so can looking into one place called Endicott illuminate the larger national picture. Little places—little stores and farms—are tied to the whole of an economy, because even if they are mostly subsistent operations, they are that way for a broader reason. There were no discrete places in the middle of nowhere in America during the Great Depression; in fact, there is never such an entity as a single human location. We are all intertwined through the exchange of ideas, language, goods, and DNA. In this case, people were drinking Endicott's corn in liquid form as far away as Chicago. And where did the corn come from? It was, we might argue, a locally produced, value-added product made by mountain producers that any "locavore" (local-food advocate) might applaud as part of the solution to our food problems today. But before that, corn originated in Mesoamerica and moved thousands of miles to become the staple of Saponi agriculture in the Blue Ridge long before Europeans arrived. It's fascinating to imagine how corn made it to Endicott in the beginning and how these settlers from Ireland, Scotland, Wales, and elsewhere married their barley-distilling heritage with a crop that their ancestors had never seen before. In these ways, corn was already a global crop traded across borders millennia ago. As profit became more important than purity, sugar began to displace corn as the main ingredient, and this made moonshine even more international as cane sugar came in from Barbados, Jamaica, and Haiti for distilling liquor in America. The laborers may have been from the mountains, but the raw materials they used were imported and exported by ship and rail and then brought in on horse and wagon to Endicott.

So a host of influences inhabit this history of moonshine, local and national. Well before the twentieth century, through immigration and trade, outside influences were at work on Endicott and Endicott's influences worked on other places. Understanding such facts takes the story of liquor production out of the realm of jokesters and myth-makers who continue to depict barefoot hillbillies dressed in funny hats driving race cars down back roads and whooping it up and puts the history in a context that actually makes sense. Sure there were drunks and fast car driving at times in Franklin County, but how is that different from where anyone lives, then or now? They were on the road hauling whiskey not for fun but because people elsewhere wanted what they had; indeed they couldn't get enough of it. And, shockingly, too many were on the road in Franklin County because the law told them to do it.

My grandfather's life and many others like it have taught me that moonshine was a last-ditch stand on many mountain farms and for some a way to buy or save them. As mountain land holdings dwindled through successive generations of inheritance and subdividing within families, and as railroads and banks began to facilitate the growth of agribusiness in the breadbasket we know today, farmers on the fringes and left out of that development because they had relatively few acres with which to work turned their cheap crops of corn and sometimes apples and peaches into comparatively profitable liquor. There were good reasons for some farmers like Pete Thompson and Luther Smith to build stores on their land and to carry sugar and five-gallon cans to sell to their neighbors. It was a sound farm strategy in the absence of any other help. And all this came into being because there was a market for liquor, and people were selling it because the money could be made and used, as the mountain ballad goes, to shoe someone's poor little feet and to glove their hands. It was used for schooling and for taking care of the "old folks back home." It was illegal money—that much is true—but it was

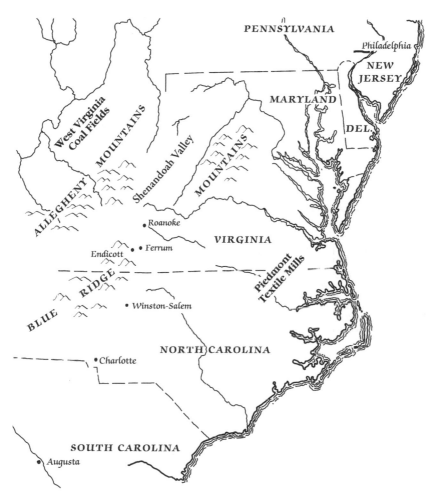

Endicott, located in Franklin County, Virginia, was both remote, as its roads were unimproved and the mountains around it steep, and interconnected, as its liquor made it to locations far up the eastern seaboard and to points westward as far as Chicago.

money made from sweat. That sweat money made liquor bosses rich, but it also bought and preserved small farms, keeping people out of the mills and mines and on their own land for a generation or two longer, leaving people some independence to determine their own directions and to change their families' futures, ultimately making possible my schooling and my privilege to write about history and culture of this place and its people. The spirits of the many who made those sacrifices surround me as I write.

Spirits of Just Men

1   Conspiracy Trial in the Moonshine Capital of the World

Government had long been to them a thing far off. They got no benefit from it. Roads were poor and there were always government men interfering. They sent men in to stop their liquor making. They wanted to collect taxes. For what? —SHERWOOD ANDERSON, *Kit Brandon*

IN 1934, THE ROAD UP Thompson Ridge was red dirt or mud, depending on the weather. No road grader or state gravel had ever touched it. After a rain or snow, people parked their roadsters or trucks, the few who had them, that is, at the foot of the hill and walked home. Sometimes they used their teams of horses or mules to pull the stuck vehicles up the hill to their farms. Sometimes they just left them at the bottom of the hill by the store until the road dried out.

Pete Thompson's store sat at the foot of that hill on level ground where two different roads intersected, one that wound back out to Long Branch Church and the other that wended toward Ferrum the back way. It was a good location for conducting local commerce. There were other stores in the broader community of Endicott then, including the Bryant and James store that housed the post office and was the center of the community a few miles away, but Thompson's was that hollow's store, and people went to it in part because it was too hard to go anywhere else. For some it was also a decent place to get the essential ingredients they needed for making whiskey without having to let too many know their business. Old Man Thompson didn't keep written records, at least ones just anybody could access, and he didn't talk about others' dealings. Keeping quiet was part of surviving, economically and otherwise, particularly for store owners, who couldn't help but hear or overhear news and gossip.

In good weather, the store's front porch was a gathering place. In winter, people moved in around the stove. Little stores like Thompson's were places to buy maybe a strawberry soda or a can of potted meat and some crackers and sit and talk about the weather and maybe intimate just a little of their predicaments to a neighbor struggling in the economic bottom we now call the Great Depression. Few would reveal much, particularly about the businesses that kept Pete Thompson's store in the black. More than a few barns had been burned down after someone said too much to the wrong man. But people who knew each other well did hint around and gave each other clues. Sometimes people have to talk—at least among people they think they can trust. A boiling pot, even of the best copper, has to give off steam or it will explode. Indeed, sometimes there had been explosions and there would be more.

If we squint, we can see the men sitting at the store in their patched overalls, cracked brogan shoes, hats with salt lines dried on their crowns, maybe one of the men whittling an oak stick, making curled shavings that fall at his feet, maybe another spitting tobacco juice every so often, each of them knowing the folds of the hills surrounding them nearly as well as the lines of their own hands, but none of them having a firm hold on their livelihoods. At least they found some solace, and pleasure, in sitting together for a spell. They farmed the same crops: corn, potatoes, beans, apples, and tomatoes, to name the most common. Almost every one of them raised hogs and milked a cow or two and shared the same weather as their neighbors, and this common work and experience would start and end most conversations. But every so often, talk turned more serious, to themes of their common plight: too little income and too little land and what they were trying to do about it. But few let on much about their pain. Even when they did speak a few details about their worries or plans, it was often in the form of a joke or in hushed talk or with encoded words we might not understand at first. This was especially true for men engaged in the illegal business they called blockading.

Though there is no store there today, and not one business anywhere near now, dozens of upturned flagstones along with a few granite markers lined up in family cemeteries up on the ridges, the overgrown farmsteads surrounded by zigzagged chestnut rails slowly rotting into soil, the metal and wood parts of old stills now rusted and rotten along creek beds, and the ruins of the store with a rusted Nehi sign all show that people once lived, worked, conducted business, and died near there. It is remarkable how many hundreds of them did given how quiet the ridges and hollows seem today. If we strain to hear them, their voices echo from the oral histories of their kin, the words still

FIGURE 6. Bryant and James Store and the Endicott post office, circa 1915. Author's personal collection.

passed along in conversations at the car lot or the feed store or from the ruins of the places themselves.

Farmers talked about the weather, as farmers will always do. In the summer of 1934, there was too much rain. Some of them had never seen so much water: Just when a man's trying to get his hay cut and put up! My corn's laid over by that wind, and I don't know if it will ever stand up again. And on top of that, I'm supposed to have a load of you know what ready to haul out. Them lawmen is breathing down my neck, and don't they know I've done bought plenty of sugar on credit here and I need to make a dollar same as anybody else? Loads of sugar coming this way from down at Ferrum Mercantile is like gold—all them store owners buying it up and prices going higher. Hard to say how many thousands of pounds of malt and everything they're unloading down there at the train depot. Somebody's making a killing, but it sure ain't me or any farmer I know.

There was talk among kin, and some of Pete's customers were his kin. Every now and then anger would make them say more than they planned: You got to pay for the things and pay to send it out the other direction, too. They complained about getting caught up in the mess. I wish to God I'd never seen that lawman Jeff Richards coming toward my place. Twenty-five dollars just to run a batch! Now I feel like a duck shut up in a pen, nowhere to run or fly, just scooping up grain and fattening up for the slaughter. I dog if it's worth it, but what else can you do, sit there and starve? I guess you could get deputized like old Luther Smith done and start getting paid to go after the bootleggers. I heard he quit them crooks, though.

What about you, Pete? They turned to the crotchety man with his elbows propped on the counter. You're sitting here at the store getting rich, ain't you? It was a common joke as everyone knew no one was. But among his most trusted friends, he would've talked back a little, mentioning the racket all of them were caught in.

Hell you say, boys! What if them federal lawmen start cracking down on the sellers? And you're forgetting one thing. I'm using some of the cans and sugar, too. I'm in it with you. And if one of us goes down, we all probably will. And people are talking. What about sheriffs and hotshots taking money from the little man? Don't the federal government think about that? But don't you know if they get to pushing, it's the little man's that's going to pay?

When they thought it really safe, Carter Lee's, the commonwealth attorney's, name came up. A few jokes circulated about so-called law. Somebody's wealth all right, but it sure ain't common, one of them said. Lord knows they run them caps and worms out the back door of the courthouse to a bootlegger as fast as the deputies bring them in the front. And I've paid them big men near as much as I've brought in. I just wonder how long it can last. Too many's got into it. And the big ones has got too big.

We folks here don't know the half of how much they're making off us. They've got it running up to Washington, even Chicago. They've got it going down south. Our county's the hub of something big. Them runners heading to Roanoke and Winston are just the start of it. We sure ain't ever been on the map before, but we sure are starting to look like a mighty big part of this here business. It can't last like this, boys. Something's bound to change.

The neighbor men would sit awhile, everyone knowing that they were playing with fire. A few would load up some bags of sugar. Some could pay cash after a run and some couldn't but instead would buy on credit until the still was run. After visiting a bit, some procured square-sided five-gallon cans and loaded them onto a truck bed and covered them with a canvas tarp.

But they weren't hiding much from those who lived there. Everybody knew everybody's business. This was protection and vulnerability sewn into one backdrop.

Even the children knew, but they were told to keep away from the places back in the hollows where the men gathered during the night, lanterns burning and steam rising up through rhododendron and hemlock branches, unless they were needed to help. Everyone could tell a still was running, sometimes by the thumping sound or the smoke or when the hogs and cattle coming upon spent mash would stumble around fields or when the men gone to drink would walk the roads staggering, too. The children of the mean drunks knew especially well. Sometimes people could tell by a man's extra money he spent at the store when a run was done.

The most serious of the liquor makers either refrained from drinking while working or kept away from it altogether. There was too much at stake to run a still while under the influence. They knew that some of those around them had done time. Being sent to jail meant even less money for the family. So they set up a network for notifying people that when alerted spread faster than a car could drive. Stillers usually knew that the law was coming to make a bust perhaps an hour or more before they arrived. There was a system of warnings: might have been a series of shots or shouts, a farm bell or a child running down a path to a neighbor's homestead, or notices relayed from as far away as Ferrum that told of strange cars or people headed their way. The whole community, regardless of age, worked together to protect this livelihood, even if they didn't do the work itself. They knew why their men and women had to make liquor; it was no less a necessity than having to get up on dark winter mornings to break ice out of springs or to feed and milk the cows. Turning corn into liquor was a farm chore, and just about the only one that yielded cash in that time and place.

A few outsiders who used the old red road caused no alarms when they did so. Two of them were Miss Ora and Miss Maude, the women missionaries who lived up at St. John's on the other end of the community, in what the local people called the Rock Church. The two sometimes made their way in the mission's car up into the back hollows to tend to the sick and to women giving birth, walking or riding horseback if they had to and arriving in the homes with baskets in hand and with mud-caked shoes. The granny midwives were often the first to arrive for birthings, but the missionaries were usually close behind and welcomed when they made it. They had medicine and later even visiting doctors who worked with them. Another frequent visitor in the early years, the most regular of all when he carried the mail in his horse-drawn jumper, was the Primitive Baptist preacher named James Goode Hash. Most called him affectionately Elder Goode, as he befriended and tried to help most everyone in Endicott and neighboring communities for miles around, sometimes catching a ride with relatives or neighbors and going on foot to make his rounds. He was often the preacher called on to talk with the sick and dying, read them the Bible, and help bury those who succumbed. Besides those few, and the occasional musicians who would come through to play a house dance, most everyone who came through on horseback, in wagons, or in motor vehicles lived there.

That is, except for the bootleggers from out of county and even out of state, like the Duling boys from West Virginia, and other buyers that people didn't know at all, who started showing up in the dead of night to pick up a load, or convoys of drivers from outside the community, from places like Floyd and Roanoke, came roaring in unannounced and left out at speeds too fast for most drivers on a dirt road. Then there were the lawmen who barreled into the community, sometimes two or three carloads at a time, guns readied, in an attempt to surprise some unsuspecting crew at their stills, as well as the other lawmen there to collect fees for protection from busts.

With the community's warning systems at the ready and informants as far away as Ferrum calling in once phones came, few raids or even visits occurred without prior knowledge. But as traffic on even the worst roads increased and unknown vehicles went there for business or to try to break it up, people lost their ability to know every car owner and to name who went up or down the road. The Endicott roads, as bad as they were, became busy with commerce and its regulation, even if most of the dollars traveling them were destined for pockets elsewhere, including the pockets of the lawmen themselves. The traffic was a clear sign that change had come, and the cars were harbingers of a world of consequences about to break in on Franklin County with full force.

▪ ▪ ▪

In January 1934, Federal Agent Col. Thomas Bailey, a decorated World War I veteran, drove alone into Franklin County, Virginia, where Endicott is located, to work undercover. While serving in the 111th Infantry in France, Bailey, then a lieutenant, crawled on his belly a hundred yards through a no-man's-land of trenches and barbed wire. He then sneaked another two hundred yards behind German lines, gaining what his Distinguished Service Cross citation called, "Information of the greatest value, making possible a subsequent and successful attack."[1] Bailey also won medals as a sharpshooter. Some two decades later, at the height of the Great Depression, the territory Bailey penetrated was domestic. This time the colonel's orders came from the Alcohol Tax Unit of the U.S. Department of the Treasury. His assignment was to infiltrate and prosecute perhaps the biggest hot spot of moonshine production in the Virginia Blue Ridge. He had no idea when he set out just how hot it would be.

Prohibition had ended in March 1933, ten months prior to Bailey's arrival. President Franklin D. Roosevelt signed the Twenty-first Amendment to the U.S. Constitution only two weeks after his inauguration, repealing the Eighteenth Amendment, or the Volstead Act, that had made the manufacture, sale, and distribution of alcohol illegal. The Eighteenth, which had passed in 1919, was the only amendment to ever be repealed. The reversal brought to an end the harrowing work of the Bureau of Prohibition, made famous by Agent Eliot Ness and the Untouchables. But the repeal did nothing to lessen the government's interest in ending illegal alcohol production. Instead, the government's tax collection responsibilities intensified.

By 1934, licensed breweries and distilleries, mostly well-financed larger businesses, were beginning to make a comeback in some parts of the country and starting to pay their taxes, just as the Tax Unit wanted them to do. Yet, with illegal distribution channels already well entrenched, underground alcohol continued to flow, particularly from places where jobs were scarce. With unemployment running higher than 25 percent nationally at that time, and with some areas like the Blue Ridge much higher, jobs off the farm were scarce as hens' teeth. On top of that, for broke consumers who needed a drink, alcohol made and sold without the hefty taxes added by the state and federal governments was several dollars cheaper per quart. And likely just as important, homemade liquor had a loyal following that was hard to break, particularly among those who had little access to government Alcoholic Beverage Control stores: people living in dry communities and residents of poor communities from the West Virginia coalfields to the Philadelphia inner city. Once people had gotten used to white liquor, the store-bought stuff just didn't have the zing.

Thus the Treasury Department had a nearly impossible assignment just one year after Prohibition's repeal. Though the Tax Unit agents' job was no longer the idealistic effort to put an end to alcohol consumption as Bailey's forerunners had attempted, they still had to catch people avoiding taxes on alcohol and, through stamping out illegal operations, attempt to systematically direct people to legal production and consumption. They were revenuers, tax men, and their mandate was to help clear up corruption and to bring in funds to help run a strapped government. Since the Whiskey Rebellion of George Washington's day, taxes on liquor had been a matter of life and death. This assignment was not for a bureaucrat; a military spy was perfect.

By the time of Bailey's arrival, Franklin County's reputation had already gone national. Even by the 1920s, tales of fast liquor running and moonshine blockades in the Virginia mountains had reached the press, and myths about the place abounded. Some of the gullible believed every single inhabitant, regardless of age or gender, was involved. Rumors spread about armed hillbillies ready to blow your brains out if you got lost and veered too close to a still. Starting at the turn of the century, a whole literature had sprung up about Appalachian mountain life, and as the nation read the exaggerated stories, mesmerized by people living as pioneers of old, misinformation about mountain lawlessness and depravity metastasized. Things got even more ridiculous as comics in print and on radio caricatured the Snuffy Smiths of the hills, men with an aversion to work and with a gun in one hand and a jug in the other. Even people from the county seat of Rocky Mount were afraid to venture into the mountains in their own county, adding further to the problem of neglect of roads and schools in the region. No one had stopped to think of providing economic aid to mountain farmers, alternative jobs, or even that perhaps legalizing the small-scale stills could be a means of curtailing illegal trafficking.

While exaggerations abounded about the people and how they lived, one amazing statistic was true: Millions of gallons of whiskey were being produced and sold out of Franklin County every year. This truth intermingled with overblown reputations and lies, locally and all the way to Washington's Treasury Department. Thus Franklin County showed up on the federal radar and, with the agent's arrival, would become the first big example Bailey's department used to teach others throughout the Blue Ridge a lesson.

As for the boys down at Pete Thompson's store and the many small-timers in Franklin County like them, Bailey was not much interested in catching and prosecuting them—not this time. It was clear that lawmen had already busted hundreds of stills in the area, and this wasn't the outcome he wanted from his investigation. The approach had done little to stem the moonshine tide in the first place. So Bailey turned his attention to prosecuting the masterminds who had made Franklin County's production possible on such a large scale. It didn't take him long to realize that trainloads of sugar, cans, malt, and even corn were coming into the county regularly and that millions of gallons of hooch were going out. Only slowly did he begin gathering evidence about the ringleaders, but when he did he knew he had uncovered a grand liquor scheme that involved even the county's most powerful elected officials. He called on the small-time sellers as informants, and he would eventually use hundreds of them as witnesses before the grand jury, but his targets would be higher up in the pyramid—all the way to the top of the law enforcement community, in fact. Specifically, Bailey had set his sights on Carter Lee, commonwealth attorney, along with the sheriff and his deputies.

■ ■ ■

It all seems naive now, but for decades antiliquor campaigners believed alcohol would go away if only the government could make it hard enough to make and buy. It was their generation's "just say no" crusade, and for fourteen years the whole nation had been absorbed by its Prohibition's moral power. Relentless preaching by teetotalers, including the National Women's Temperance Union, Prohibition Party, and the Anti-Saloon League, succeeded in convincing enough lawmakers, if only temporarily, that the government could legislate away social problems by simply outlawing the liquid spirits. Preachers and their followers had begun their antiliquor crusades as early as the 1840s, and by the 1900s states were beginning to do their part to stop sales. The crusaders fought saloons and public beer halls, believing that if they could close legal watering troughs they could help restore alcoholic fathers back to their families, sober up drunks, and end the rampant crimes associated with drink—everything from traffic accidents to murders.

The antialcohol forces, usually allied with religious leaders, believed that if people first said no to booze, they would next say yes to things moral and Christian. Their best-known spokesperson in the early twentieth century, evangelist Billy Sunday, preached tirelessly. "Whiskey and beer are all right in their place," he said in his famous sermon in Boston, "But their place is in hell."[2] Legalization and control were not enough; the prohibitionists sought eradication. However, the antisaloon and temperance forces backing Prohibition never dreamed that their crusades would unleash a different kind of evil and that legal liquor's eradication would create a new hell for the government men. The crusaders, in retrospect, seem to have been blind to the raw power of intoxicants to draw their own adherents and ignorant that liquor would be strong enough to make men and women break laws and sometimes even kill for what alcohol could do to their brains and pocketbooks. So, even as they won their battle in Congress, the antisaloon proponents began losing everywhere else, from the backstreets to the backwoods.

Virginia, like most states where local temperance societies and Bible-thumping preachers were most active, was one of the states that chose to rid its territory of strong drink before the Volstead Act passed in the U.S. Congress. Decades prior to Prohibition's passage, Virginia had sixty-three active chapters of the Women's Christian Temperance Union at work. By 1900, the teetotalers had succeeded in drying up twenty-seven of Virginia's one hundred counties and parts of twenty-eight more. Their goal was to eradicate liquor consumption one municipality at a time. By 1911, nearly all saloons had closed in the state. In Franklin County in 1894, there had been seventy-seven licensed distilleries and dozens of watering holes. By 1911, only one Franklin County establishment selling whiskey by the glass remained. Six years later in 1917, even that one was gone.[3]

Prohibition eradicated public sales all right, but in reality it kept strong drink only out of the hands of the few with no means of finding it from bootleggers. Meanwhile, Prohibition created a haven for lawbreakers and put hundreds of millions of gallons of untaxed and unregulated liquor into the hands of people at cheaper prices. Despite government crackdowns and much lip service to cleaning up America, sophisticated liquor distribution networks developed everywhere in the country. Speakeasies, as illegal drinking spots were known, proliferated in both urban and rural areas. The demand for illegal whiskey gave rise to alcohol kingpins such as Chicago's notorious Al Capone and his rival Bugs Moran and made their mobs rich through liquor trafficking. Capone ran more than ten thousand backroom speakeasies in Illinois alone and ruled much of the business on the East Coast as well, helping fuel the Roaring Twenties. So instead of saving America, eliminating the heartbreaks of alcohol, and ridding communities of the immorality associated with it as the Anti-Saloon League had preached, the prohibition of strong drink pumped life into a non-tax-paying, corrupt shadow economy run by organized crime. Instead of helping their cause, the antiliquor groups helped create and feed a new monster known as the Mob.

Prohibition also gave rise to corrupt officials seeking to make a killing off their own citizens' whiskey in many locales, including Franklin County. The county that had once been known as a bastion of legal production, with widespread sales of brandy made from water out of the clear streams and ample supplies of apples and peaches. Thousands of small producers had long made whiskey for their home use and for sale locally. By the late 1920s, prompted by Prohibition, corrupt officials had capitalized on that local tradition, creating with their marketing savvy and production controls what people still call the moonshine capital of the world. When long-held local expertise mixed with a national supply chain organized to meet a heightened demand—all in an area with no other employment opportunities—the growth of a black-market economy was inevitable. The equation makes complete sense: Demand drives supply. But what was not so obvious at first was that the main suppliers were no small-time mountain producers acting independently as the literature about the quaint mountain people had told the story, but rather an organized syndicate headed by powerful local men to whom each local producer paid a tax to the men at the top for making or hauling. These big shots, including lawmen, had used the power given to them by the state to exploit their citizens' desperate need for income, and it worked. Millions of gallons were flowing, with most of the profits going into a few hands.

As with many other unregulated industries at the time, producers at the bottom were taking most of the risk and getting only a few dollars in return, while the heads of the conspiracy were raking in thousands of dollars every week. Colonel Bailey's investigation of Franklin County was meant to send a scare through the region, but what he would uncover instead was a conspiracy so grand it became national news. Rather than arresting Snuffy Smith and Li'l Abner holed up in some hideaway, Bailey would indict the very officers the state and federal government had counted on to uphold their laws, men bearing some of Virginia's history in their heritage who would show up in court wearing three-piece suits with phalanxes of lawyers at their behest.

Bailey posed for months as a moonshine buyer. Nowhere in Franklin in 1934 could he have bought a legal bottle; there were no ABC stores in the county and no one had means of buying any legal whiskey without driving in a car, if one had one, a good distance and then paying a heftier price. He only had to talk with a few people before learning where to buy clear homemade alcohol at just a few dollars a gallon; eventually he began to learn about how to procure any number of five-gallon metal cans—rectangular containers easily stacked and hauled—all full and ready to transport. With the federal taxes on legal whiskey at five dollars a gallon, the local price was about half the market value of legal liquor, and by doing the math, he knew pretty quickly that someone was getting rich.

Bailey used all his best spying skills. He befriended bootleggers; got to know those who made and sold still parts; learned the places to drink locally in Franklin, like the back room in the Blackwood Station near Calloway; recorded the names of the rumrunners who hauled liquor out of the county; and studied the routes they took. He ate meals with moonshiners, sat around and listened for hints at country stores, and visited backroom bars. As the bootleggers increased in number and the strangers in town became less an anomaly, Bailey blended in. He had gone to a place where people still did say hello to strangers and more often than not people would ask to stay for meals.

Many cooperated even after they knew he was an investigator. He told them he was after the men at the top and that if they cooperated he would not go after them. No one liked being a snitch and people were afraid to say much, but Bailey offered protection in the federal courts. The threat of jail time was enough to get people to say more. We don't know how much liquor he drank to get the information he sought, but we do know he succeeded in getting his information. He learned enough to write in his final report that the county was "one of the most lawless in the United States" where "a majority of the population . . . was either directly or indirectly involved in illicit liquor traffic."[4] He left the county with enough evidence to fill a forty-page report and a list of more than two hundred names that he would call as witnesses before the grand jury. Many of the witnesses would be people from Endicott and communities like it. The indicted would come from all over, including former Prohibition agents and others sworn to uphold the law who'd instead decided to cash in on the easy money.

Every law enforcement man in the county, he wrote, had some hand in moonshine production and protection. They had operated together a protection scheme in which the supposed enforcers of the law coerced hundreds of backwoods liquor producers not only to get into the business but to pay them a fee to do so—either that or face time in jail. Moonshiners were no independents for the most part, but employees of sorts or pawns of a syndicate—all of whom worked through the night for a one-sided scheme. The deputies provided copper still parts and protection against arrest. The producers agreed to pay the deputies a fee in exchange for nonintervention, twenty-five dollars for each still and ten dollars for each load hauled. Full compliance by the producers was nearly guaranteed given the alternative. As the scheme got rolling, millions of gallons were flooding out of the county, while millions of potential tax dollars were bilked out of the federal budget and diverted into the pockets of a few schemers. Store owners pocketed a few extra dollars profit, raw materials haulers and moonshine runners alike were being paid, but most of the money made it to the top. The commonwealth attorney, the sheriff, and most other lawmen, who organized and then "taxed" the liquor trade without as much as having their clothes smell like smoke, pocketed the proceeds from a thousand stills. Meanwhile, the distillers themselves remained poor, giving their all to a clandestine business that would never be unionized or controlled for risk to its employees—and would certainly never pay them their due.

For obvious reasons, Bailey avoided using the local deputies or even state men as allies. Eventually, as the task grew larger and more witnesses surfaced, three other feds entered the picture to assist him. They combed the county together collecting depositions to use to make their case to a federal grand jury. In their preliminary report to the acting deputy commissioner of the Alcohol Tax Unit on July 31, 1934, titled "United States vs. Charles Lee, Et Al.," Bailey and his coinvestigators wrote the following:

> In Franklin County, Virginia, commencing in 1928 and continuing from that time until the present, an organization which extends its scope into the surrounding counties, which has for its purpose the manufacture, transportation, sale and possession of non-tax paid liquors and the protection of members of this organization by the Commonwealth Attorney's office of Franklin County, the sheriff's office, state prohibition officer, and certain men who now are or formerly were federal officers engaged in the enforcement of liquor laws.
>
> In the fall of 1928, Charles Carter Lee, the Commonwealth's Attorney for Franklin County, Virginia, and Sheriff Pete Hodges called the various deputy sheriffs of Franklin County into the office of Pete Hodges, singly and in pairs, making them a proposition to divide the County up into districts for the purpose of assessing illicit distillers and bootleggers a certain amount (from ten dollars to twenty five dollars) per month for the privilege of operating with the protection of County officers.[5]

The investigators urged that a "Grand Jury be called in the Western District of Virginia at the earliest practicable date."[6] The grand jury obliged, called more than two hundred witnesses, and found the allegations worthy of prosecution. Their findings were made public on February 7, 1935, and were compiled in a single major indictment against thirty-four individuals and one corporation. They charged that the defendants did "unlawfully, willfully, knowingly, and feloniously conspire, combine, confederate, and agree among themselves and with each other . . . to commit certain offenses against the laws of the United States of America; that is to say . . . while engaged in carrying on the business of a distiller, defraud, and attempt to defraud the United States of America of the tax on the spirits distilled by them."[7]

■ ■ ■

Whiskey making has been a part of the county's experience since the arrival of the first European settlers in the 1740s. A century before the American Civil War, many Franklin County residents had produced brandy and other drinks legally, a great majority of it for local sale and consumption. This became a regular source of income for those selling to travelers passing through the county on the Carolina Road. After war broke out, whiskey was outlawed in the Confederate States. While many wounded Confederates surely needed whiskey as a painkiller and disinfectant, with many troops going hungry the Rebel generals demanded that the precious corn crop be used for food only. Though farms in the Blue Ridge sections with mostly small subsistence farms and few slaves to fight over had little to spare in the way of provisions for the war, mountain fathers and sons went in great numbers to join the cause not only for reasons of loyalty but also because of the pay offered by large landowners and the consequences brought by the bushwhackers if they refused to go. After the war ended and the country slowly reunited, the U.S. government got into the business of taxing liquor in every state, a move that brought deep resentment from the farmers who had lost most everything they had already and who could scarcely cough up a whiskey tax payment when their crops and fields had been neglected or perhaps destroyed by marauders during the war. Taxing liquor and shutting down the wildcat stills took force. In the 1870s, President Ulysses Grant's Commissioner of Revenue Green B. Raum sent raiders into Virginia to wipe out illegal stills and force the opening of licensed distilleries that the government could, in turn, regulate and tax. The strategy appears to have succeeded, as over the next two decades ten Franklin brandy distillers were listed in the Virginia business directory and, by 1893, seventy-seven different Franklin County distilleries had followed suit and purchased Virginia licenses.[8] Most of the distilleries were small, farm-based operations.

Today, such a high number of small legal distilleries cropping up in a single location would make national news and send connoisseurs of local food and drink flocking there. Unfortunately for those of that bent at least, by the first decade of the twentieth century, the temperance movement had nearly eradicated all legal whiskey production in the county. By 1911, only R. F. Rakes's distillery at Shooting Creek and his Rocky Mount saloon remained open. By 1916, even Rakes's establishment, literally the last chance saloon, was out of business.

Perhaps some of the whiskey drinkers frequenting such places across the nation, upon hearing the antiliquor ranting, saw the waywardness of their ways and quit drinking, replacing their habit with something more temperate. Many did not. In Franklin County and thousands of places like it, even as the legal distilleries took their businesses off the books, others were firing up illegal operations in clandestine places.

As the licensed producers went out of business, the temperance-era Endicott moonshiners found their popular liquor in greater demand than ever. Shooting Creek and other Franklin County whiskey-producing locations became famous almost as soon as the saloons began shutting down. One writer who signed his name only as "J. L. G" to a series of articles in the *Roanoke Evening News* wrote of his explorations in the Shooting Creek and Runnett Bag areas of Franklin County in 1904. He exclaimed that the Endicott area provided "Ideal localities for moonshining and blockading. . . . Situated in the foothills of the Blue Ridge, the country covered with a dense growth of laurel and ivy, permeated by numerous streams of the clearest, coldest water, apples and corn in abundance, nature seems to invite you to 'jist make a doublin' or two for your own use.'"[9]

Especially with coverage like this, people began looking for the Franklin County product, and these laurel-shaded hollows with their crystal water continued as a haven for moonshine making even as the laws changed around them. For many desperate to find some brandy they could trust, this was a godsend. Now, even if off the books, the distillers continued to draw in much-needed farm income with the sale of a half gallon or two here and there. In the beginning, such local sales meant a dramatically different market than would eventually come to pass. But it didn't take long for the kingpins to start organizing and consolidating the profits, a move that would eventually gain the county a reputation where it did not want one—Washington, DC.

In 1931, some four years prior to Colonel Bailey's foray into the county, a mention of Franklin County whiskey made it into a federal document. It had all started when President Herbert Hoover, in an effort to salvage the work of the Bureau of Prohibition, appointed the National Committee on Law Observation and Enforcement, known as the Wickersham Commission after its director, George W. Wickersham. Hoover charged the Commission with identifying the causes of criminal activity within the liquor trade and making recommendations for appropriate public policy solutions. In their report issued in January 1931, the Commission first documented the widespread evasion of prohibition and the numerous ill effects liquor was having on American society. They admitted Prohibition's dismal record of enforcement of dry laws, saying "few things are more easily made than alcohol."[10] However, instead of recommending Prohibition's repeal and a new plan as many had assumed they would, the Commission took a last, though futile, stand for temperance. Director George Wickersham's personal statement attached to the report argued—though he used a double negative, perhaps tipping off his uncertainty—that the country fight against the odds: "Despite the well financed active propaganda of opposition to Prohibition and the development of an increasingly hostile public opinion, I am not convinced that the present system may not be the best attainable, and that any substitute for it would not lead to the unrestricted flow of intoxicating liquor, with the attendant evils that in the past always were a blight upon our social organization."[11] With these words, the Commission called for retrenching the government's efforts, by increasing "the number of agents, storekeeper-gaugers, prohibition investigators, and special agents."[12] Then it singled out the Blue Ridge Mountains as one of its hardest law enforcement challenges and mentioned Franklin County by name: "In one county, Franklin," the report reads, "It is claimed 99 out of 100 people are making, or have some connection with illicit liquor."[13] Thus, in Prohibition's last years and as whiskey became legal again, federal and state agents, with the Wickersham report in hand, zeroed in on Endicott and other area locations. But they made little headway. As Bailey's sleuthing revealed a few years later, not even these government agents remained unscathed by the corruption. Given the revenue officers' pay of less than one hundred dollars per month and their having to risk their lives with every raid, bribes became too tempting for many of the agents to pass up.[14] While some agents were axing stills and perhaps slowing production, others were taking bribes and warning stillers of their arrival. It was a losing battle for the feds, as agents joined in the illegal activities directly.

Many already knew the temperance war wasn't winnable, and by the time Wickersham first issued his quixotic report, he and his allies were already losing their support in Congress. In Hoover's last years as president, opposition to Prohibition reached a fever pitch, particularly as the blues of the Great Depression began to take effect. By 1932 when Franklin D. Roosevelt was voted into office, Americans had lost their patience with liquor-induced organized crime brought on by Prohibition, and a sizable percentage of citizens were fed up with forgoing legal drink. Roosevelt's outspoken opposition to dry laws helped him ride the nation's discontent with Hoover to a landslide victory. As his administration took office in 1933, the Wickersham Commission was eliminated, and a month later Prohibition itself was overturned.

The new administration turned its attention to ending organized crime associated with liquor as well as to collecting whiskey taxes as an attractive source of much-needed revenue to help the nation rise out of economic ruin. The burden of alcohol regulation shifted from the Bureau of Prohibition to the Alcohol Tax Unit of the Treasury Department, taking whiskey out of a moral battleground and placing it in a fiscal management arena. The new attitude was that having the state and federal governments make money from alcohol was preferable to their spending great sums trying to prevent a drinking public from having their vice and losing their political support in the process. Happy days were here again in more than one sense of the phrase, but for Colonel Bailey and the other federal alcohol tax agents like him, corruption and vice would continue to make collecting liquor revenues a deadly business.

■ ■ ■

In response to Bailey's lengthy report, the federal grand jury agreed to schedule a hearing in Harrisonburg, Virginia—a location well removed from Franklin County in the northern Shenandoah Valley—for October 19, 1934. Federal marshals began serving subpoenas in Franklin County, and people immediately started talking among themselves. The fact that the conspiracy ring was the target meant the deputies were on the hot seat for a change. So some of the deputies started talking; most vocal among them was Deputy Sheriff Thomas Jefferson "Jeff" Richards, known locally as the treasurer of the conspiracy. Richards told a number of people, including his wife, that he thought the rest of the conspirators wanted him to take the rap. He told his confidants that he wasn't about to go down alone.

According to Richards's wife, who was never identified by first name in the transcript or newspapers, Richards told her he was going to cooperate with the investigators. He was "going to tell what he knew," Mrs. Richards said, but he also threatened that, "He wasn't going by himself."[15] When word got out and Richards started getting nervous, he further endangered himself. He told people he knew that his life "wasn't worth a thread" because he was going to be "bumped off."[16] Some might have thought he was exaggerating.

On October 17, 1934, Jeff Richards left his constant working companion, former Prohibition Officer Edgar Beckett, also one who would be indicted as a coconspirator, heading past the Antioch Church of the Brethren on his way to transport a prisoner to jail. Richards and Beckett were together so often people joked about them as the comic strip characters Mutt and Jeff. They did all their work together, but someone wanted Richards alone that time. Five minutes after he left Beckett and drove away in his squad car, Richards was ambushed and shot multiple times with both a shotgun and a .45 caliber handgun. His car was riddled with buckshot and bullets; the windshield looked like someone had used it for target practice. Richards and his prisoner were both found on the ground some yards from the car. Apparently, both had survived to run a short distance before falling in the spray of bullets. The investigating physician, Dr. George Booth, said that both Richards and Mr. Jim Smith, his African American prisoner, died of multiple gunshot wounds from "persons unknown."[17] This suspicious act, just seventeen days prior to Richards's scheduled testimony before the grand jury, got little attention from the county. Bailey, however, was incensed as Richards likely would have been the government's key witness and potentially Carter Lee's undoing. But the wheels of investigation cranked slowly, and the murder was still far from prosecuted even by the time the moonshine conspiracy trial would begin in Roanoke, Virginia, in early 1935. The investigators and prosecutors had suffered a significant setback, but they proceeded with their investigation anyway, summoning hundreds with relevant information to Harrisonburg. Bailey knew this trial could not wait for more witnesses to appear or, for that matter, to die. Richards's case would have to be shelved in order to go after the conspiracy writ large, even though the two were likely intertwined.

The grand jury met twelve days after Richards's murder and continued deliberations through the rest of 1934, concluding with the last witnesses in December and finally issuing its findings at the end of January 1935. The press was kept in the dark until the official release of the indictment on February 7, 1935. In anticipation of its release, however, an Associated Press dispatch from Harrisonburg the previous day predicted that the jury would reveal "an alleged conspiracy in Franklin County." Thousands awaited word. When the document finally went public, newspapers plastered on their front pages details from a written indictment more than twenty-two pages in length that named over eighty persons in all, thirty-four of whom were considered the primary actors. The headlines in Roanoke were nearly three inches high: "Grand Jury Indicts Franklin Officials." The indictment charged that the conspirators not only had engaged in distilling but they also had defrauded the federal government of the United States. Sixty-eight specific overt acts were named in the document, including particular payments made to Charles Carter Lee by specific individuals, including Roosevelt Smith, on specific dates and at specific locations. The investigation was no half-baked job. It seemed airtight. The trial was set for late April.

On April 22, 1935, the lead article on the front page of the *Roanoke Times* reported that as the court opened for the seating of the jury, "the courtroom was packed to the doors when Judge Paul mounted the bench . . . and the halls outside were jammed with spectators unable to get inside." The clerk read out the case: the *United States v. Edgar A. Beckett.* Those mentioned by name included Charles Carter Lee, Robert E. Lee's self-proclaimed grand nephew and Commonwealth Attorney of Franklin County; Edgar Beckett, Jeff Richards's sidekick and former prohibition inspector; Sheriff D. Wilson Hodges; and almost all the county's deputies. Thirty-one other people, along with one business called Ferrum Mercantile Company, were arraigned. Fifty-five more were listed as accessories to the crime.

The courtroom was built for a maximum of two hundred fifty people, though as many as seven hundred tried to cram into the courthouse. Many had to remain in the hallway and outside. In attendance were farmers in their best creased overalls and white shirts, along with storekeepers dressed in suits, most of the spectators from rural parts of Franklin County. Some traveled there on dirt roads in Model A Fords, Buicks, and Studebakers. Others traveled by train. A few still drove horses and wagons out of the Endicott hills to get to the Ferrum train station. This was a huge spectacle, of course, but also many people attended because their livelihoods depended on this trial.

In the audience were what some called the "little people," many of them waiting to be called as witnesses, who had been forced to pay these big shots for the right to make and sell whiskey to make a dollar. There were young men and women whose livelihoods depended on their ability to outdrive the deputies who pursued them trying to shoot out their tires.

As the men took off their hats in the post office on the first floor and climbed the marble stairs or took the elevator up to the second floor federal courtroom, one could tell the farmers by their two-tone faces, the white foreheads where their hats covered and reddish brown on the lower parts where the sun beat down daily. They were the ones who when they stood and grasped the seat back in front of them you could see their brown hands were larger than an office man's and rough enough to twist the corn off a dry cob in a single pass. Many sported mustaches; a few had beards; and most kept their hair short, usually parted straight and greased down flat to their heads. Many of the farmers dressed alike in the uniform of the yeoman: a clean and pressed shirt tucked into bibbed overalls, shined shoes, and a felt hat for dress. Others wore suits and ties. The women were fewer in number at the trial, as was customary with many public events at the time. Even in most churches they remained silent. Many rural women wore clothes they or their relatives made themselves; their dresses, sometimes made from printed flour sacks, hung well below the knee. If they had one, they wore their best store-bought dress to court. These were proud women. Their hands, too, were those of workers who washed and ironed by hand, screwed on jar lids when canning vegetables and meats, carved off ham and bacon in thin slices, yet who rubbed those same hands with lard or lanolin and sewed beautiful patterns of quilts and combed babies' hair. These were people who raised most of what they ate and made 90 percent of what they used. The little cash money many of them made to buy the 10 percent they did not make or raise was the subject of the trial. They would not want to miss it.

It was corn planting time in Shooting Creek and elsewhere in Franklin County when the trial started. Corn was planted around Easter and hoed all summer in plots on the sides of hills so steep, some joked, you had to shoot the seed into the ground from a rifle and tie yourself in the field to keep from falling out to harvest it. Franklin D. Roosevelt's newly minted Soil Conservation Service would discourage nearly every ground breaking in the entire area in the 1930s. Too much soil would be lost from row crops in such terrain. Better to grow trees. Eventually, many would be paid to take their

FIGURE 7. Luther
Shively carrying
a turnip still near
Endicott, Virginia,
circa 1920. Photograph
courtesy of the Blue
Ridge Institute of
Ferrum College.

hillside crops out of production and to replace them with white pines, but
not yet. In 1935, every field was still in use because every family was barely
getting by with what little they could scrape from the soil.

Cornfields left by the displaced Saponi were their mainstay. Where wheat
and barley would not grow productively, these European descendants found
a way to raise a different, more prolific grain. It became their main bread,
with wheat bread reserved for special occasions, and their main source of
grain for alcohol as well. They raised potatoes, sweet as well as Irish. Many
harvested poke salad and wild greens to go with the mustard and turnip
salad they raised. Their livestock—cattle, hogs, and only a few sheep and
goats—grazed in small pastures and in woods, feeding off a mixture of grass
in small pastures, chinquapins, acorns, and tree leaves from the forest. The

meat animals fed on corn and hay only when fattening for slaughter. The milk cows and mules, usually one or two of each per family, fed on a daily ration of grain along with their forage, when it was available, because they needed extra calories. Outbuildings in the Blue Ridge were made of logs and siding from trees harvested off the mountainsides: everything made by hand, everything made to last, every farm building gray as wood grays with the streaks and cracks of time in the open air. These hands that grasped the hand railings and court benches were the hands that chopped down locust and chestnut, hauled the logs to sawmills or pit-sawed it by hand, and drove nails into barn siding. This was after the coming of the chestnut blight, the disease discovered in 1904 that had wiped out nearly every chestnut tree in America by 1940, but much of the majestic timber still stood dead and gray in the forests in the 1930s, and people found even the deadwood the best for building buildings and fences. It was wormy chestnut if after the blight and chestnut clear of wormholes if harvested before the devastating scourge. They had used everything off the land. Rocks for foundations and chimneys so beautifully carved and laid that some still stand intact in the woods without any mortar—just ingenuity and well-manipulated gravity to keep them from falling. And their barns and fences have remained as well. You can find them in overgrown woods. Many log cabins they dovetailed and laid together are still standing, with some of the log work hidden beneath aluminum and painted wood siding today.

Despite their ingenuity, they had too little money to buy adequate shoes for their children in the 1920s and '30s. Most were able to provide only one pair per child each year, if possible, because that kind of purchase took cash, and many didn't have it. This meant the children needed to go barefoot most of the year just to save up the good leather for special days. And snow fell a lot during the winters then. Rags tied on feet and stuffed into men's old boots sufficed for many. Shoes for children are merely one example for explaining how desperate people became as they tried to improve their incomes. These people were not ignorant; they were not doing without because they failed to know about the wider world. They knew what others had, even as close as their own county seat and certainly in Roanoke: health care and education, housing and heat, water and septic tanks, and aid for the elderly. Yet all of these were unavailable for them, impossible to obtain at that time and in that place. Electricity had not made it to Endicott either, especially up the difficult terrain of Runnett Bag and Shooting Creek. The life they made without these amenities that urban Americans, even those moving to textile mill towns, already considered givens, either made a family tough or it killed them.

Those people had a stake in the outcome of the moonshine conspiracy trial, at least as it related to their ability to make money. And they came in droves to witness it. There would be high drama to keep them coming back, though it would be the longest trial in the history of Virginia jurisprudence.

For the next two months, reporters would scribble away as the evidence mounted against the conspirators, particularly Carter Lee. Because of his power and what the assistant attorney general of Virginia called the "considerable political and other pressure . . . brought to the case," the Virginia office had asked the Federal Bureau of Investigation to investigate and vet the jury. The prosecution would call more than one hundred fifty witnesses to build their case; so many, they believed, that no defense, no matter how well-funded or sinister, could discredit them all. Readers who could not attend the trial would be riveted by the regular front-page articles in the morning paper, the *Roanoke Times,* and its evening counterpart, the *Roanoke World News,* with their regular in-depth coverage and photographs. The Roanoke papers would assign their best reporter to the case to be sure they got it right and to prevent libel suits.

Other reporters from outside Roanoke would also cover the trial, including Sherwood Anderson, the famous author of the novel *Winesburg, Ohio.* By then, Anderson had settled into Ripshin, his new home in the mountains of Southwest Virginia a hundred miles from Roanoke, from where he would drive to see for himself what the hubbub was about and to seek an angle on the story of the common man. Out of his explorations would emerge an essay on the trial for the national periodical *Liberty Magazine,* the *Life* magazine of its day. Sitting at the trial scribbling away in his notebook and then afterward interviewing some of the people involved, he would quickly recognize the national significance of the trial in which the federal government would go after the most powerful bosses of this one moonshine county named Franklin and what it would mean for the not-so-powerful ones as well. He would write the following opening to his *Liberty* article: "What is the wettest section in the U.S.A., the place where during prohibition and since, the most illicit liquor has been made? The extreme wet spot, per number of people, isn't in New York or Chicago. By the undisputed evidence given at . . . the United States court at Roanoke, Virginia, the spot that fairly dripped illicit liquor, and kept right on dripping it after prohibition ended, is in the mountain country of southwestern Virginia—in Franklin County, Virginia."[18] Anderson's creativity as a writer would be rekindled by the Franklin County story, not only because this would be a sensational tale of the nation's biggest moonshine-producing place and would therefore draw a wide readership, but also because of a subtler message that would emerge from within it: a message for and about America's working people and their future.

Indeed, at precisely that time as President Roosevelt urged Americans to work their way out of the national tragedy we know as the Great Depression, the nation would begin to understand that it was in the midst of a new era of rapid change. World War I had destroyed the optimism of the new century, and a decade later the Depression had ripped security away from Americans on their own soil. By 1935, even most pious Americans had to admit they couldn't legislate morals through Prohibition, and no matter how temperate they were, they couldn't hold to the past. Most everyone had lost faith in banks and free enterprise's moguls, and their only faith was in a future they had not yet seen. Americans would soon forgo any false security they might have held in their pastoral past, as small farming would quickly give way to industrialization and specialization, and assembly lines and tractors, rather than sledgehammers and pitchforks, would slowly become the new symbols of American productivity. This change was painful and didn't come without ruined people and places left in its wake.

During the Great Depression, many had returned from Main Streets to the farm to seek security, and the farm population actually blipped up around the mid-1930s, but now we know that was a last-ditch stand. What many who returned found living down on the farms was a way of producing their own food and a sense of common good as they avoided starvation; however, with fleeting profits and dwindling opportunities for those without adequate money and good land to expand their operations, millions would soon learn they could not hold on. As the government pushed modernization, farm youths on the smallest of holdings would know there was no future for them in agriculture. Sharecroppers, like John Steinbeck's fictional Joads and Dorothea Lange's migrant mother, had early on hit the road in search of jobs on big farms. Hundreds of thousands of farm owners, young and old, would soon join them in the exodus from their lands and head into manufacturing, though that sector would not begin to give people much security until the next world war. A much smaller percentage of farmers, those left after the great sifting out of growers, would begin to buy mechanized equipment, buy up more land, and be responsible for feeding ever larger numbers of people in the rapidly urbanizing nation.

As this upheaval took place, subsistence farmers still left on their little farms—those who had learned special skills as intricate as reaching into the uterus of a cow to rearrange the legs of a breech-birth calf, how to repair harnesses and make hinges for doors, or how to butcher their own meats and build barns from timber on their own land—would be told they were unskilled in their search for off-farm jobs. Their choices would be to hang on where they could at least manage their own time or sell themselves to an ungrateful industrial world. Some went willingly off the farms. Others remained and instead turned to the ingenuity they had always relied on.

In the midst of this radical national change, we find a rural county whose citizens had tried to survive the best way they knew how—in an industry that had provided their ancestors some spending cash but whose laws had by then driven them into hiding. Through Prohibition and its messy aftermath, moonshiners like those in Franklin County were caught between needing to make money and needing to keep quiet about it. This put them in a predicament of perfect vulnerability into which the unscrupulous could enter and take advantage. And they did.

Though few would recognize the significance then, the trial of the big men in the county provided a picture of the last days of mountain self-reliance and its transition to a particular market economy pushed by government policy. Actually, the county had already entered the age of modern organization of industry through the moonshine conspiracy with its own intricate plan for transport and distribution; it was simply an economy no one could boast about. As the trial would draw out of the witnesses, a tale emerged of how a small group at the top of a moonshine pyramid had created wealth for themselves at the expense of many who were trying to hold onto farms and

FIGURE 8. Early twentieth-century Franklin County farm scene. Hand-hewn rail fences and hand-built structures dotted the small-farm landscape at the time. Photograph courtesy of the Blue Ridge Institute of Ferrum College.

who were willing to work for low wages. The stillers sought, in the absence of any other outside help, survival even if it meant breaking the law. The captains of the new moonshine industry were eager to oblige.

The trial would provide a window into these crises, both individual and collective, that the great transition caused, even in a community located a day's travel from the closest smokestack. In what would turn out to be a series of three interrelated trials, the prosecution would reveal just how entrenched some of the county's powerful men were and how widely their web spread, and thus how difficult it would be to bring certain ones to justice. The transition symbolized by the showdown in the Virginia courtrooms in the months and years to come would not be pretty, but indeed these trials would be worth witnessing. Being there would be like watching the bloody birth of a new age.

2 Wettest Section in the U.S.A.

Involved in the trial at Roanoke were some of the solid men of the big mountain county. There were merchants, automobile salesmen, liquor financiers, sheriffs and deputy sheriffs, a member of the state prohibition force, a federal revenue man—makers and more makers of moon—and the charge on which these men were tried was not that of liquor making, but of a conspiracy to beat the government out of the tax on liquor. Carter Lee, a grandnephew of Robert E. Lee, was up there, facing a possible prison term, and the South was shocked. —SHERWOOD ANDERSON, "City Gangs Enslave Moonshine Mountaineers"

ASSISTANT U.S. ATTORNEY GENERAL Joseph B. Keenan, one of the prosecutors of the conspiracy, knew right away how formidable his Franklin County opponents would be. On April 12, 1935, ten days before the trial was to begin, Keenan wrote a letter to his boss in Washington, DC, calling to his attention how the Wickersham Crime Commission had singled out Franklin County as "the most notorious spot in the country for liquor violations." Then he added that during the latest Treasury Department's investigation of the county, "Considerable political and other pressure has been brought on the case, the Government's witnesses intimidated, and one or two killed." He warned of further trouble, particularly that the jury could fall prey to the same bullying. Before writing the letter, he had telephoned lead prosecuting attorney Frank Tavenner Jr. to ask him what he thought of the situation. Tavenner admitted that he was unfamiliar with the territory and therefore "greatly handicapped" in the selection of the jurors. Knowing this, Keenan asked his home office to seek help from the FBI.

The attorney general's office immediately relayed the request, and just days later FBI Director J. Edgar Hoover rushed a memorandum to Keenan, signing it himself. Hoover promised an "investigation of the jury panel at Roanoke, Virginia." Noting that the trial would begin in four days with a real possibility of jury tampering or worse, Hoover promised to expedite his department's work.[1] But that's as far as the investigation went, as presiding judge John Paul refused to bow to the pressure from Washington and declined to give out

FIGURE 9. Luther Smith (second from left) and fellow deputies pose with guns during the heyday of the moonshine raids in Franklin County. Smith's jurisdiction was near Endicott, Virginia, circa 1920. Author's personal collection.

the names of the potential jurors. Only slowly would the feds realize how decisive Judge Paul's move would prove in the outcome of the trial.

At a few minutes past ten o'clock in the morning on April 22, Judge Paul rapped his gavel and called the court to session. He then asked the forty-five potential jurors sitting in the front rows to go to the jury chambers for group questioning. When they had filed into the room, he read the list of defendants and asked the jurors whether they knew any of them. One man stepped forward and said he owned a farm next to a defendant's father. One from Rocky Mount said he knew nearly every one of the defendants personally. The judge excused those two, along with seven others who told him they'd already formed opinions about the case from what they'd heard or read. From the remaining group, all of whom claimed no prior knowledge of the defendants or the case, the defense struck two and the government one, alternating turns, until they reduced the number to the requisite twelve with two alternates.

There is a photograph from the *Roanoke Times* of all fourteen of the jury members and alternates posed alongside the deputy marshal in charge of their supervision. For the picture, the fifteen men wore suits and ties and most wore fedora hats with wide bands or had removed them for the picture and held them in their hands. All were white. From the court's jury list, we know that none of them were from Franklin County, but all were from adjacent counties: Craig, Montgomery, Botetourt, Patrick, and Roanoke Counties. Of the jurors and the alternates, ten of the fourteen were farmers, with four living in small towns. With all the men in one posed shot made in front of the courthouse, they present the viewer with no clues about themselves. Their faces are blank as they all stare straight ahead at the camera, seven of the men squatting, eight standing, each of the well-dressed men seemingly as earnest as the others.

It would have been impossible for Tavenner and his team of prosecutors to know that the man standing fourth from the right in the back in the photo, the smallest of his row, with his dark hat pulled low over his eyes, was the son of a big bootlegger from nearby Floyd County, a place also drenched in the production of whiskey and liquor trafficking connected to Franklin County. Of course no one could tell from the photo or likely from his face how Mr. L. E. Marshall might react if someone connected to the Franklin County liquor business came to him to ask a favor or what kind of pressure or profit it would take to persuade him to help out a defendant. Maybe the FBI could've dug up that kind of inclination in a man if they had investigated, but Judge Paul prevented that from happening.

The jurors and the alternates—Marshall mixed in the number—listened as the clerk read the list of the indicted thirty-four individual defendants, a corporation, and fifty-five coconspirators. These names had never been read aloud in the same breath in this way before—the county's most powerful men, some of them businessmen, some of them lawmen, some of them listing their occupations as farmers, all in cahoots with one another. Even some schoolchildren in Franklin County knew how the conspiracy worked, but it took an outsider to bring it to light. There was no one local who could have touched them. These liquor bosses had even wrangled Prohibition officials sent to clean things up into their ring, and so the list included not only county but state and federal men as well. They had things sewn up, they had nearly everyone working for them, and no one had any power to bring them down—until now. And in the federal courtroom at the end of April 1935, they sat together, all of them dressed in their best, looking none too cowed, but sitting there dutifully nonetheless.[2]

As the clerk continued down the list of names, from the high sheriff on, just hearing them read aloud would strike fear in some who had been coerced to work for them. Just speaking their names together would mean that hundreds of others connected to them would be immediately implicated, particularly the hundreds who had given them money, many of whom were there sitting in various parts of the high-ceilinged courtroom, waiting to be called as witnesses, thinking about their futures, wondering just how much telling the truth would actually set them free or set them against the power brokers ready to come after them at their first chance. None of the witnesses who had already given their affidavits in Harrisonburg could have felt at ease. This was their county on trial, after all. And they would have to live there when this was over.

The last three named defendants were dead men. Deputy Thomas Jefferson (Jeff) Richards, Deputy Charles Rakes, and former Sheriff J. P. "Pete" Hodges were considered central to the conspiracy against the government, but now all of them were silent; their testimonies, as damning as they might have been, were lost. Rakes had died of pneumonia less than two weeks before Richards and his prisoner were found shot dead. Hodges had died four years before that but had been from day one a ringleader of the conspiracy, and now both his sons, including his eldest, D. Wilson Hodges, the current sheriff, were on the list of the indicted. Richards in particular would have been invaluable to the prosecution's case had he lived. He had been the treasurer, many said, and had kept the records on money coming in and going out. He knew who paid and who got paid and how much each received. Even in his absence his name carried weight, and the indicted would throw his name around regularly in the coming days as proof of both guilt and innocence, but the use of his memory was only weak consolation for the government team. They knew they had lost their best witness and could only hope their huge numbers of subpoenaed liquor buyers, sellers, deputies, and family members would be enough to sway the jury in his stead.

After reading the names, the clerk began to read aloud the twenty-two-page indictment. The document zeroed in on the seven-year period beginning in September 1928 and lasting "continuously thereafter up to and including the date of the indictment." It charged that the defendants conspired to commit offenses against the federal laws in an attempt to "defraud the United States of America of the tax on the spirits distilled by them." The language reminded everyone that this was not a case against distilling per se, but a charge against those who had taken tax money that belonged to the federal government. It meant this conspiracy was an assault on the coffers of the United States—a theft of the people's money.[3]

Yet not everyone in that time and place would have seen it that way. This charge by the feds had come to bear on the same South that had lost the American Civil War only seventy years earlier, a region that had in no wise recovered from that devastation, or from the resentment of war for that matter. At the top of the list of the indicted was the name Lee, whose great-uncle, Robert E., was perhaps remembered most for his dignified surrender at Appomattox, Virginia, and who had remained a symbol of pride for Virginia even in defeat. Dragging the name Lee down again would be wrought with symbolism that some would never countenance. With Lee mixed in the indictment, creating a scene laden with both sore memories and vaulted reputations, more would be at stake than the men on the list. On trial was the very idea of southern mountain pride.

This trial also came at a hardscrabble time. On top of the regional plight in the greater South, there was also particular suffering in the mountain economy. The places in the mountains where tobacco, cotton, and other row crops would not grow well remained the poorest. The Great Depression made the already devastated region even worse. While President Franklin D. Roosevelt had done much to soften southern hearts toward the federal government with programs like the Works Progress Administration and the Civilian Conservation Corps, his government programs had been no panacea for the acute problems in the region. In places like Endicott, people there saw little difference in the poverty before and after the coming of the Depression.

"We didn't have nothing before, so we didn't miss nothing after it came," said Lane Boyd, who grew up there in that time. And even fewer would have said their lives in 1935 were any easier than in 1929. In that tough economic and political climate, moonshine makers were considered affectionately as both rebels and survivors.[4]

The main snag in the widespread view of survival through moonshine was that all the people involved in it were not equal; they were not under siege together as one, no matter whose name was at the head of their army. Rather, the vast majority of moonshiners during the Depression were people who had risked much but gained little from it. In Franklin County, the rank and file in the moonshine business had faithfully made, transported, and sold liquor, but in doing so they had been pulled into a pyramid at whose apex sat the county's most powerful men who had gained at the their expense. Those taking the risks at the bottom had little to show for it. In fact, they had paid out much of it to the ringleaders to avoid arrest. Their labor and risk had gone to enrich the few.

The prosecutors were up against much more than the indicted thirty-four. They would have to take on the challenge of local culture and politics as well. The big questions of the trial would be whether mountain loyalties, southern loyalties—along with simple values that said a man's business is his own and perhaps fear of reprisals when this was over—would keep the witnesses from speaking against those moonshine bosses. Could the federal government build a case, using the testimonies of the little operators against their own big shots, which could persuade mountain jurists that a greater wrong had been done? Those issues were in essence why so many packed the courtroom.

The outcome to these huge questions would lie in the hands of the few chosen to serve on the jury. Those jurors could not help but be aware of the gravitas of the case. The swarm of reporters showed them how many others would be waiting for the outcome of their decisions. It was a sobering responsibility. Yet despite how serious their federal court responsibilities were, the jurors had to think about other pressing matters as well. For as the trial got underway, they started to realize it would not be over soon. They realized they would be giving up much of their spring planting season and perhaps the summer, too. The farmers on the jury were especially worried about their loss of time and income, and Judge Paul knew this. He had already moved

FIGURE 10. The Joel Quinn family at their mountain still site near Endicott, Virginia, circa 1930. The box on the right is called the flakestand. It was filled with running spring water, and the copper worm passed through the water to condense the hot alcohol-laden steam. Photograph courtesy of the Blue Ridge Institute of Ferrum College.

to protect the jurors once from zealous investigators from Washington, and now he was concerned that they were in danger of losing money and time, all in the service of justice. So he let the jurors go home early that day. As he dismissed the court, Paul told the jurors that he had considered sequestering them, but given "the length of time the trial will require and knowing the hardship it will work I am unwilling to impose this condition on you unless necessary." A few got home that evening in time for their chores that day, to feed the animals, milk the cows, maybe even plow a few rows or plant some of their gardens. The problem with letting them go, however, was that now other things could be planted in their minds as well. The wheels that made the conspiracy run set to cranking again that night.

■ ■ ■

In February 1935, Charles Carter Lee, upon hearing about the grand jury hearing and the coming indictment, announced that he was "not going to resign as Commonwealth's attorney but will continue to hold office and be a candidate for re-election in the coming election."[5] He showed no fear or remorse or any sign of guilt. Arrogance is more like it. Regardless, the U.S. government attorneys decided to go after Lee, thinking if they could get him, they'd send a message to the entire region, if not the whole country.

On the second day of the trial, the prosecution gave its opening statement. The lead prosecutor, Sterling Hutcheson, spoke first. "The conspiracy began in the fall of 1928, when Sheriff Hodges and his deputies, along with State Prohibition Officer Beckett, agreed to divide Franklin County into districts," he said. "D. Wilson Hodges succeeded his father in the conspiracy, and Carter Lee directed activities from the Sheriff's office."[6] Lee had overseen it all, Hutcheson said, even back to the beginning when the late Sheriff Hodges had been there. Lee was their prize buck, and the prosecutors had him centered in their sights.

He would be no easy prey, though. Nine defense lawyers hovered in protection around the commonwealth attorney and his cohort. These, after all, were rich men, and they could afford the best and as many lawyers as they needed. Stephen Timberlake from Roanoke was one of them. He gave the opening argument for the defense. "I represent Carter Lee," he said. "He is the grand nephew of Robert E. Lee, being a grandson of the elder brother of the South's immortal leader, and he has a name to uphold which would not permit him to stoop to the things that the government charges."[7] It was a brazen defense, as though birthright would make a man immune from breaking the law, as though ancestry would prevent one from engaging in a pyramid scheme or worse. Then Timberlake, after mentioning the most lauded son of the South, went after Col. Thomas Bailey as a "federal sleuth sent here from Pennsylvania." He might as well have said it was an act of northern aggression against General Lee himself.

Prosecutor Tavenner called Deputy Lewis Bridges as his first witness. Bridges testified that as a former deputy he had been asked to join the conspiracy, along with his fellow deputy Luther Smith. He said that Sheriff Pete Hodges had called the two of them to a meeting and explained how the deputies were going to divide the county between them, charging ten dollars for transporting a load and fifty dollars per month to operate a still. Bridges said that Carter Lee was in the room through the entire meeting, though Lee didn't say much. "[Hodges] told us to go out and advise people to make whiskey and boost business. He told us to raid the stills of those who weren't paying."

"Did you do so?" Tavenner asked.

"I did not," replied Bridges.

"What happened?" Tavenner asked.

Bridges replied that the sheriff asked him, "How many stills you got going? I told him, 'None,' and he said, 'Why not?'"

Tavenner asked Bridges what more the sheriff had to say while Lee was in the room. "He said there was an old still, cap, and worm in the clerk's office, and 'they would leave the door open.' I was to get it out. A man would meet me and give me $50 for the still and the other equipment."[8]

Jeff Richards, the gunned-down deputy, was everywhere as the treasurer and main messenger of the whole ring. When Tavenner called J. R. Underwood and asked whether he had ever engaged in the Franklin County liquor trade, for example, Underwood showed how intertwined Richards had been in a number of his business deals. "Well, I fooled with it a little, never did very much. I haven't fooled with none, I reckon, fifteen year or more until I moved down there [to a farm Jeff Richards sold him]."

"How did you happen to start back at it," Tavenner asked.

"I was told to," was the reply.

"Who told you to?"

"The man I bought the land from."

"Jeff Richards?"

"Yes, sir."

Tavenner pried further: "Now, when the whiskey was sold, what was taken out?" Underwood: "Well, there was a little taken out for the 'granny fee,' is what they called it."

"Who did that go to?"

"I suppose it went to Jeff."[9]

Deputy Jeff Richards was present whenever there was money to be collected, it seemed. Yet as common as his name was in the trial, there was one striking omission in this case. No one was ever asked to connect his death, which had occurred only six months earlier, to the conspiracy trial. As the prosecution called witness after witness who mentioned Richards as the one who was there to take the money, the lawyers left out his brutal murder, as though his getting bumped off was immaterial to the case at hand. The murder had come up numerous times in Bailey's investigation in preparation for the grand jury hearing in February. But with the murder case still pending, no suspects yet arrested, and no proof of its relationship to the conspiracy yet proved, the whole incident was set aside and excluded from the conspiracy trial altogether. Yet the omission, as huge as it was, was only half of the story. Stranger still was the fact that Richards's murder was simultaneously being investigated by none other than the Franklin County commonwealth attorney's office, headed by Carter Lee himself.

With the murder just half a year in the past, no newspaper connected the murder to the conspiracy trial at hand. No official questioned whether there might have been conflict of interest for Lee. Fearing objections, no government prosecutor dared bring it up in the Roanoke courtroom. Nonetheless, there was the fact of the deputy lying in his grave, his murder unsolved, swirling around the courtroom like a ghost. The ghost was there when Carter Lee and the other defendants took the stand and blamed Richards and when witnesses spoke of him collecting fees. The silence about his murder screamed with questions of injustice. Keenan already had connected the murder and moonshine in his request to the FBI for an investigation. Leaving it out entirely made its specter all the more haunting.

Though they were allowed to say nothing about the murder in the trial, the feds had a strategy to connect the two later. First, the prosecutors would paint Carter Lee as the very kingpin of the conspiracy case in general. If they could succeed at getting a guilty sentence against Lee, that conviction would have made him ineligible to investigate the murder in the pending Richards case. And if his guilt could be proved in the big conspiracy, perhaps it could have a domino effect on the murder trial. Instead of the investigating commonwealth attorney, he would become a prime suspect. First things first, they thought.

The prosecution had very good witnesses against Lee as the prime moonshine conspirator. Thomas Cundiff, a codefendant who entered a guilty plea at the trial's beginning, was just one of those who provided damning testimony against the commonwealth attorney. The following took place on May 20, the twenty-first day of the trial. Cundiff, wearing wire-rimmed glasses and dressed in a black suit and tie, stepped into the stand. Tavenner asked him about his relationship to Willard Hodges, another defendant, a store owner with the same last name as the sheriff, and, through him, Carter Lee. Cundiff testified under oath that Hodges told him that, "If I would pay Carter Lee a small amount he could keep the Rocky Mount law off me."

"Did you ever see Mr. Carter Lee," asked Tavenner.

"Yes, sir."

"Tell these gentlemen [of the jury] the circumstances."

"Mr. Hodges went with me up there a few days after that, and he talked with Mr. Lee private."

"Privately?" asked Tavenner.

"Yes, sir," replied Tom Cundiff. "And then they called me in the little back room and Mr. Hodges brought it up, and he says—Mr. Lee kind of held back, wouldn't say nothing—and he said, 'Ain't any danger in Tom, Tom knows all I done told him.' The agreement was I was to pay Carter Lee $10 a month, and he was to keep the Rocky Mount law off me, so I could operate at the time, though I wasn't operating regular."

"Now you say that in this conversation that Mr. Lee, at first, didn't want to open up and talk?"

"Yes, sir; it seemed like he was scared to talk in front of me, and Mr. Hodges told him, says: 'It's all right,' says, 'Tom knows it all anyway.'"

"So then what did Mr. Lee say?"

"He agreed to take $10 a month and keep the Rocky Mount law off of me. I wasn't making liquor regular, I explained that to him, I would go make up a bunch, I had a small trade at the time, and then afterwards I got to making more, of course."[10]

Bolstered by dozens of testimonies just as powerful as Cundiff's, the prosecution built what seemed to be an airtight case for conviction of Lee and the rest. Witness after witness told of working for and paying off the sheriff and his deputies and of Carter Lee's involvement in the scheme, often just out of the picture, lurking in the back room, or meeting people in service station speakeasies on a country road to Roanoke. Examined alone, the evidence all started to fall into place for the feds, and the case against Lee seemed to be mounting to the point of tipping the balance toward conviction. But then there were the defense's strategies, most of which had nothing to do with evidence or alibis.

Old-boy loyalties only worked in one direction in that courtroom. When they benefited Lee and his cronies, defense attorneys were glad to exploit them, but they didn't hesitate to tear down the reputation of their neighbors in Franklin County when it worked in their favor either. From the first cross-examination of Bridges, the defense began systematically trying to make the dozens, then even the 150, who testified against the conspirators into a bunch of disloyal liars and crazies. On the first day, the defense accused former deputy Lewis Bridges of holding a grudge against Lee and of constructing his story merely to get back at him. "Didn't you make the statement that you didn't care a damn what happened to the Lee family?" Timberlake charged. It was as though every witness that came forward was on trial, and in this case the insinuation was that Bridges had forsaken the Lees, the whole Lee family. This was just the beginning.

As the prosecution brought witness after witness to the stand, the defense would attempt to tear them apart. It seemed the only strategy they had. They not only attacked the witnesses with cross-examinations, but they also brought witnesses to testify against the government's witnesses. The *Roanoke Times* headline from May 31 gives a sample of how the whole month went: "Defense Again Attacks Veracity of Witnesses: 27 Take Stand to Declare Many Persons Testifying for Government in Conspiracy Trial Had Bad Reputations."[11] After witnesses recounted how Carter Lee personally took money from them or stood by as the moonshine corruption connections unfolded, the defense attorneys shot back with blistering character assassinations. One easy target was a black janitor named Bud Saunders, who worked in the Franklin County jail. His name was reported in the Roanoke paper only as "Bud." Saunders testified that he saw the conspirators unloading goods in one door and taking them out another before the next morning. But then the defense hit him with accusations about taking a drink from the evidence himself.

Dalton Dillard, defense attorney, asked Saunders, "Didn't you take some of that liquor out of there that was saved for evidence?" Reportage in the *Roanoke Times* worsened things by using stereotypical dialect and spelling that made the witness seem ignorant and a liar. They wrote: "Negro addressed attorney as Mistah Dalt" and continued with the following.

"Who me?"

"Yes, you."

"Naw suh!"

"Didn't you put water in a half-gallon can when you had drunk the liquor and Mr. Lee went into the courtroom with water for evidence?" pressed Mr. Dillard.

"I don't know," replied Bud Saunders, and then he lapsed into silence.

"I think we can safely say he did," broke in Judge Paul with a chuckle. He halted the questioning there, leaving Saunders humiliated.[12] In the Jim Crow South, Mr. Saunders could not have talked back without risking being lynched.

White witnesses received scarcely better treatment. William Christie, a white man from northern Virginia, testified that he had bought liquor from the defendants and that Carter Lee had sold him whiskey himself, but before his cross-examination was through Christie had been accused of running houses of ill repute and of being mentally deranged. Flustered, all he could say was, "No, I don't" and "No, I'm not"; but merely bringing up such a possibility planted seeds of doubt among the jury members, even if an objection by the prosecution was sustained.

As the case wore on, the defense painted the whole group of government witnesses with a single brush of malice, arguing they were "as disreputable a group of witnesses as ever breathed the breath of life." The *Roanoke Times* of June 28 ran the headline "Trio of Lawyers Assail U.S. Witnesses: Claim Case Built upon a Foundation of Hate and Malice."[13] Judge John Paul permitted such behavior in his court, denying objections from the prosecution at every turn. That, of course, was the outcome the defense lawyers sought, and the witnesses succumbed to the withering attacks as Judge Paul looked on.

Despite the hostility, the government's evidence continued to mount against Richards, both sheriffs Hodges, father and son, and Lee, in particular. Witnesses they summoned also told of how Peg Hatcher, Roosevelt Smith, Nick Prillaman, Luther Burnett, and Herman Shively divided the granny fees garnered by the top men. Witness Lee Guilliams told the court how the term *granny fee* came to be: "The old mountain grandmothers who acted as midwives received payment." Later the term was used "when a still was ushered into the world," he explained. With detailed information—names, places, and times associated with the thirty-four, along with evidence that Ferrum Mercantile employees had been selling fourteen-inch copper caps and worms, galvanized cans, and millions of pounds of ingredients for years—the prosecution chipped away at the defendants. Even as the defense lawyers did their best to fend off the testimonies of the witnesses and tear down their character, the government kept bringing more, like waves of reinforcements against an enemy stronghold. Sooner or later, the defense's ammunition of derision would have to run low, they reasoned, and they kept the onslaught coming. And those looking on, particularly the jury, had to start wondering how so many witnesses, over two hundred all told, could all be liars with axes to grind against Lee and his friends, as the defense continued to claim.

■ ■ ■

Sherwood Anderson made two visits to the Roanoke courtroom, one in May and one in June. In the first visit, he zeroed in on Carter Lee right away, noting how "shocked" the South was that Robert E. Lee's very own grandnephew was facing a possible prison term. But Anderson was unimpressed with that pretension. What he really cared about was the exploitation of small-time moonshine producers, as the title of his article for *Liberty* magazine would reveal later that year. The language he would use in the piece is as strong as it gets: "City Gangs Enslave Moonshine Mountaineers."

"City gangs" these local Franklin County leaders were not, however. The idea sounds good on paper, but the largest town in Franklin County was Rocky Mount, and no one would've called that a city. They wouldn't today, either. We have to guess that Anderson was tying the case in Roanoke to the broader sensationalized story of gangsters in big cities, who were known for trafficking in illegal liquor, after all, and whose crimes likely gave business to the local producers. Liquor from the Blue Ridge Mountains surely helped enrich the coffers of many gangsters as it made it to major cities. Also, just the year before, in 1934, feds had killed or captured many famous gangsters—Pretty Boy Floyd, Bonnie and Clyde, John Dillinger, and Baby Face Nelson, to name a few—and the term *gangs* would have rung alarm bells in readers' minds. *Enslaved* was even stronger. The title certainly grabbed attention nationally, even if it didn't ring true in Franklin County.

Sherwood Anderson was no misguided newcomer to the place or the topic of moonshine when he arrived in the Roanoke courtroom. By 1935, he had considered the region his home for a decade. He moved from New Orleans in summer 1925 and traveled with his wife by logging train into Troutdale, Virginia, a high mountain community of farmers and moonshiners. The Andersons stayed first in a guest room owned by a local farm family, from whom Anderson also rented an old log cabin to use as his writer's retreat. His cabin was in a "corn field beyond a hillside apple orchard in a little hollow in the hills. . . . It had not been occupied in years," he wrote. Having grown up in farm country in Ohio, Anderson was excited to write in the middle of a working mountain farm, and the simple conditions were perfect. "The cabin stood in tall corn. It had no windows. For years the dust had blown through the openings where the windows had been and through the open door. It was a foot thick on the floor."[14]

The farm's owner, Mrs. Caroline Greear, sent her boys to do the heavy work of cleaning up the cabin and moving Anderson in. Anderson wrote that "a troop of boys"—there were five to be exact—"came with shovels and brooms. They cleared it out. They built in a rude table at which I could sit. They brought a chair from the house." He would use the cabin for weeks on end and write his novel *Tar* there.[15] To test the sound of his prose, Anderson would often step outside and into the corn and read his words aloud amid the stalks, in private so he thought. That cornfield would be one of his first intimacies with the makings of moon. There would be more.

After spending mornings in the cabin and cornfield, Anderson set out with a rented horse and buggy most afternoons. As he drove the rig through the mountains over the dirt road, he put the reins up on the dashboard and read a book. He let the "old beast" find his way along the road. Even as he tried relaxing, Anderson was self-conscious about how he looked to his neighbors: a grown man reading and passing the time in broad daylight with no particular place to be, no physical work to keep him occupied. "What sort of fellow is this?" he knew they must be asking. He soon found out when one of the Greear boys finally told him what people thought. Anderson recounted: "'They were watching you, quite sure you were a revenuer,' he said. He explained how people came to the Greear house asking. All of this was during the time of prohibition and the business of making moonshine was flourishing."[16] The Greear boys defended him, "He's a writer. He's writing a book." But few believed it. "You didn't look like that to us," one of the neighbor men told Anderson later. They had sent people to find out for themselves. "He told me they sent men through the corn, creeping toward my cabin. It may be that they heard me, spouting in the cornfield. It may have saved me. They perhaps thought I was crazy."[17]

Despite his strange appearance to others in Troutdale, almost immediately Anderson "felt at home" with the area and the people.[18] By 1926, the Andersons had purchased a farm in Troutdale about five miles from the Greear place. He searched "many miles over the country" before finding land owned by a woman whose husband had been killed in the West Virginia coal mines.[19] The widow needed to move away to find a job to support her family, and she finally agreed to sell the farm to Anderson after several meetings with him. He named the farm Ripshin after two different creeks flowing through the property, according to some biographies, or as Mrs. Greear told it, it was because getting there through the brambles ripped your shins.[20]

That farm also had a log cabin complete with windows, fireplace, and a wooden floor. He set up his office there. Wanting a larger home for his wife and their guests, he called on many skilled neighbors to help build a rock house using local fieldstone and oak timbers from a nearby sawmill. The result of their work was a beautiful two-story home situated next to a rushing stream and surrounded by the tallest mountains in Virginia—as idyllic as any setting in the Blue Ridge. When Anderson and his wife Elizabeth moved in, he began to farm a little on the side. The new place gave him a feeling of community he hadn't experienced since he was a boy.

> My house was my house. It is true that I had to go on a lecture tour to pay for having it finished and, when it was finished, I had to close it for two years, being unable to support living in it. But there it was.
>
> It was a place for my books. It was a place to come and to bring my friends. It was, I thought, a beautiful house and in building it I had got into a new relationship with my neighbors. They were John and Will and Pete and Frank to me, and I was Sherwood to them. I was no longer a man apart, a writer, a something strange to them. I was just a man. I had a farm. I planted corn and kept cows. They had found out that I was far from the millionaire they had at first taken me to be and I had found my land.[21]

FIGURE 11. Sherwood Anderson seated at his writing desk in his office at Ripshin in Troutdale, Virginia. Photograph courtesy of the Newberry Library, Chicago. MMS Anderson, Box 108, Fl. 3453.

Yet Anderson also knew he was in a community where most people possessed no cash money at all, let alone for extravagances like his home. They lived in log cabins and simple frame houses; they had no cars and survived by trading labor. His neighbors didn't quite get Anderson's lifestyle. Mountain people knew about travel, of course, as they sometimes had to live in the coalfields or work in the mills in the flatlands. But travel to create or promote his books as Sherwood had to do in order to buy his land was completely new to them. Most continued to think him rich, even as Anderson struggled for cash at times. He knew he would never be from the mountains, and to his credit, he readily admitted those times when he failed to understand life there.

He wrote of one "little old woman neighbor," a widow, who passed by his house on the way to grind her corn at the nearby gristmill. Seeing she was nearly bent double from carrying the corn on her back, he asked her to "come sit with me for a spell." As she rested, he gestured with pride to the half-completed walls where his neighbors were busy laying stone and asked her what she thought of it. "Do you not think it is going to be a beautiful house?" Anderson asked.

> "Yes," she said. Her eyes were looking steadily at me. . . ."I guess we are glad to have you come in here and build your house. . . ." She mentioned the fact that I was giving men work. They earned cash from working for me.
> "But there is something else," she said, "We were all poor together in this neighborhood before you came."
> So I had set up a new standard of life, had changed things, perhaps I was profoundly disturbing a way of life that has its own values. I could not answer the woman. I sat looking at the ground by my own feet. What she had said sent a queer wave of shame down through my body.[22]

He let her go on her way to the mill without giving her a response, just thanking her for stopping. She had revealed American inequality in a couple of sentences and put Sherwood in his place. Scenes like this made him all the more determined to say in writing what he could to make those people real to his readers. He sought a way of telling the "lives of people" in all their intricacies in order to correct some of the misinformation people outside Appalachia were getting about his neighbors, whiskey making and all.

▼ ■ ■

In February 1935, a letter arrived for Anderson marked with the official seal of the United States.[23] It had come from Herbert E. Gaston, the assistant to Henry Morgenthau Jr., the secretary of the treasury. Anderson soon learned that Morgenthau had initiated the contact with Anderson just two days after being notified about the grand jury indictments of the Franklin County conspiracy. Morgenthau sought Anderson because he hoped Anderson would write about the "human side" of the trial, hopefully to offset the hype such spectacles were sure to produce in the print media.[24] It was the middle of the Great Depression after all, and Morgenthau knew that while illegal whiskey was a source of graft and corruption and had to be shut down, it was also a cottage industry that he knew people used to make ends meet on farms. One side of the story would be readily available to a public primed to read sensational stories about gangsters and crime. Morgenthau needed a counterbalance from Anderson and paid Sherwood's expenses to go to the trial in order to get it.

Becoming interested in agriculture while in college, Morgenthau had worked during World War I for the U.S. Farm Administration and was appointed head of the Farm Credit Administration when Franklin D. Roosevelt came to office in 1933.[25] The agency handled most of the New Deal's efforts to aid debt-ridden farmers. Because of huge declines in farm prices following World War I, hundreds of thousands of farmers had succumbed to foreclosure and bankruptcy through the 1920s and '30s. No one in government knew better than Morgenthau how farmers bore the burden of the failed economy. Though Morgenthau lobbied for the secretary of agriculture post so he could do something about the agricultural crisis, Roosevelt appointed him instead to head the Department of the Treasury when the previous treasury secretary retired suddenly. Morgenthau's passion for helping farmers remained, even as he went on to navigate the nation through the Depression and the next war from his Treasury Department post.

As Morgenthau took the oath of office as a new Roosevelt cabinet appointee in 1934, prohibition's last vestiges were fading, even as agents like Col. Thomas Bailey were fanning out into the hinterlands to bring illicit whiskey makers to justice. As Roosevelt shook Morgenthau's hand, congratulating him on his new post, Morgenthau took direct responsibility for the conspiracy Bailey had begun uncovering in Franklin County. Nationally such crackdowns would mean bloody confrontations between G-men and gangsters and the closing of thousands of speakeasies in back alleys in cities through America. But locally in communities like Endicott, Virginia, with Morgenthau at Treasury's helm, the crackdown would also raise farm questions, human stories.

Sherwood Anderson had already met Morgenthau and others in the Roosevelt administration, including Rexford Tugwell of the Resettlement Administration and Henry Wallace, then secretary of agriculture, and had written to his brother Karl that he had "got rather fond" of all of them.[26] He had also expressed his strong support for the New Deal and its leaders in a series of essays. When he received the request, Anderson wrote back to Morgenthau and agreed to take the job, saying that while he lacked the skills to get and tell the facts as quickly as some crackerjack reporters could, "the human side of such a tale I can I believe often dig out."[27]

• • •

By Anderson's second visit to the Roanoke courtroom, his attention gravitated to a female rumrunner named Willie Carter Sharpe. He would write that she was a "rather handsome slender black-haired woman of thirty" often seen driving through the Franklin County seat of Rocky Mount at seventy-five miles per hour leading a caravan of liquor haulers.[28] The *Roanoke Times and Evening News* printed that she admitted to hauling or piloting over 220,000 gallons of whiskey, much of it from the Shooting Creek section of Franklin County, between 1926 and 1931. "She was the 154th witness to take the stand," the Roanoke reporter wrote. She told the court that she gave up her job at a five-and-dime store to wed Floyd Carter, son of John Carter, the bootleg king of Roanoke at that time, and that she had hauled 110 gallons or more every day into the city. Most of her job was piloting the caravans in the front-running but empty car. "I haven't hauled so awful much myself," she said.[29]

Anderson visited Willie Sharpe outside the courtroom, interviewed her about the moonshine-running business, and even met some of her family. He drove through Franklin County to see the lay of the land. He learned that some of the county was a rolling place where bucolic fields and dairies and orchards were interspersed with mixed hardwood forests, but that down in the southwestern corner there was a place where the hills got significantly higher and steeper, the roads worse, and the possibilities for making a living off farming slim, similar to Troutdale both in its beauty and in its lack of money.

The next year Anderson would publish a book loosely based on Sharpe's life, giving her the pseudonym Kit Brandon, also the book's title. *Kit Brandon* was a rich treatment of the story of Willie Carter Sharpe, though Anderson's portrayal of her departed from the real character altogether. The fictional Kit is a moonshine runner driving at the head of furious whiskey convoys, just as her real-life counterpart had been, but her family circumstances and other details vary widely from what Anderson learned in the trial. Never considered one of Anderson's best novels, some reviewers also panned it for its blatant politicizing and lack of narrative flow. In the book, Anderson had much to say regarding the politics of farming and moonshine and veered into a scathing critique of big coal and big timber as well. It tells a human side of the moonshine conspiracy for sure, and it also preaches.

Anderson used the story as a critique of the larger society, making lawlessness and violence in the book societal as much as individual.[30] Structural inequalities had become a theme in his writing. For example, in June 1935, while the trial was in progress, Anderson published a short piece for *Today* magazine entitled "Give Rex Tugwell a Chance." In the article, he argued for stamping on the toes of those destroying small farming communities and called on readers to support Tugwell's land-reform ideals. "We have to begin to think more of America as a whole," he wrote. "There are all sorts of big new things to be found out concerning the land . . . and what is America but the land? Factories, towns and cities go, but the land stays. . . . [Tugwell's plan] is going to be, as I understand it, the big beginning of an attempt to fight back at the land destroyers, big and little. . . . It is going to take patience, perseverance, brains. . . . Little toes and big toes will be stepped on."[31]

Anderson struck similar chords in *Kit Brandon*. Going further than mere defense of the land alone, in *Kit* he launched a sharp assault on extractive industries in the mountains that had impoverished the region's people and forced them to turn to moonshine production. He wrote that the timber industry had cut and hauled away nearly all of the region's virgin trees, the Blue Ridge's greatest treasure: "It is true that modern industry had done something to, if not for, the hill country. The great lumber kings had invaded the country. There had been thievery of great boundaries and ruthless cutting and slashing. An old story, the whole country may some day realize what a tragic story."[32] Throughout the novel, Anderson was able to show his true colors, which he referred to elsewhere as "radical," even "revolutionary."[33] One of his reviewers panned his writing style in *Kit Brandon* as that of an "indignant reformer."[34]

There was nothing like living in a hardscrabble place like the Virginia mountains during the Great Depression, even if as a spectator, to make one indignant. Anderson learned that in part because of his new wife. By 1935, he had divorced and remarried; his new wife, Eleanor, a Virginian and an unapologetic reformer herself, took him to textile labor strikes and to the coalfields to meet coal miners. Anderson saw firsthand how little the people of the Virginia mountains got from their labor at that time and why the hill farmers trying to survive on too little land had to resort to something to add value to their measly crops. In one of his essays that followed, he linked the life of a mountain farmer to his need to make moonshine: "Back in the hills somewhere he owned a little strip of land . . . on which he raised corn. Most of the corn, I fancied, went into whiskey. A man who has fourteen children and but twenty acres of land has to scratch hard to live. I imagined the coming of prohibition and the rise in the price of moon had been a big help to him."[35]

From his life in Troutdale and excursions through the region, Anderson knew the disparity between the mountains and the wider America he had traveled in. He knew that electricity had not yet arrived in any Virginia mountain communities, though the Rural Electrification Administration and Tennessee Valley Authority had come into being elsewhere. He wrote that "life, modern life, with its high-powered swift machines, new comforts, in clothes, houses, food—all of the modern conveniences of life—these [passed them] on by."[36] Though someone in Troutdale had tried to start a factory, he says, "it had failed, impoverishing the little mountain village. The chimney, that has furnished the power for the factory, seemed to leer at you as you went past it on the dirt road that led over the mountains to the prosperous land beyond."[37] He wrote that as the owners departed the damaged region, they said, "Let the land and the people of the land go to hell."[38] So Anderson's Kit Brandon engaged in hauling liquor because she "lived in a country long out of the path of *so-called* American progress, a *country long forgotten.*"[39] Kit had tried working in a textile mill, but with nothing to show for it she began driving fast cars and hauling untaxed liquor.

In writing *Kit Brandon,* Anderson also consciously battled stereotypes about the Appalachians, which by then were rampant. The comic strip characters Li'l Abner and Snuffy Smith, both steeped in images of moonshine, had come into being in 1934, for example. Most of the travelogues and literary writing about the region was little better. With the proliferation of these materials, Anderson believed that misguided tourists were tooling daily through the mountains of Virginia in their cars, already having formed their opinions about the place before seeing it. "Tourists in Fords, Chevrolets, Buicks, Packards went whirling along roads and through the hills . . . [and] the tourist going along in his car looked about. What a desolate country! [They were] mistaken. . . . As always happens, the mind of the man out of another world too much influenced by the reading of newspapers, popular magazines, and novels could not differentiate. The mountain men were thought of, by tourists passing swiftly through the hills, as all of a type. They were dangerous, secretive, sly. They spent their time hunting 'federals' or shooting at each other. It was of course all nonsense."[40]

It *was* all nonsense, but when Anderson found himself in the courtroom during the moonshine conspiracy trial, complete with lead-footed drivers, rum-running in fast cars, and shootings, he knew the story would be fraught with misconceptions before he wrote the first word. He had to address those problems first, but the social problems swallowed some of his prose. His goal was to show Kit Brandon's family as a pragmatic people making choices out of necessity and making and selling homemade liquor to pay their bills, not to fuel their violence or help them get out of work. In some of this writing in *Kit Brandon,* he succeeded, particularly as he made the people around Kit into individuals like those everywhere else: neither all bad nor all good. "They were of every type, incipient poets, honest hard-working men, killers, horse traders, liars, men faithful to friends unto death, stupid ones, smart ones, God-seeking ones."[41]

His description was on the money for the different witnesses he had seen in the trial. Without a doubt, some were honest and hardworking and made whiskey for some cash money for their families. Others were out for profits well beyond a simple living. Some spoke poetically and with passion. Some lied, but many told the truth about their involvement. Some protected their friends by refraining from ratting on them, while others brought a list of coconspirators. Anderson knew the fight there was malicious nonetheless. It was likely when he heard the lawyers go after the witnesses and how the moonshine mountaineers were treated there that Anderson began thinking of using the word *enslave* for his article.

■ ■ ■

After nearly two months of hearing from witnesses, the prosecution gave its closing statement in the last week of June. Prosecutor Frank Tavenner spoke for nearly seven hours in all, calling the case "one of the most important . . . ever presented to any jury in the state of Virginia."[42] "Evidence fits like a glove fits the hand," he said. "You could wipe out the testimony of ten or twelve men and it would not affect your decision in this case." He pleaded for prosecution of all the defendants, saying that "no conspiracy could be proved by more overwhelming evidence than this evidence of the people themselves, and I submit to you that on that issue there can be no doubt in your minds." He said the 61,960 pounds of yeast alone "astound the imagination." If this yeast were used to make bread, he said, "The loaves laid end to end would stretch 1,245 miles, or from here to Omaha, Nebraska." The sugar sold by the conspiracy was enough to supply every inhabitant of the county with two tons. The cans "if flattened out . . . would roof 2900 homes 40 by 40 feet."

Tavenner again named every conspirator and showed how each was guilty, some much more than others. About Carter Lee he said, "He was in a position by reason of the position he occupied as [the] Commonwealth's attorney to know everything there was to be known about conditions." The lawmen, with Lee in the lead, had stolen the very county away from its citizens. He closed his argument by pleading with the jury to "Return that county to its people."[43]

Five lawyers retaliated for the defense. They brought more of the same kind of character assassination they had used throughout the trial. They feigned disbelief that the indictment had been issued in the first place. Lawyer Stephen Timberlake said in his closing argument that, "I have to rub my eyes to make sure I'm not dreaming, when I think of the utter folly, foolishness and futility the government has brought here against Mr. Lee and the others." Then he went to his favorite tactic: the hero-of-the-Confederacy defense. "Charles Carter Lee comes from the distinguished ancestry in America. His grandfather was the eldest brother of Robert E. Lee, the gentlest, noblest figure in American history, who stands with Washington." Then he used Lee's youth as an equally unconvincing reason that he couldn't be guilty of a crime: "Lee was probably the youngest prosecutor that any county or any other political subdivision in the state ever had." Timberlake left out the fact that Lee had succeeded his father in office. Nepotism wasn't mentioned. But Timberlake did imply that youth is why the prosecutors and their witnesses had tried to tear Lee down. "Never in my life have I witnessed a more merciless or heartless prosecution of a man such as the government waged against this boy. . . . Every hostility and hatred against him has been uncovered."

Timberlake's colleague Dalton Dillard added in his lengthy statement that Carter Lee was the "victim of a frame-up" by the witnesses, "every one of whom had something against him."[44] It's true that a substantial number of the government witnesses had been convicted by Lee in earlier cases, but they were now coming to court at the behest of the government prosecutors, not because they faced conviction. Most of them likely wanted to stay clear of the government and only appeared because they had to. But by the time the defense lawyers finished, it was as though the witnesses had engaged in a conspiracy of their own against the defendants. The *Roanoke Times* called the defense's closing arguments a "bitter and scathing assault on government witnesses," reviling them as "convicts, ex-convicts, and inmates of insane asylums."[45] With that harsh closing, the defense attorneys rested their case.

At the end of the trial's second month on June 25, following days of the defense's withering questions to the last of the government's witnesses and their own presentation of counterwitnesses, who spoke mainly of the untrustworthiness of those presented by the defense, and then the lawyers' final statements, the judge finally charged the jury with their responsibilities for deciding the case. Through forty-nine days of trial, the jury had heard from rumrunners and moonshiners who outlined their illicit trade in detail. No one doubted after the longest trial in Virginia history, if they ever had before, that Franklin County was the capital of the moonshine world. But this, of course, was not the goal sought in the indictment. So Judge Paul in his charge to the jury differentiated between the facts of liquor making and the conspiracy as charged. He instructed them that they were not to judge whether millions of gallons of liquor had been produced. That was a given. What they had to do instead was to decide who profited from the sales and how. His statement was twenty-two pages in length. A few highlights follow:

As I have previously stated, you will have little doubt, I presume, that various persons in Franklin County were making liquor in large volume and were disposing of it to and through other persons who were transporting it out of the county. Where, in any case a manufacturer or dealer in liquor sold it to someone out of the county or some one else, the person involved in each of these had agreement between them, but it is not independent or separate agreements of this sort that are the subject of this charge. . . .

The laws of the United States which these defendants are charged with conspiring to violate are those which make it illegal to manufacture whiskey without paying the tax imposed by the United States government, operate a distillery without having given bond to engage in such business, registered with a collector of internal revenue, and several other offenses of a similar nature which are charged in the indictment and all of which are made offenses against the revenue laws.[46]

These laws seem merely fiduciary when stated in this manner, but the people in the courtroom knew Judge Paul was talking about charges over which people had been killed and many more had been injured in a variety of ways. Their meaning would only grow more strident as the lawyers began their final statements.

The jury filed out, their heads filled with facts and fictions, as the judge instructed them to remember it all as best they could. They likely also carried with them trepidation about getting the verdict right and of reprisals either way. As they left and shut the door, the courtroom crowd of hundreds, many of them waving fans in the sweltering late June heat, breathed a sigh of physical relief and then flooded into the hall and down the stairs, some out to the nearest shade to recover and wait for the verdict.

Not everyone could stay. As they had done every day they attended, the farmers in the crowd had to return home to milk their cows and slop their hogs. Corn had to be hoed. Hay needed to be cut. They would spend time in the fields on Saturday as well. Here high drama met with mouths to feed, and the mouths won out. Farms had a way of always calling, especially the livestock. Farmers can never truly leave their animals behind. The trial would have to wait for the farmers in the audience. They would seek the news over the weekend, either by paper or by store or church. Jury members and witnesses, the ones who had stayed dutifully, had to ask relatives and neighbors to do their work. The others, without any federal mandate to stay, made themselves leave and got home in the early morning to prepare for their work the next day following a few hours' sleep. The jury deliberated through the rest of the afternoon and into Friday night, but they would come to no verdict.

The jury worked all day Saturday, too, even past midnight on June 29. Judge Paul kept them the next day as well. There would be no going home until they reached a decision. The jury attended three services at the Calvary Baptist Church on Sunday, June 30: the men's Bible class, the morning worship, and the evening service. Then the jury reported back to the court on Monday and continued. They were forbidden to speak to anyone about the trial, and they slept in a hotel in downtown Roanoke. Something was amiss, and the long deliberations that followed told everyone the jury was deadlocked. Word sent by the jury to the judge confirmed this. Things were not going well. Judge Paul told them to keep at it anyway.

At 4:07 on Monday afternoon, the jury finally emerged to announce they had reached a verdict. The foreman delivered the jury's decision to the judge, and every person in the room leaned forward to listen to his every word as he read the paper. The jury had found most of the individual men and the Ferrum Mercantile Company guilty of conspiracy, he reported. But three of the men were found innocent: Carter Lee and two other two-bit players— Deputy Sheriffs C. Will Wray and H. W. Maxey.

Disbelief racked the courtroom even as the defense congratulated one another on their partial victory; at least their most celebrated defendant had beaten the odds. He was the one they were most concerned about anyway. Visibly elated, Lee rose and made a statement to the court. He said he was "very much gratified at the verdict," adding that the charges "were founded on political prejudice, and anger on the part of criminals whom I prosecuted."[47] Following this, the other defendants were told to remain to hear their charges. Then Judge Paul thanked each juror individually for being members of the best jury he had ever worked with and dismissed them into the throngs who had watched.

Sherwood Anderson, in his reporting based on two trips to Roanoke, wrote simply that Carter Lee "came clear." He had gotten the news from the *Roanoke Times* and then summarized it with the following: "The jury declared he was not guilty. He is the prosecuting attorney of the mountain county and, of all the men indicted, he and two unimportant deputy sheriffs were the only ones who did come clear."[48] Unfortunately, Anderson knew little about how he did so. A little more digging may have revealed an awful truth about why the most powerful one in the room got off while nearly everyone else paid a price. Anderson was not there to see in person Carter Lee stand to make his statement of vindication before the court. He had not been there to apply his righteous reformer's mind to the fact that, while occupation and background have little to do with whether one is guilty or not, that day it had very much to do with who was convicted. Had Anderson stayed around for the end of the conspiracy trial, he would have had a major piece to write about the way the justice system worked in the mountains. But in fact no one in the press seemed to question Lee's innocence or to have any desire to probe further. The *Roanoke Times and World News* said Carter Lee's acquittal was "a relief to many citizens both on account of the name he bears and the office he holds." Maybe they were the ones relieved not to have to write anymore. Anderson clipped the editorial along with the other articles published over the two months of the trial, believing they would make important source materials for his writing, but he would write no more about Lee.

At least one fed was livid, however. Colonel Bailey knew he had been defeated, but he would set to work again almost immediately. He would seek permission from Treasury Secretary Morgenthau to stay and interview the jurors to find out what went wrong. Surely there had been something crooked there. Surely someone had been paid off, just as Assistant Attorney General Keenan had thought. Bailey would request permission to investigate. He wanted to go to visit every juror to find out what went on behind the chamber doors. Curiously, in Prosecutor Hutcheson's report a week later to his boss, the attorney general of Virginia, there was no mention of any problems whatsoever. As far as Hutcheson's report went, the case had been prosecuted well. Though he had no report to write, Keenan could not have agreed. He had seen it all coming and had even got the backing of the FBI to prevent it.

For all that Hutcheson's report of July 22, 1935, left out regarding Lee's acquittal, it did contain some remarkable details regarding the extent of moonshine production in Franklin. In addition to describing the variety of witnesses and their work, from the "moonshiner who converted into whiskey the grain or apples grown by him" to the "manufacturer who began his operations when prices increased due to National Prohibition," he outlined the extent of the production gleaned from records of rail and truck shipments.[49] While admitting his figures were partial at best, with one year's records missing altogether, he listed the sales of sugar hauled to the county by rail between 1929 and 1934 at over thirty-three million pounds, corn meal at over thirteen million pounds, and yeast at thirty-five tons. There were over 115,000 pounds of copper hauled by the N & W trains during those years and 1,250,000 five-gallon metal cans.

Sherwood Anderson used some of the same statistics for the "City Gangs" article. He focused in one section on the fact that the cans used for liquor transport had been engineered so they made no noise in transport: "Some one had invented a five-gallon non-gurgling tin can. That was an idea. Most of the liquor made in this Virginia mountain county had to be run out to some distant city, and one of the pests of the rumrunner is the gurgling sound arising from containers on rough roads. The non-gurgling cans apparently worked. And they sold. Into this one mountain county during a four-year period there were shipped 205 carloads of 516,176 pounds."[50]

It was a fascinating story for anyone to write about, even in a bureaucratic report. It showed how one industry in the Blue Ridge Mountain county of Franklin had reached amazing proportions despite the efforts of the federal government. The latest chapter reported was about how one powerful name there had gone unsullied in the process, even as the other moonshine ring-leaders went off to serve time. They were nothing like a city gang, but the network had been formidable and deadly nonetheless. Now that the trial had ended, there would be no going back to add details to the proceedings. Colonel Bailey would have to start all over again in his quest to bring down the biggest kingpin in Franklin County. The Jeff Richards case was still pending. Much remained to be done.

By the time Bailey could start working anew, Sherwood Anderson would already be back at Ripshin beginning to write his article and then on to *Kit Brandon.* All of the convicted, save the dead ones, would be in the federal penitentiary serving their time, some of them two, some five years. A new slate of officers headed by C. C. Jamison would take over the sheriff's office. And the big man Lee would already be back to running his office of commonwealth attorney and preparing for his reelection. His successes in the trial and the coming election would mean that he would continue with his investigation of the murder of Jeff Richards.

Meanwhile, hundreds of witnesses and spectators from the Franklin County hills and beyond—some of them sorely discredited in public for testifying for the government—had returned home to an eroded farm economy more precarious for them than ever. Indeed, things remained too much the same for the little producers, even as lawyers patted each other on the back and went in search of a drink to celebrate their victory. Mountain moonshiners would lie low for awhile, but how could they quit whiskey making? Maybe they would try to do it on a small scale again, but with trusts and supply chains broken, stresses would increase just getting a batch sold. Their suppliers and their distributors would have to change, and new supplies of copper would have to come in some other way. And who could afford a license to make it legally? Not those living in the middle of the Great Depression. Not after this setback.

Right away some farmers would begin to realize what many more would eventually come to understand: that those old farms their ancestors had found, fought for, and died on just wouldn't cut it anymore. Some had made their last dollar from whiskey, and other alternatives were fleeting. Over the coming years, more than one song would be written and sung about leaving the old home place and missing the old folks at home, written by and about people who packed their belongings to set out in search of a job in a broken land already overrun with too many farm refugees.

3 Appalachian Spring

The people of my adopted section of Virginia . . . came out into this fine sweet western hill country to live, and were joined out here by solid Germans from Pennsylvania. . . . The stock did not like the older colonial Virginians much in an earlier day. They felt themselves neglected, left out in the cold. They still feel that at times. —SHERWOOD ANDERSON, "Virginia"

THE ANCESTORS OF THOSE who packed into the Roanoke courthouse had moved into the western Virginia hill country generations before, seeking farms they could settle on and call their own. Finding mountain farms was a godsend for them, a fulfillment of their search for independence and a way to raise their children with the hope for a better future. Yet as the nation's economy and infrastructure began to develop during the industrial boom of the late 1800s, the people of the mountains were "left out in the cold," as Sherwood Anderson put it. But these were resourceful people, and they figured out ways of surviving despite their neglect, even as their farms paid them less than they needed. One way, of course, was through expanding what they called blockading: mountain whiskey making and bootlegging.

As the conspiracy trial showed, it was not that the Virginia mountains lacked economic activity, but that in the absence of roads, schools, and jobs, people had used their skills to invent an economy from scratch, without outside help. The problem with this strategy was that when the U.S. federal government passed liquor laws making any moonshining illegal, mountain whiskey production had to be put under wraps, and thus it became wide open to corruption. Instead of eradicating it, local government officials ended up in the middle of the corruption. So as demand rose for moonshine, all sanctioned by local government officials, kingpins took advantage of the situation and to enrich themselves at the expense of those producing whiskey for survival. When their whole pyramid threatened to come crashing down with Col. Thomas Bailey's investigation, the people who had done most of the work and made the least from it were destined to suffer most again. In other words, the ones already out in the cold were about to lose their most reliable source of heat.

As headlines emblazoned the papers in 1935 with tales of the conspiracy trial, readers became fascinated with those who made a living by distilling and hauling whiskey. But the newspaper articles stopped short of answering why hundreds, even thousands, of people in one county were involved in this trade to begin with or what history and economics had to do with it. Prevalent stereotypes and myths associated whiskey production with mountain immorality, depravity of mind, backwardness, or even a general mountain disdain for law. Thus, when the trial revealed a major moonshine scheme in Franklin County, many who followed the news jumped to the conclusion that the producers were all criminals. Federal reports accusing 99 percent of the county of being involved only worsened the reputation of mountaineers.

Sherwood Anderson was an exception. His treatment of the mountain whiskey producers, in *Kit Brandon* and elsewhere, linked moonshine with the broad national picture of business and agriculture at the time. He also sought to explore the history of mountain settlement chronologically in order to put to rest some of those wrongheaded notions of mountain inferiority. In an article in *Vanity Fair,* he linked the story of the mountains to immigration and harkened back to the arrival of whites in the Appalachians. He pointed out that those who traveled to the mountains heading down the Shenandoah River from Pennsylvania started out already quite behind eastern Virginia planters who had first received land grants. They traveled by horse and Conestoga wagon "one by one and settling there," without the assurance of land titles recorded in courthouses. He also hinted at a deeper history in Europe when he wrote that a "surprising number" of the settlers were "Scotch-Irish—so called."[1]

He got much of this history right. The settlers of the steepest mountains had trekked down the Great Wagon Road along with Germans in search of unclaimed land on the frontier. Many of them ended up on the steepest land in places like Endicott, where they picked "a place with a bit of creek or river bottom," Anderson said. "Hundreds and even thousands of cold mountain streams flowed down out of the hills. They were alive with trout. The forests were full of game. There was enough grass . . . the nutritious blue grass in the limestone hill . . . to feed a cow, a team of oxen or a horse. Pigs could be marked and turned loose to roam in the forest and in good years they grew fat on the fallen acorns."[2] In places far from the growing eastern seaboard flush with trade with England, immigrants found a foothold in a place where "Life was hard but good, too," especially when compared to what they had come from.[3]

This was true at least for those who held onto their land. But long after they had claimed and worked their land in the mid-1700s and beyond, too many farmers who had established productive homesteads were forced to leave and head west to start over again as those connected to the eastern establishment pushed them out. Anderson called it "the earliest forms of American graft." He wrote, "Even the immortal Washington got in on that racket." Even Daniel Boone "in his old age was gypped out of [his] land by some big land company."[4] The land grabs, which continued until government offices began to impose order on the situation, left small farmers in the mountains cramped with beautiful but woefully inadequate holdings. Anderson lamented that while "Appalachia meant something terribly important to the whole country," its "dream of a new conception of life and the land" had been ripped from the grasp of many who lived there.[5] That pattern of dominance in early Appalachian settlements not only echoed with familiarity during the conspiracy trial but also hearkened back to similar histories in places a world away.

■ ■ ■

Most of the families who owned land in Franklin County's Endicott in 1935 traced their ancestry back to Europe and usually mention Ireland and Scotland somewhere in their past. The Rakes, Shivelys, Trails, Quinns, Cannadays, Hashes, Boyds, Bolings, and Thompsons, for example, all have ancestors from Ireland and Scotland, and they were representative of most other settlers in the community.[6] Some just say they come from somewhere in the British Isles. Many are unsure exactly how but think that they might have Native American ancestry. Others have German and other northern European ancestors mixed in. Such a mixture of traditions and origins is not at all unusual. Americans who have taken DNA tests to trace their ancestry, thinking they'll pinpoint a tribal or ethnic past, are usually confused or annoyed by the great diversity of possible places of origin the tests reveal.[7]

Most of the early European settlers who moved to Endicott, with the exception of one or two families, were dirt poor, as were generations of their descendants. Those with few resources often have difficulty knowing their history, keeping family genealogies, or even obtaining the education to write them in the first place. Naturally, those struggling to stay alive have a hard time keeping their community stories together, particularly in writing. For that reason, whole generations of mountain settlers lived and died with no documents to their name.

Well-known missionary John C. Campbell confirmed this lack of regional written history when he explored North Carolina mountain communities between 1908 and 1912 for the Russell Sage Foundation. He found few definitive memories among his interviewees regarding their European past. He wrote the following, with his wife Olive Dame Campbell editing and publishing his work following his death: "Inquiries of the Highlanders themselves as to family history and racial stock rarely bring a more definite answer than that grandparents or great-grandparents came from North Carolina or Virginia, occasionally from Pennsylvania, and that they 'reckon' their folks were 'English,' 'Scotch,' or 'Irish'—any of which may mean Scotch Irish—or 'Dutch,' which may and usually does mean German."[8] Most Endicott family graveyards have only a few engraved tombstones even from the 1800s, and almost none before that. The few markers left, along with names on deeds, pages from family Bibles, and oral history, are all we have to construct family histories.

Parish and ship records show that from 1717 to 1775 as many as half a million migrants originally hailing from lowland Scotland left there for northern Ireland. In turn, many of those traveled from there to the Blue Ridge and beyond and made up the majority of the early European settlers there. Some call them Scots-Irish. Others call them Ulster Irish or Ulster Presbyterians or combine the migrants from Ulster with Scots, the Welsh, and other northern British and refer to the group as borderers.[9] This latter term fits because the immigrants did come from the edges of several countries and the margins of their economies.[10] The term *borderers* also allows for grouping peoples of diverse geographies and ethnicities, even those with ancient language differences, within a collective history of migration.[11] While borderers didn't all leave from the same places or times, many of them hailed from a variety of places in the British Isles that shared similar histories of displacement and migration. As they made their way across oceans, down the Blue Ridge, and mixed together in Endicott, they intermarried and built a close-knit community that lasted for generations.

As Anderson wrote, the Blue Ridge is a beautiful region filled with resources, and thousands of immigrants were elated to call it home. It took incredible energy and spirit to get there, and it took many skills to survive there. Most had farm experience along with one or more cottage skills, from milling to blacksmithing to coopering to cabinetry, when they arrived. Whiskey making was but one of their skills of self-reliance. And they were resourceful and inventive enough to survive the trip to the Blue Ridge and make it with the labor of their own hands. They began building settlements after clearing land for farming. Endicott is a good example of such a place.

By the turn of the twentieth century, there was a strong community in Endicott and several families had opened stores there. Three grist mills used water power from the creeks. Numerous cottage industries, from a casket maker to a wheelwright, had sprung up as well. But, there was still very little cash flow. Thus, by the Great Depression, every one of the families in Endicott, save two, also made money from whiskey, either from selling the ingredients to make it, providing the equipment to manufacture or haul it, or bootlegging or driving it to its destinations. Most did so because of the pressures of having to live on too little land as the local population increased and income dwindled per farm. Making whiskey was the only reliable way to make money to allow one to stay in one place at least a while longer.

Timber and coal in the greater Appalachian area had made some rich in the preceding decades, but not those who worked the forests or the mines. Their farms were not paying, either. Most farmers had already subdivided their family's original holdings into smaller parcels and divvied this up to their children. Even those with some good land had watched the agricultural markets dwindle away during the 1920s and '30s. The pressure to emigrate to look for jobs outside the Blue Ridge and in some other sector of the economy was mounting. Some Franklin County families sent members to work in the coalfields a hundred or more miles away. Others had relatives working in textile mills as far away as Delaware or, eventually, as close as Danville, Virginia, as the mills moved south. Yet in the 1930s there were too few jobs

FIGURE 12. Virgin timber in Franklin County was cut and sold to manufacturers in the Northeast and Europe. Here sawyers pose in front of John Wade's sawmill near Ferrum, Virginia. Photograph courtesy of the Blue Ridge Institute of Ferrum College.

to go around, particularly when the national unemployment rate ran over 25 percent. The lucky ones who found employment off the farm needed their families to keep hold of their land to supplement their meager earnings from their work. They returned to help whenever possible, some to harvest or even to build simple houses with the earnings they brought with them, some just to visit the old folks left behind, or some to gather homegrown food before heading back to work.

Whiskey production helped with many of these situations. When people had some moonshine to sell, having family members in mill and mining towns could help market whiskey where they worked. Whiskey funded many trips back home. And it put food on many tables when they got there.

■ ■ ■

The Depression wasn't the first time the families who settled Endicott had moved to find work and food. Similar searches began centuries before, when their ancestors were already part of a "world in motion" long before their descendants set sail for the New World.[12] By the time of recorded history, Celts had moved from what is now Ireland, Romans and Gaels had moved through Britain, and their crossings and intermingling with others had linked mainland Europe with the place later called Scotland.[13] Mainland and island peoples—the Frisians, Angles, Saxons, Danes, Norwegians, Normans, and Flemings—traveling in sailing and rowing vessels intermingled with one another there.[14] It's impossible to say how far each of those different peoples had traveled prior to that. Trade, wars, hunger, hunting, adventure, and other factors pushed and pulled at people looking for pilferage or simply for new beginnings. The result of all that movement and intermingling is that no single ethnic description could possibly encompass the Scottish, Irish, English, or any other group for that matter.[15] When writers in the early twentieth century, from explorer Horace Kephart to Presidents Teddy Roosevelt and Woodrow Wilson, represented those who came from Ulster as a distinct Scots-Irish "race," they were simply misguided by anthropological theories of their time.[16] It *is* true that lowland Scotland generated a major human flow toward America via Ireland, and they encompassed a majority of the early settlers in places like Endicott, but the push had almost nothing to do with a distinct race or ethnicity and everything to do with land and resources. Their story of migration began centuries before they arrived in America.

Heightened land scarcity in northern Britain began in the late Middle Ages when powerful feudal lords tightened fiefdoms around the peasants there. The lords enclosed lands, demanded high rents, and claimed the people as well as livestock within their borders as their property.[17] Through brutal wars, conquerings, and religious conversions of kings and queens, that network of fiefdoms became Scotland, and the line dividing that country from England came into being. But its boundaries were far from stable. The Scottish peasants were forced to divide and reunite within these shifting political and religious boundaries numerous times. Except for a privileged few, the people remained landless, subservient, and poor. They were forced to pay any income they earned to landowners, church, and Crown. They developed a common hatred for the Crown of England as it lorded over them in political and religious ways without providing protection or services in return.[18] Landlords and the Church of England were no better.

They called the form of Scottish tenancy forced up upon them by the land-owners rack-renting, evoking the medieval torture device to describe the excessive charges for land payments and interest. Rack-renting squeezed out land squatters and sold land to the highest bidder, forcing tenants to compete with one another, the lowliest with the wealthy absentee landlord. Even for the families long established in one place, the lords inched up the rent each year, milking tenants for everything they had, even making them borrow against future crops. Like sharecroppers in the American South two centuries later, they remained in debt from one season to the next, always unable to own anything.

Having no money to invest in homes or land, the rack-renters were forced to live in makeshift shelters. Their farming methods changed little over the centuries because farmers had no resources to upgrade. As population increased and farmers couldn't rotate their crops because of having too little land, productivity dwindled. By the 1500s, the Lowlands were nearly treeless as the population grew and farmers cleared the last of the forested acreage, either for their own plots or at the behest of the landowners. Often landowners ordered the peasants to harvest the timber and then sold it off, leaving only the brush to the tenants to burn for fuel. The soil, with little replenished fertility, gave back less with each passing year.[19] As soil fertility declined, the renters raised sheep and wool, barley, and oats, but at only subsistence levels. Many survived on oaten cakes supplemented with a few wild greens and homemade ale.[20]

Somehow through all of this, people continued to think beyond their misery toward a better life.[21] One reason for this perhaps was that by the 1550s thousands of Lowlanders had begun converting to the Calvinist or Presbyterian faith. Their new beliefs encouraged what Max Weber termed "this-worldly asceticism," a belief that frugality could improve their lives in this world and please God in the process. Their dreams of controlling their lives in these small ways fueled their will to look for other futures as well.

Partly for their own levity and partly for income production, the Scots developed ways of distilling malted barley over smoldering peat, a drink that eventually became widely known as Scotch. Mixing religion and liquor was never a problem for the Catholics, and in the early stages of Protestant history in the British Isles Calvinists continued to imbibe, too. Though John

Calvin encouraged moderation in drinking in Geneva by placing Bibles in taverns, he refrained from preaching that believers should abstain from drink altogether.[22] So whiskey consumption was one common practice Protestants and Catholics could both agree on, and they embraced it heartily.

■ ■ ■

In 1601, King James I (also known as James VI in Scotland), the only son of Mary, Queen of Scots, announced his Irish Plantation scheme. His plan was to resettle Scottish landowners and their tenants in Ulster. It was a good way to encourage Protestantism—which he had been influenced by after his mother's death—in what he deemed an overly independent, Catholic, and wild island. That the lands were already inhabited and farmed didn't seem to hinder him. James confiscated lands belonging to the Celtic chieftains of Ulster—the lords of Tyrone and Tyrconnel—and offered the territory in the north to English and Scottish planters.[23] His goal was to "plant" English and Scottish farmers in the northernmost Irish province—only twenty-one miles across the Irish Sea from Scotland—and to displace the rebellious Catholics with people not only loyal to Protestantism but also beholden to him.

No foreign king since the time of Scotland's Robert the Bruce in the early 1300s had been able to subdue Ireland and impose national law there, so James's strategy had to be drastic.[24] His goal was to impose order through Protestant religion and organized agriculture, and to use violence if necessary. Writing to Sir Arthur Chichester, both the architect of the Plantation of Ulster and the founder of Belfast, King James said that the plantation would "establish the true religion of Christ among men . . . almost lost in superstition."[25] Ultimately, his goal was to quell political rebellion. He told one advisor he wanted the settlers to be "God's bulldogs . . . to bite the wild Irish" into submission.[26]

Willing planters from Scotland and England, called undertakers, had to agree to place on each thousand acres they received to settle at least twenty-four Protestants households from at least ten different families.[27] Three-quarters of the settlers became tenants or sharecroppers, but the promising news for the renters was the new leases were to last decades, not the yearly rack-rents they had known.[28] The Lowland Scots began packing their few belongings.

James I granted land to twelve London companies as well as to 205 individual English landowners. The remainder of Ulster he set aside for individual Scots who would, in turn, seek settlers from their homeland.[29] Hearing exaggerated promises of ample land, low rents, and bumper harvests, thousands of Scots readily left their "racks" to make the journey, some of them risking their lives in uncovered boats to cross the narrow but rough and frigid Irish Sea.[30] Over the following decades, 200,000 migrated.[31] As their king had planned, the Calvinist Scots left for Ireland with their faith intact.[32] He did not plan, however, for the pervasive sense of this-worldly justice they would cultivate in the process, a trait that would eventually send them packing again.

In the beginning, the Scots became the most aggressive farmers in the province. They believed they could improve their lives through labor.[33] Yet soon they realized that no matter how hard they worked at increasing Ulster's population and productivity, they remained landless and indebted. With the rich still holding the deeds to property, most grew dissatisfied and restless. With increasing pressure on the land and even the good leases starting to fade, the settlers lost faith in the plan.

On top of that, religious tensions, even among the Protestants, began to mount. Anglican landlords found their Calvinist tenants' beliefs in equality made them "troublesome, defiant, and likely to be involved in agrarian dissent."[34] After the Crown established the so-called Episcopalian Church of Ireland, it passed new penal laws known as the Test Act of 1704 to control the Presbyterians. The laws prohibited the construction of non-Anglican churches, annulled marriages performed in kirks, and even forbade military or public office for anyone outside the established church. Being Calvinist turned into a serious economic as well as political liability.[35]

These predicaments worsened when the land ran out. Farmers had cleared the forests and drained wetlands as they had done in Scotland, yet again there was quickly too little land to go around in Ireland as well. As births and new immigrants increased the population, demand for land further increased and rent competition intensified. Again, rack-rents appeared, quintupling payments on some plantations in just twenty years.[36] The Irish Catholics refused to leave and continued to compete with the new immigrants. When the king imposed fines and doubled the rent in an attempt to clear up the problem, some of the Irish managed to pay up.[37] They were not about to go away quietly.[38]

When land pressures were at a boiling point, economic and natural disasters took their toll as well. In 1717 and 1718, the linen industry, which had been Ireland's mainstay, began to fail economically. This was followed by three bad crop years between 1725 and 1729. Then in 1740 and 1741, famine struck Ireland and more than 400,000 died—a whole century before the infamous Irish Potato Famine. Things only worsened with a second multiyear drought between 1771 and 1775.[39]

Those disasters came just as shifts in agricultural and trade policies killed farm profits in Ireland. England, seeing growing competition from Ireland in wool and other livestock products, passed the Woollens Acts in 1715, which proclaimed that Irish farmers could export no other animal product except wool and that even the wool could be sold only to England.[40] England then restricted trade of Irish grain products. Linen, which had already experienced huge setbacks, became Ireland's only export crop. With legal trade options down to only one product, more and more cottage weavers were forced to compete with one another for work.[41]

▪ ▪ ▪

With strong Irish and Scots traditions of whiskey making already in place and a strong demand to go with it, Ulster renters turned to homemade whiskey to help pay their bills. The story is one that would be repeated again and again both there and across the Atlantic. It goes like this: With the price of farm products too low to provide an income, with markets in decline, and with grains in relative abundance, people turned to making illicit distilled liquor to increase their farms' profitability and, likely, the farmers' emotional ability to weather the economic storms. They took a tradition and made it into a cottage business.

When in 1661 the Irish parliament placed an excise tax on legal liquor sales, creating what became nicknamed "parliament whiskey," a whole new world of sales opened up for the boys in the bogs. They called untaxed whiskey poteen (pronounced "pot-cheen," meaning "little pot").[42] With every downtick of the economy or turn of the legal screw, the sale of poteen increased. According to Irish economist K. H. Connell, "Many a tenant paid his rent only because he, or his neighbour, made poteen."[43] Any criticism of the poteen maker, he wrote, would be better focused on "the folly of excise legislation that was unenforceable as well as unpopular."[44]

Whiskey distillation in Ireland predated the time of the plantation by perhaps a millennium. According to legend, St. Patrick himself brought a simple still to Ireland. Monks likely did introduce whiskey to Ireland as early as the sixth century. And it caught on quickly, making the words *Irish* and *whiskey* quite comfortable in the same phrase. Even the word *whiskey* is said to have originated in Ireland, and the current spelling is an Anglicization of the first word of the ancient Gaelic term *uisce beatha,* which translates as "water of life."[45] After the introduction of the simple distilling technology, thousands of home distillers began to experiment, and later a number of licensed distilleries started up as well. In Ulster, for example, the Bushmills distillery, whose product is sometimes termed "Protestant whiskey," started operating in 1608 and has continued since that time to produce whiskey in the same location in County Antrim in Ulster.

Poteen became a mainstay not only because of profit, but also because people thought it tasted better than the taxed drink.[46] They also liked the mystique surrounding homemade liquor. Small distilleries provided convenient and cheap gathering places for neighbors after their farm work hours.[47] When the police began patrolling, poteen makers began brewing by the light of the moon, so nighttime gatherings, maybe with a fiddle or a penny whistle to make the wait lighthearted, were common. *Moonshine* became a common nickname during that time.

As the conditions worsened from natural and man-made causes, even with poteen sales most tenants were unable to get ahead and, in the end, few had any desire to remain on the dwindling holdings their ancestors had worked so hard to get. When high rents, drought, and famine started killing their weakest neighbors and draining everyone's resources, even brisk linen or poteen trades weren't enough to sustain them.[48] Under these dire circumstances came the call of a land where rent would be unnecessary, where the climate was sunnier, where virgin lands awaited clearing and planting, and the knowledge that one could pay his or her ship's passage by labor alone.

◆ ◆ ◆

Propaganda about passages to America began circulating in Ulster as early as the 1710s.[49] With receptivity in Ulster higher than most places, agents for shipping companies fanned out to markets and fairs in the region to post public advertisements and bark that in "America they can get good land for little or no rent."[50] Importing human labor was a lucrative business, and the more takers the more profit. As more ships began making the transatlantic voyage, Ulster tenant farmers jumped at the chance to join the exodus, even those with no resources at all.[51]

Tens of thousands of Protestants, in contrast to their Catholic neighbors in Ulster, decided to leave immediately. Protestants were more likely to go because, as in England, Protestantism was the established faith in the colonies and settlers there harbored strong prejudice against Catholics. Early in colonial history, William Penn, the Quaker from Pennsylvania, had recruited heavily in Protestant areas, and the pattern had continued since. The Protestant focus on internal piety more than on local shrines and pilgrimage sites likely made it easier for Protestants to leave their churches behind and establish churches on new soil.[52] Plus, the Calvinists of Ulster had already been transplanted to new soil once. And the huge numbers of their fellow church members and kin began talking of going together, which likely added extra incentive.

Contrary to common belief, however, the Protestants' migration from Ulster at that time was not primarily a flight from religious persecution, but a move of economics. A search for land and a new start financially were the primary motivations. Even when a Presbyterian minister at Ardstraw in County Tyrone wrote to ask his presbytery permission to leave for America, he said only that he lacked the "necessary support" from his job. He tallied that the congregation owed him over eighty pounds, but he said nothing in the letter about America being a freer place to practice his faith.[53]

In the period from 1717 to 1775, hundreds of thousands left their homes and made their way to the docks of Belfast, Londonderry, and other port cities, ready to leave for America when the opportunity arose. Many put themselves into voluntary servitude in order to escape, selling themselves into a class just above slavery.[54] The times were desperate and the promise of change exaggeratedly huge; that combination has set emigrants afoot throughout the ages and still does.

Only one out of ten could pay his or her way to America.[55] In order to board a ship, those migrants without adequate money for passage had to agree to offer themselves and their families as servants to ships' captains and others who would, in turn, market their labor upon arrival. Some of the migrants were sold at auctions on the American docks. Many were offered for sale as skilled craftsmen. But thousands of laborers were sold as farmworkers. Most of the laborers were already indebted to landlords back home, and they reasoned that there would never be a way to afford their freedom otherwise; a few more years of bondage to others in order to gain land and a new start were worth the sacrifice.

Many died before they made it to land. Three ships filled with Ulster hopefuls went down. Untold thousands, forced to lie in close quarters in unsanitary conditions for weeks, succumbed to any number of diseases and were buried at sea. Even if they made it, some never escaped the poverty they found themselves in upon arrival in America. Leaving for America was a huge gamble. Getting there was no guarantee of success.

The process was dehumanizing. The sight of people being auctioned horrified many contemporaries. An army officer just arriving in Philadelphia, by far the most frequented port of entry for the Ulster emigrants, wrote to his father in Ireland of watching indentured servants being sold. "They sell the servants here as they do their horses, and advertise them as they do their oatmeal and beef. . . . Such of the unhappy natives of that part of Ireland, as cannot find employment at home, sell themselves to the masters of vessels, or persons coming from America to deal in that species of merchandise."[56]

Though treated as chattel, many of the indentured steeled themselves to their years of work that followed and remained unbroken by the experience. As with enslaved peoples from Africa, many new Ulster immigrants maintained their resolve, even if in private, and continued to dream of freedom. Of course, the difference between the indentured and the enslaved was the former needed to overcome only economic obstacles in order to leave. Unlike the Africans held in bondage, no laws in America made the indentured stay in servitude once their debts of time and work were paid.

Many of the immigrants were skilled workers and carried trades with them.[57] Often new arrivals were unmarried, and having fewer family obligations, they were ready to launch into their new lives at the height of their ability to handle hardships physically and emotionally. If they happened to own a little personal property before leaving Europe, they were able put that to use immediately and start building toward independence quickly. But even the best-off immigrants usually needed to work for someone else first, if just to earn money for tools and a horse before leaving in search of land. The cost of the Atlantic passage was as much as nine pounds. Those who intended to farm in America needed at least ten additional pounds for rent, tools, seeds, and transportation. Most arrived with nowhere near that much cash.

In addition to the indentured servants who were sold for a length of time, usually seven years, another class of borrowers known as redemptioners could purchase their freedom at any time by redeeming the cost of their loan. Their obligation would end anytime payoff occurred. In contrast to the indentured servants, who were beholden to their bosses for the term of their indenture, some redemptioners borrowed from wealthier cotravelers on the same voyage and paid the loan quickly. Some counted on relatives who had already arrived to buy their freedom upon their arrival.[58] No matter how they arrived, or what means they worked off their debt, the desire to own property in America was nearly universal among these travelers.[59]

■ ■ ■

The majority of the Ulsterites arrived in Philadelphia because their ships' captains preferred to trade there. The usual pattern for these immigrants was to work off their indebtedness in the city for at least awhile.[60] For that reason, between 1740 and 1774 the Philadelphia population increased more than six-and-a-half-fold. This caused rents and the prices of goods to rise rapidly while depressing wages, so new immigrants sought ways to leave the city as fast as possible. Having come from plantations already, most Ulsterites looked for work in the rural life they knew and ultimately for land of their own in the countryside. As soon as they were free to do so, many moved to where kin or church created communities or simply where the available transportation routes led them; in the beginning this was mostly toward western Pennsylvania.[61]

As increasing numbers of landless settlers moved west, their competition with one another for land, along with speculators who bought land merely to resell it, continued to drive prices higher and settlers farther west. Farmers sometimes had to move three to four times to find land they could afford. Speculators advertised for new settlers in distant places and offered bargains on property in the hinterlands.[62] Some targeted their enticements to Ulsterites in particular.

The Ulster immigrants, already thought to be stalwart Protestant defenders of Ulster's territory in Ireland, began to develop a reputation as the bravest settlers on the frontier in America. Colonial leaders promoted their reputation and deliberately encouraged these new immigrants—the borderers—to push the American boundaries. Ulster Protestants, after all, had been used to tame an Irish land with wild natives and had waged a famous victory against the invading Catholics on the northern coast of Ireland.[63] They could be used that way again, as James Logan, the provincial secretary of Pennsylvania in 1720, surmised. He wrote, "it might be prudent to plant a settlement of such men as those who formerly had so bravely defended Londonderry and Inniskillen."[64] Virginia Senator Jim Webb's 2004 book *Born Fighting* shows the reputation of the Ulsterites as fighters continues to today. In his book, Webb celebrates their readiness to defend their territory and wrote that the Ulster Calvinists "took the land no one else wanted." Then he admitted that perhaps others *had* wanted the land, which, he said, makes their settlement "difficult . . . to sell in today's politically correct environment, since in many eyes they took it from the Indians."[65]

Even as the Ulster settlers took land from those who had lived there for millennia, and the English governors justified it based on the superiority of whites, there was another kind of prejudice at work. It showed up in land settlement patterns as well as in language, such as the term English Americans called the Irish American settlers: lubbers. The term had been used in Europe and among seafarers, usually as an insult about someone clumsy and rude. *Lubbers* was probably first used in writing to describe the Ulsterites by William Byrd in the early 1700s. He used the term to refer to those living outside boundaries not only geographically but also culturally. The word was the "redneck" or "hillbilly" of the day. It came into existence as rumors circulated about backcountry people forming communities with Native Americans and even escaped slaves. Sometimes the Irish Protestants were considered simply "curiosities," though often the English considered them simply "savages," even as they were encouraged to drive off the Indians.[66]

To some they were hard-fighting heroes with guns helping stretch America farther westward, and to others they were a wild, violent, and even subhuman group of savages not a whole lot better than the ones they drove off.

The origin of prejudice against the people heading into the American backcountry predates even William Byrd. In the early 1700s, the first Ulsterite settlers had gone to New England, where they thought their fellow Calvinist Puritans might accept them. But, as historian James Leyburn wrote, "The Puritans liked neither Scots nor Irish." They disparaged them for "illiteracy, dirtiness, slovenliness, and their notable divergence from Puritan customs, habits, and outlook."[67] Pennsylvania Episcopalian clergyman William Beckett, writing in 1728, was perhaps the first to pen the term *Scotch-Irish*. He used it in a letter to a Boston colleague as a means to differentiate the Ulsterites from English whites. "The first settlers of this county were for the greatest part originally English, but of late years great numbers of Irish (who usually call themselves Scotch-Irish) have transplanted themselves and their families from the north of Ireland into the Province of Pennsylvania."[68] In a letter written in 1730, even James Logan admitted to Thomas Penn his growing dislike of the newcomers. Though from Scotland himself, Logan argued that while "they are of the Scotch-Irish (so called here) of whom J. Steel tells me you seem'd to have a pretty good opinion but it is more than I can have tho' their countryman."[69]

Few among the newcomer community had adequate money to buy land close to English settlements anyway. Rather, as most Ulster immigrants began their lives as servants or redemptioners in America and none had received free land grants, they started out behind in American society. Their lack of resources made them unseemly to the English gentry who held property given them by the Crown, attended schools maintained by the colonial government, and dressed in the styles of their day.

Both poverty and prejudice contributed to the push of the Irish Calvinists westward toward the southern Pennsylvania border with Maryland and beyond. While some of the Ulsterites earned government military permits by fighting in the French and Indian War, giving the right to claim land, these permits allowed them only the right to settle on unclaimed land.[70] Even the veterans were forced to move beyond English borders.

As the settlers reached the Allegheny Mountains in Pennsylvania and

Maryland and settled along the natural barrier toward the west, the next wave turned and headed south. Some began to rent from speculators who had claimed huge tracts in the hinterlands early on. Others without military permits or the ability to pay for land became squatters. Their search for land carried them down the Wagon Road, once a Native American trading path, but by then a road originating at Market Street in Philadelphia and heading toward present-day Gettysburg and on toward Carolina. Leaving Pennsylvania, and putting up with ever worsening road conditions, they forged on into the Shenandoah Valley of Virginia, often traveling alongside Germans who had also found no welcome among the English.

Even as the Ulsterites moved into the backcountry of Virginia and beyond, they failed to escape prejudice. Edmund Burke's "Account of the European Settlements in America," written in 1757, shows how the aristocracy of Virginia shunned the newcomers. Using the term *Scotch-Irish,* Burke treats this entire population as lazy and unable to farm as well as their German neighbors.[71] He wrote, "The number of white people in Virginia is growing every day more numerous by the migration of the Irish who, not succeeding so well in Pennsylvania as the more frugal and industrious Germans, sell their lands in that province to the latter, and take up new ground in the remote counties in Virginia, Maryland, and South Carolina. They are Presbyterians from the northern part of Ireland, who in America are generally called Scotch-Irish."[72]

How did these disparaging attitudes, which often turned into verbal or even physical abuse, affect the Ulster Scots? What did it mean for them to always be on "the fringe?"[73] Some believe they turned their anger toward those lower in society, especially the Indians and blacks.[74] Perhaps it created a disdain for authorities who disparaged them. Maybe disdain for them made them better fighters, as Teddy Roosevelt believed. Maybe none of this is true. But certainly others' beliefs about their being different did help push the Ulster Protestants toward those who resembled them in dress, speech, and income. People tend to group together with those whom they don't have to apologize to or fight.

For decades, writers such as James Leyburn have argued that the Scots-Irish were in fact good citizens and that their reputation among the elite for being disorderly or savage was just a myth made up by a prejudiced English-based society. Leyburn, among others, showed the Ulsterites were strong supporters of orderly government and that upon their arrival to America already knew and respected standards of morality and property with what he calls the "same laxity and rigidity as any society." Being already willing to head to Ulster as tenants and to remain stalwart Calvinists in the process, they came to America not to escape authority but for the promise of economic freedom and inclusion in society.[75] That Leyburn still felt the need to argue this in 1962, however, shows just how persistent bias against the Scots-Irish had proved to be.

As with the Palatinate Germans—who despite their ingenuity were also victims of prejudice in the early colonies—discrimination against the Ulster Scots along with poverty made them not only keep their distance but also rely on one another for everything from birthing to burying.[76] Some began using the term *Scots-Irish* as a means to self-identify their community, in part because it sounded closer to English than the term *Irish* alone. Grouping themselves under a single banner also became a way of strengthening their community against prejudice. The term also differentiated them from the Catholic Irish, who were then considered nonwhite.[77] Becoming a distinct group, even if the identity was an amalgam of borderers and migration histories, allowed them to stick together for protection emotionally as well as physically. Many other immigrant groups past and present have taken similar measures. In addition to a common name, one way people stick together is to cling to their traditions. The Ulster Scots had Calvinism, music, whiskey distillation, and much more.

■ ■ ■

Whiskey making, while rare in southern England, was highly developed in both Scotland and Ireland by the time of the Ulster emigration. We can credit the Ulster immigrants for helping introduce the tradition to America. Through their influence, whiskey making became commonplace everywhere in the new colony, particularly on the frontier. Frenchman Marquis de Chastelleaux observed that it was the only drink served in the American backcountry.[78] In the Pennsylvania backwoods of the 1700s, everyone made and drank whiskey, no matter their standing in the community.

The newcomers built both farm-based distilleries and larger-scale commercial operations in the cities, and they had a ready market for their products.

From the Philadelphia elite on down to the redemptioners who worked for them, nearly all the easterners downed alcohol with meals, though those who could afford it also purchased imported rum and wine. Men, women, and often even children drank whiskey at various times of day, and the beverage enlivened nearly every kind of gathering, from church meetings and elections to dances and prize fights.[79] With this kind of consumption pattern among the English, they had little room to ridicule people of the western mountains as habitual drunks. But they did so, even though their words rang with hypocrisy.

In fact, it was whiskey's popularity among the English that gave the back-border farmers impetus to produce more than they could consume and haul it back East to sell. Whiskey became the first frontier cash crop and the main source of income when the supplies of animal furs dwindled as woods gave way to farm fields. Whiskey made small loads on a single packhorse profit-able, whereas grain alone or most any other farm product could barely pay for the trip. On the western Pennsylvania and Virginia frontiers, whiskey sold for twenty-five cents a gallon. In the more populous areas, a gallon of rye could bring as much as a dollar. No entrepreneur would bother to transport sacks of grain by horse and wagon across mountains when it could be reduced in volume through distillation and bring in more money in the process.[80]

As people moved into the backcountry, it was common to see settlers with copper worms and small still pots slung under their Conestoga wagons or on their packhorses. Some took with them only the knowledge of how to build a rig. Coppersmiths soon set up shop in the mountains and built and sold stills to their neighbors to supplement their farm earnings. Those who had made poteen in Ireland needed only equipment and grain to get started. Those who had no prior knowledge worked with neighbors and learned by doing.[81] Soon nearly every community had stills and nearly all the farm families had some way of making or procuring whiskey. Eventually distillation spread to other areas of the colonies.

On plantations throughout the colonies, a still house was a common outbuilding in which barrels of whiskey were distilled and aged. By inde-pendence, small distilleries were everywhere. Even three of the first five U.S. presidents—George Washington, James Madison, and James Monroe—owned distilleries. Jefferson, who favored wine and beer, was the only one to frown on hard liquor. John Adams had no distillery on his farm, but he wrote that he drank hard cider made on his place nearly every day of his life. For presidents and nearly all their fellow citizens, distilled whiskey became the indispensable and ubiquitous American drink. Even with other regions joining in the business of distilling, frontier whiskey continued to hold a good reputation in cities back East for both its taste and its price. Good water was another reason, as were the local ingredients they used to make it. The farther south the farmstead, the more likely it would have shifted from producing oats, barley, sheep, and cattle, common in the British Isles, to wheat, pigs, and corn.[82] Corn became far and away the primary grain of the Appalachians as well as the main ingredient for the liquor produced there. The corn varieties—called Indian corn by most—developed by the first peoples were perfect for the climate and rich in taste and carbohydrates, which made for higher alcohol content per bushel and a sweeter product. As settlements shifted from hunting and trapping to sedentary farming, all the ingredients for stilling this new crop were present in one place. Making liquor where the corn was raised added freshness to the flavor as well.

On the frontier as well as back in the settlements, few had any moral problems with whiskey consumption. In fact, hospitality and courtesy of the day required offering liquor. Failing to serve it would have created a serious breach of etiquette. Custom was to furnish whiskey in liberal quantities at all community gatherings, particularly workings such as house-raisings and corn-shuckings, as well as to laborers at harvest time, haying, and fruit gathering. Whiskey also was one of the few medicines available. People used it for rheumatism, malaria, snakebite, and a variety of communicable diseases from colds to gonorrhea.[83] Whiskey was good for helping work, sickness, pain, as well as for making festivities more joyous. Many a song paid tribute to its transformative power. To most it was considered a God-given right.

▪ ▪ ▪

In 1794, when Alexander Hamilton and other leaders proposed raising internal revenue for the struggling American government by taxing whiskey, the plan met with open revolt. Farmers who had fought against the British, specifically against taxation without representation, wanted nothing to do with the tax. The Whiskey Rebellion of 1794 ensued. The uprising was best organized in Monongahela County in southwestern Pennsylvania, where Protestants from northern Ireland had settled. The protesters made counterresolutions, staged tax protests, and intimidated, even beat, revenue collectors. Tarring and feathering the revenuers was common. When the rebellion spread into northwestern Virginia and the rest of the mountain region, it became what historian John Alexander Williams called "one of the few expressions of 'perfect unanimity' in the mountain region's entire political history."[84] Though President Washington sent troops to Pennsylvania and quelled the uprising before it managed to get out of hand, the insurrection caused the government to drastically redraw its tax policy. While a whiskey tax remained on the books until the 1840s, the feds stopped collecting it for decades to come. Congress could find no one desperate enough to take on the job.[85]

Resistance to the whiskey tax politicized and united many local communities in ways that no other issue had before. Even as Secretary of the Treasury Alexander Hamilton was oblivious to whiskey's centrality, the whiskey rebels

FIGURE 13. Still site hidden in a rhododendron thicket in the Vesta area of Patrick County, Virginia, 1912, approximately 15 miles from Endicott. Photograph courtesy of the Blue Ridge Institute and Museum of Ferrum College, Patrick County Bicentennial Collection, Patrick County Historical Society.

showed Americans that citizens had to be involved in their own governance. Whiskey had linked farmers politically, and through protests they made it clear that whiskey was their only source of cash and their way out of debt. Taxing that main means of escape from dire poverty made people fight as if their lives depended on it. Indeed, they proved Hamilton's assertion to Congress that a whiskey tax was a luxury tax had been simply wrong. Instead, the whiskey tax had pushed people with no money too far.[86] Had the whiskey rebels got something back from their taxes, say access via roads to greater markets or maybe economic help, they may have seen the benefit of paying them and behaved differently when the collectors came calling. But no government services were forthcoming on the frontier. As Sherwood Anderson pointed out in *Kit Brandon,* these whiskey rebels had to wonder, "What was all this business about taxes? What has government done for us that we should pay taxes?"[87]

■ ■ ■

Well before the Whiskey Rebellion began, the search for land pushed the settlers along the Great Wagon Road beyond the Shenandoah and on toward present-day Roanoke, then called Big Lick for the salt deposits there. At Big Lick, many took the Carolina Road as it turned southward, passing through what is today Franklin County.[88] The first European settlers reached the Blue Ridge by this route as early as the 1740s, some of them paying for their new opportunity with their lives, as Indians retaliated against them for encroaching on territory they had long hunted and planted. But the borderers weren't the first Europeans to arrive there; speculators had already claimed much of Virginia by then.

The first Europeans to enter the mountains were enticed there by Virginia Governor Alexander Spotswood in 1716. That year, the governor himself led a group of wealthy men into Shenandoah Valley and the Blue Ridge, where he set up camps and plied the participants with food and drink. While at camp, he gave each participant a gilded horseshoe and welcomed each into a new elitist society he coined Knights of the Golden Horseshoe.[89] Fearing French encroachment from the north, the English colonial government was eager to get settlers into the rich lands of the Shenandoah in particular, and their goal was to find recruiters to entice them.

The Golden Horseshoe speculators bought very little land with cash, but they claimed much anyway. They took advantage of a 1730 law that granted each a thousand acres for every family from outside Virginia who settled west of the Blue Ridge. Through this law, many obtained vast grants of ten thousand to one hundred thousand or more acres."[90] Seemingly overnight, they joined Lord Fairfax, who held over five million acres, as the landed elite of Virginia. Absentee owners held titles to a great portion of land by the time settlers arrived. But they needed settlers to solidify their gains and help push out the native inhabitants, and the landless Scots and Germans answered their call.

Teddy Roosevelt contrasted the early Scots-Irish settlers heading into the Virginia mountains with those who settled Jamestown in 1607, referring to them as people "from their great breeding ground and nursery in western Pennsylvania."[91] He extolled their perseverance and hard work on the frontier, writing that:

> "Every acre . . . had to be cleared by the axe and held with the rifle. Not only was the chopping down of the forest the first preliminary to cultivation, but it was the surest means of subduing the Indians, to whom the unending stretches of choked woodland were an impenetrable cover behind which to move unseen. . . . The axe and rifle were the national weapons of the American backwoodsman. . . . Salt and iron could not be produced in the backwoods. In order to get them each family collected during the year all the furs possible, these being valuable and yet easily carried on pack-horses, the sole means of transport."[92]

To Roosevelt, they seemed quintessentially American: Neither cowardly nor ready to seek a truce, they fought to victory or death. "They were relentless, . . . revengeful, suspicious, knowing neither ruth nor pity; they were also upright, resolute, and fearless, loyal to their friends, and devoted to their country."[93]

These frontier settlers were never separated commercially from the East, however. They traded furs for necessities at outposts, and nearly from the beginning, traveling merchants took their wares into the mountain frontier and exchanged them for the goods found on the perimeter.[94] They used animal hides as the primary means of exchange in the beginning, as the term *buck* tells us. Yet as the settlements spread to the west and farmers cleared land and built homesteads, whiskey became the most common currency for trade and barter. Maybe they should've nicknamed the dollar a "dram," a small drink of liquor.

Though the settlers coming down the Great Wagon Road from Pennsylvania increased the production of Virginia whiskey, they were far from the first to distill corn in the colony. The first record of corn distilling in America is actually from the 1620s along the James River in Virginia. There Capt. George Thorpe, a Cambridge University scholar and missionary among the Indians, first experimented with whiskey production using the indigenous American grain.[95] He wrote to his cousin in England that "Wee have found a waie to make soe good drink of Indian corne I have divers times refused to drinke good strong English beare and chose to drinke that."[96] Though the English weren't known for it, Thorpe had somehow learned the craft of distilling before setting out on his mission. As we have seen, other colonial English, including the famous Virginia founding fathers, later followed suit.

While the first settlers, including some who arrived in Endicott bearing their stills with them, may have helped perfect the American whiskey trade, they were no anomaly in the new country. In fact, had they been teetotalers they would have stood out as strange. The main difference between Blue Ridge settlers' livelihoods and those of the larger plantation owners to their east was their need to rely so much on the product for their survival. The Blue Ridge settlers' location far away from larger towns and major trade routes had afforded many settlers the ability to buy their land or to become squatters to begin with.

Yet their location was rarely helpful in any way except for affordability. While it afforded privacy perhaps, living in remote places made making a living their greatest challenge. Though the Blue Ridge Mountains' isolation from roads and commerce would one day provide struggling mountain farmers an advantage in producing whiskey secretly, being out of the way in the first settlements made farming for cash sales harder, and thus their location kept many in the whiskey business even as other agricultural regions diversified to other products, particularly tobacco. The Blue Ridge had always been a good place to produce whiskey, but to make a whiskey dollar, one had to transport the product long distances.

Blue Ridge settlers from the beginning hauled the liquor away and brought home the goods the whiskey money bought on their return. They often cut their own trails. You can picture them with Sherwood Anderson: "a little caravan of mountaineers [traveling] over stony winding mountain roads, half trails." These early settlers were going in two directions, to and from their homes. "The men carried axes to cut underbrush away. Up and down mountains they went, a team of oxen pulling a covered wagon, a few dozen jugs or kegs in the wagon." They had let the corn whiskey mature before hauling it. They "didn't hurry it." This was their lifeline to the larger economy. "A man and his family wanted sugar, salt, tobacco, snuff. The women and children had to have clothes."[97]

As soon as the settlers arrived in what is now called Endicott and cleared their land in the 1700s, as soon as they got the corn growing on the hills, they were already thinking about making their way back East to trade. Back to where people would soon know their mountain liquor was as good as they could get anywhere, made with the best water, carefully by hand, and delivered and vouched for by the very people who made it.

4 Elder Goode

Primitive Baptists paid no preachers. Their preachers, like the members of the congregation, were farmers. —SHERWOOD ANDERSON, "I Build a House"

REELING FROM THE ACQUITTAL of Commonwealth Attorney Carter Lee, Col. Thomas Bailey, now working with coinvestigator C. S. Roth, received permission from the Treasury Department to continue his investigation. He headed into Salem and the rural counties surrounding Roanoke to talk with the jurors who had sat through the long weeks of the case and the closed-door deliberations. He met first with the jury foreman, E. H. Carlton, on Carlton's farm in neighboring Montgomery County. The head juror was quick to speak his mind. Like Bailey, he, too, had been deeply disturbed by what he had seen and heard at the conspiracy trial and was willing to say so in writing.

Carlton provided Bailey a sworn affidavit claiming that one of the jurors, Edgar T. Marshall, the son of a Maryland bootlegger himself, had not only resisted any reasoning in the jury room but refused anything less than the acquittal of Lee and the two others. According to Carlton, there was strong reason to believe Marshall had been bribed by a certain Mr. John Moore, of Moore's Milling Company in Salem, Virginia, and perhaps several other parties, to hold out for Lee's acquittal and to hang the jury if he had to. Carlton added, "I do not want the impression left that I was unwilling to convict the head of the conspiracy—Carter Lee. I made the statement to the jury that I thought Lee the guiltiest one of the bunch and the other jurors said the same thing." He closed his statement, written with Bailey's help, by recommending the government "make a thorough investigation of the cause of juror Marshall's attitude, as I feel it resulted in a miscarriage of justice, and I have been subjected to much criticism by my friends on account of the jury's failure to convict Carter Lee."[1] Ten other affidavits from the remaining jurors corroborated this statement by their foreman. Eleven men had voted to prosecute Lee and the others, and they agreed there had been a breach of justice and said so in writing. Bailey got others to sign papers as well, including some original conspirators who said they colluded with Carter Lee.

Knowing he had a good case, Bailey sent these statements to United States Attorney Sterling Hutcheson for his review. Though Prosecutor Hutcheson's first report on the trial had failed to mention any sign of jury tampering, Bailey and Roth's formidable collection of affidavits, both from the jurors and even those convicted in the first trial, were too much to ignore. Hutcheson agreed to take the case again to the grand jury in Harrisonburg. Bailey's persistence had paid off—at least in part.

On March 9, 1936, Hutcheson presented the papers to the grand jury and laid out the details of Bailey and Roth's findings. Lee's involvement was the centerpiece of the docket. Several of those convicted in the conspiracy swore statements that Lee had been involved in their dealings. He not only had run the conspiracy, they said, but had bought off the corrupt juror, too. Peg Hatcher said in his affidavit that Herman Shively told him that "Lee put up $1000 to help fix the jury in the Franklin County case." Charles Guilliams's signed statement said, "I heard Carter Lee say, in fact he said to me, that he had spent more than $8000 on the trial of the Franklin County case."[2] Others pointed in the same direction; Lee's name was all over this case. It looked to Bailey as if he had his man this time.

FIGURE 14. Primitive Baptist Elder James Goode Lane Hash (1881–1959), third from left, holding a Bible, was a farmer and civic leader in the Endicott, Virginia, community. Photograph courtesy of the Ora Hash family collection.

The grand jury heard the case formally on March 31, 1936, and concluded there was just cause for a trial. With additional evidence from dozens of other witnesses, the grand jury indicted twenty-four men, several of whom, including Roosevelt Smith, Edgar Beckett, Charlie Guilliams, and Claude Shively, had been on the original list of conspirators in the first trial. One of the three acquitted from the first trial—C. Will Wray—ended up on the new list of suspects. Yet, much to Bailey's disappointment, along with that of all those who supplied Bailey their detailed affidavits, the name Carter Lee was nowhere to be found on the list of the indicted. According to Frank Tavenner, a lead prosecutor, there was insufficient evidence to sustain such a conviction. Apparently the grand jury agreed.

Though Lee's name and image had been splashed all over the papers during the long conspiracy trial the year before and eyewitnesses who said they'd seen and heard Lee discuss fixing the case, his name was never mentioned in the reporting on the new trial. The press again seemed somehow reluctant to drag Lee's sacrosanct name through the mud. He would never face the courts again as a defendant.

There was no question that there had been jury tampering. There were reams of papers and willing witnesses ready to prove that the moonshine conspirators "unlawfully, willfully, knowingly" conspired with others "to influence the verdict of the said petit jurors" in the first trial in order "to return a verdict adverse to the said United States of America," as the court documents put it. Twenty of the twenty-three indicted pleaded guilty or nolo contendere right away. One distraught defendant, Claude Slusher, committed suicide. But three defendants pleaded innocent, leading to their trial by jury in federal court, with the twenty others leaving their fates to the mercy of the judge who would pronounce his decision on their case at the end of the jury trial. The three to be tried were Amos Rakes, Edgar Marshall of the Marshall Milling Company, and David Nicholson. The Honorable John Paul was called on to preside again in the same federal courtroom as before.

As the six days of trial ensued in the Roanoke court starting on May 18, 1936, the same clear details emerged about further moonshine dealings and payoffs. The commonwealth attorney still seemed to be at the middle of everything, though now he was out of the fray. Lee was in the room, having been called as a witness against Amos Rakes and others, but he sat there a free man witnessing a trial that had his name written all over it. With Lee ready to testify against them, those fighting to prove their innocence didn't stand a chance.

Lee wielded magnetism over the court when he spoke, and no one in the justice system seemed to want to question his word. Having him sit there was enough to send shivers up the backs of witnesses. Most had said, at least in writing, that they had worked for the man, and bosses have a way of brandishing power without saying much. Many had seen him take money or heard him talk about paying it out to buy a juror. But this time Lee wasn't a defendant fighting for his own innocence. He was there to testify against others instead. How much more influence could he wield over the lives of those in the courtroom now that he was exonerated? Lee was a force for the prosecution now, and they used him to convict some of the very ones who had claimed Lee was involved. He had won, and Bailey had lost, before the trial began.

Attorney T. X. Parsons was Amos Rakes's lawyer from Roanoke. He had represented some of the conspirators in the first trial ten months earlier. But now Parsons, along with the attorneys for the other two defendants, was forced to prove his client's innocence not only against a justice system eager to prosecute him, but also against a formidable government foe eager to clean up his own reputation and to distance himself from the conspiracy once and for all. By the time the government called Lee to testify, Parsons already knew that getting Rakes off was next to impossible.

According to his own testimony at least, Lee had shown up at just the right times to know others were guilty but never got too close to be sullied with a crime. He was squeaky clean even as he found himself surrounded by those engaged in illegal activities. At least that's the way he told it. Yes, Lee had been to Rakes's house just as he had spent time with so many other bootleggers and in places liquor and stills were stored, but he testified that he didn't actually talk with Rakes. Never mind that in his testimony Rakes referred to Lee by his given name, Carter, with all the familiarity of a business partner. Lee claimed he had always told anyone discussing jury bribing to shut their mouths, that he would not be in the presence of anyone discussing such crimes. Lee was as clean as a whistle, at least according to him. He spoke with the confidence of a man with little to worry about. He wasn't on trial this time.

Defendant Amos Rakes was from Shooting Creek, just up the hill from Endicott, across the Patrick County line. Amos and his brother Caleb, usually
called Caley, built and moved into one of the largest houses in Endicott, a
two-story, whitewashed home with porches across the length of both stories. Scrollwork adorned the railings and posts. Their mother lived with
them in the house until she died. Amos was married and had children. His
brother remained a bachelor but lived with the married couple, often sharing
meals with the family. The two brothers, born in poverty, had worked mules
together on their parents' farm but as young men, calling themselves the
Dukex (pronounced Duke's) Mixture, had become bootleggers, along with
starting other businesses. From these businesses they built a sizable nest egg.
They invested their earnings in their farm and home and started a logging
business. They remained good members of their community, helping two
different churches financially.

FIGURE 15. Amos and Caleb (Caley) Rakes (far left and third from left) pictured with
two friends in the group they called Dukex Mixture. Photograph taken in front of the
Rakes home in Endicott, Virginia. Photograph courtesy of Sylvia Bowling.

Though he had not been indicted in the conspiracy trial of 1935, Rakes admitted before the court in the second trial that he was a large producer of moonshine in that community and had ties much beyond. He readily told the examiners that he sold whiskey to a variety of men mentioned. The prosecution zeroed in on that. They argued that this farmer, logger, and merchant, with sales of sugar, malt, and yeast along with direct whiskey sales outside the county, had good reason to keep the conspiracy going for his own gain. They showed that indeed he had recently put seven thousand dollars in his wife's name in the bank. They contended Rakes had much to gain by helping the defendants in the first trial, out of self-interest if nothing else. But there was little direct evidence of this. How he might have been influenced by other conspirators, including the one found innocent, Carter Lee, and whether it was he or others who most forcefully tried to pay off one or more of the jurors, we will likely never know. But even if Rakes did happen to be one of the guiltiest, as the court did find, we can be sure he did not work alone.

■ ■ ■

At least four different character witnesses for Rakes were summoned to the trial and swore that Rakes was not the type to bribe a juror. One was Frank Mays, the sheriff of Patrick County, just inside the border of which the Rakes farm sat. The counsel for the government, in cross-examination, asked Mays, "Where do you live?" Mays replied, "Stuart, Virginia."

"How far is that from where Rakes lives?"

"About twenty-five miles."

"You know, don't you, that Amos Rakes is a big liquor dealer?"

"I have heard that."

"Was Amos Rakes ever arrested in Patrick County?"

"Not insofar as I know."

"Did he pay for protection?"

"Not to my knowledge," replied the sheriff. "Somebody's business had been worked on by my deputies and federal agents. We cut many stills along the Franklin County border [where Shooting Creek runs]. My deputies and I destroyed a still said to have been owned by a man; a little later he was made a deputy." [Laughter]

"How long did you say you'd been sheriff?"

"I'm in my twentieth year."

The sheriff, likely inadvertently, showed just how pervasive the corruption was. Lawmen ran stills, and distillers became lawmen. How was Amos Rakes to be singled out in such a world?

N. B. Hutcherson, former mayor of Rocky Mount, Virginia, also testified that both Rakes and D. A. Nicholson were citizens in good standing. The *Roanoke Times* and *World News* made note of two additional character witnesses for Rakes, both quite unlikely types of people at the trial. Both were residents of Endicott, and both were religious leaders, pillars of their community.

One was James Goode Hash, a Primitive Baptist minister, the pastor of the Long Branch church that had been established there in 1824. As a pastor, a married man, and a father of eleven, he knew the community of Endicott perhaps best among all who lived there. No one was better known. The Long Branch Primitive Baptists moved each weekend to one of four locations, rounding back to their home church once a month, with each member attending the others' churches whenever possible. One Saturday and Sunday, they met at Long Branch. The next Sunday, they moved just across the Patrick County line to Charity Primitive Baptist, then to County Line on the border of Floyd and Franklin Counties, and so on. Elder Hash moved with the congregation to the different locations, staying with families along the way. He never learned to drive a car and either rode his horse and buggy or caught a ride with one of his congregation wherever he went. In these ways, he became a familiar face in territory much beyond a day's horse ride.

Hash knew the community first as a mail carrier. With his horse and buggy moving at a horse's pace through Endicott, Hash was often the source of news as he carried the mail one house to another. He told of sickness, deaths, fires, and, if he knew, of arrests and the outcomes of trials. After his ordination, Hash ministered to the sick and dying and planned with families how and when, for example, he might return to read the Bible to an old man on his deathbed. Several times, he married some young people waiting for him at their mailboxes. In Roanoke in May 1936, this man of the church, a church that preached against dancing, fiddling, and drunkenness, put his reputation on the line for a known bootlegger.

FIGURE 16. County Line Primitive Baptist Church, one of four churches where Goode Hash served as elder, located near the headwaters of Runnett Bag Creek in Endicott, Virginia. Photograph 2005 by Charles D. Thompson Jr.

Another character witness mentioned by name in the newspaper was Miss Ora Harrison, a missionary of the Episcopal Church stationed in Endicott. She had grown up in Rocky Mount, some twenty-five miles from Endicott yet a world away in terms of income and privilege. A voice had spoken to her as a teenager as she gazed off toward the Blue Ridge. In response to that calling, she had pledged even before finishing high school that she wanted to go to those mountains to teach. Barely twenty in 1911, she had taken the train as far as Ferrum and then rode a mule led by a young boy whose last name was Rakes up into the deepest hollows of the county. Despite experiencing hardships, she had never imagined when she set out that she would live there the rest of her working life. But she stayed, and though committing a few errors after she got there, she had persevered in the community, making the place and its people her life mission, struggling with them through the Great Depression on a few donated dollars sent from the North to keep her dream alive. When she and her fellow missionaries, all of them women, decided to build a rock mission, members of the community pulled together. Children picked up rocks and threw them into wagons, then all these fieldstones were collected and laid by the community's stonemasons. An old farmhouse was purchased and moved onto the grounds. Men with their mules rolled the house along on logs and placed it on its new site.

Helping on this community work crew was Amos Rakes, an expert logger. He became a regular visitor to and supporter of the mission. He and other neighbors played Rook cards with Miss Ora some nights. Once he fought off some drunks he thought wanted to do her harm. As far as she was concerned—and she was far from naive regarding whiskey making—Rakes was a stalwart community member. Miss Ora, a lifelong church worker and teacher who had sternly shepherded many in the community into teaching careers, was also willing to put her reputation on the line for Rakes. Clearly, she knew more about Amos's story than whiskey and corruption. In the end, however, these testimonies were not enough to free Rakes.

▪ ▪ ▪

After taking the stand in Roanoke's federal court in May 1936 and testifying on behalf of his friend Amos Rakes, Elder Goode Hash took off his dress hat, threw his cane up onto the floorboard, and folded his lanky and stiff frame into the family's truck and headed back to his Endicott farm with his twenty-year-old son, Amos Hash, at the wheel. He relied on others to drive him anywhere he needed to go outside the community. Inside Endicott, he still drove a horse and cart, long after motorized vehicles began to show up.

When he was just starting out as a farmer, he had supplemented his farm income by delivering the mail using a two-wheeled jumper. After his horse memorized the daily mail route, Elder Goode took the time between houses to read his Bible. He read and wrote letters daily and, as his children recall, always seemed to be studying. Many relied on him to help them fill out papers and make sense of the letters they received. Traveling at a horse's pace through the community, he took time to speak to neighbors, help them decipher their mail, and spread any news he learned from them from farm to farm as he went. At times he gave thanks for the glorious weather. Other days he suffered the elements as he negotiated the ruts and mud through rain and snow, soaking wet, cold, and miserable as the winds blew through every clothing layer and blanket he could carry. Elder Goode worked for the postal service from 1910 until 1929, and he used his salary to pay for a small piece of land down the Ferrum road, several miles from Endicott. He later traded his land for his parents' farm and moved there with his wife, Nannie. It was the same farm his grandparents had owned.

The mail route gave Goode many opportunities to minister to the sick and stop to help others. If someone was ill and alone, he alerted neighbors, and meals and firewood would soon begin arriving. He sometimes took his family's canned goods back to needy families, even as his own children watched him leave home with some of their favorite foods under his arms.[3] If someone was dying, he'd return to read the Bible later, preparing people spiritually and planning with them the funerals he was often asked to preach. He married several young couples who waited at their mailboxes for him to do the honors. He knew every family in the entire area this way, those clear up into Cannaday's Gap, across to Hurd's Branch, and then up Shooting Creek. When he conducted the U.S. census in his community, he likely had to ask few names. When the moonshiners—hidden in a hollow near the road—heard his cart coming over the ridge, they knew he was not a lawman and kept working. He knew what they were up to and let them be.

Goode was a faithful mail carrier until his career ended abruptly one afternoon. As he concentrated on memorizing yet another Bible verse, a car sped up behind him and crashed into the jumper. Hash was knocked unconscious. He injured his back and received a severe concussion. His recovery took months, and he walked with a cane the rest of his life. With time, he was able to farm and preach, but he could never again sit all day in one position, and thus ended his work for the postal service. He continued to rely on the buggy or farm wagon for a variety of farm and church tasks, and he sold his last horse-drawn vehicle, a double buggy, in 1954.

The accident also ended Goode Hash's steady income. Even while a mail carrier, Goode Hash farmed for a living, especially because his ministry was almost all unpaid. As was his denomination's long-standing custom, he received no salary. His ministry was a calling, and his most important one, but it did not pay an income. So, with no money from the mail route following the accident, he had to redouble his efforts to coax his income from the soil, and farming had to pay most of his bills. Once, church members

FIGURE 17. James Goode Hash as a young father reading the Bible with his two sons, Amos and Abram, on the porch of their farmhouse in Endicott, Virginia. Photograph courtesy of the Ora Hash family collection.

bought the preacher a new suit, but typical donations amounted to a few coins or a dollar slipped into his jacket or passed during a handshake as people could afford it. Given that his people had so little to begin with, donations were sparse. The Primitive Baptist Church, whose members were rural and predominantly farm families, contributed labor when the church building needed repairs, and members always helped one another when they could, but they collected no tithes or offerings at services.

Ministering at four different churches at one time, Hash often had to rely on others for transportation. With the income from the farm and the mail route, the family purchased a truck around the time of the accident. Following the wreck, it became the family's primary means of getting to and from the train station and, of course, a way for Elder Goode to attend meetings outside the community. Amos or other family members drove their father to church when the weather permitted. At times they could make it only partway, so he made arrangements to ride as far as the car would climb, walk over the steep or impassable parts of the road, and then have someone from the neighboring church meet him with a vehicle on the other side of the mountain.

■ ■ ■

Leaving the courthouse in downtown Roanoke, Amos drove with his father the twenty-five miles over a paved and then dirt two-lane road to get to Rocky Mount, the county seat, and then additional miles of rough country roads. They passed over the same route where rumrunners like Willie Carter Sharpe had driven in caravans of up to forty cars. In dry weather, the traffic kept the road smooth, and at times the whiskey haulers in their souped-up cars topped a hundred miles per hour, at times running at high speeds bumper to bumper, so close that no deputy could break in the line to pull anyone over. When necessary, the last in line, known as the tailing driver, swerved back and forth across the road to prevent lawmen from passing the caravan in order to set a roadblock up ahead. On this highway through Roanoke and on toward West Virginia, they ran, often with the deputies shooting at them until they crossed the state line. The poor radio systems back then helped the rumrunners.

You could hear the roar of the oncoming pack sometimes for minutes before they arrived. Sometimes they sped through the county seat of Rocky Mount going seventy-five. Millions of gallons traveled this way to North Carolina, West Virginia, and eventually all the way to Chicago, Philadelphia, and beyond. In town, people knew to stay out of the street when they heard the big motors. They were fortunate that the rumrunners traveled mostly at night, sometimes running without lights at those high speeds, while the majority of the people slept. The moonshine haulers were the most skilled drivers around. And their mechanics knew how to install high-horsepower engines—some with as many as twelve forward gears—into light car and truck bodies to make them faster than anything coming out of Detroit. They were faster than anything the sheriff could buy. Some of the cars were equipped with a second gas tank just for hauling liquor. Others had false backseats under which ten or more five-gallon cans were stacked. Extraheavy springs kept the overloads from weighing the cars down and the wheels from swerving too much around curves—or the sagging loads from showing up as the cars passed by law enforcement officials. Some were equipped with hand brakes used for locking down the rear wheels and setting the car into a spin to reverse directions. A driver had to be brave and skilled to maneuver those cars. Those who didn't haul moon were aware that not every rumrunner made it around the curves or stayed in the lane. Not everyone was as lucky as Willie Carter Sharpe had been. Dozens of people from the surrounding area had been killed in crashes already, a lot of them young.

▪ ▪ ▪

Amos Hash steered his family's Chevrolet carefully, keeping on the lookout for any dangers ahead as he and his father talked about the case. By the time they reached Rocky Mount, the news was running the grapevine all over Franklin County, and the reactions were strong. Them boys were just trying to make a dollar, and I don't see how providing food for a growing family is wrong, people had started saying. And they had to wonder about the lawmen that got caught. Elder Hash, who had been known for his political savvy, might have told Amos: We're not talking about just any lawbreakers here, son, these were the most powerful men around these parts. You know how in the first trial all those witnesses talked about Carter Lee and Sheriff Pete Hodges and how they brought in witnesses from all over, and still they

FIGURE 18. Amos and Caleb Rakes built and lived with their mother in this home in Endicott, Virginia, into their adulthood. Photograph by Charles D. Thompson Jr.

didn't pin anything on Lee? That's money talking. Bribing a juror was the least of what they done. It just wasn't right that Amos Rakes and them had to be the ones to pay for something a whole lot of other folks got involved with.

As reporters covering the big conspiracy trial the previous year had broadcast stories about Franklin County moonshine as far away as Richmond, Washington, and beyond, the county had become even more notorious than ever for being the biggest moonshine-producing place in the United States. Going to court as a spokesman from Franklin County had now taken on a new sense of mission for the elder. There was so much about living in those hills that people outside it didn't understand. He had preached numerous times on the Ten Commandments, including "Thou shalt not bear false witness against thy neighbor and love thy neighbor as thyself." Had he done this? Had he told what he knew in a way that helped his neighbor? He never quite believed he measured up. That was the way of the mountain Calvinists; they never knew if they were among the elect.

The Hashes were neighbors with Amos Rakes. They knew about his moonshine dealings, too. They knew how Rakes had been mixed up in a few messes in his day, ever since he and Caley had run with those boys they called Dukex Mixture back during Prohibition. But they knew more than that. They knew Rakes had always been good to his mother and had helped build her a house, that big white house that looked like a hotel to some. Rakes had made out a little better than some in the community, but he worked hard for a living. He was always bouncing up the road in his logging truck. In fact, he had just given Goode a ride to town the previous week in the big truck on his way to haul logs to the sawmill in Ferrum. People up north wanted all the big logs for furniture—veneer logs they called them. Some of them went to trim in the fine homes. Few of the best logs stayed in the county. Earlier that year, Rakes had delivered the Hashes' lumber and hadn't charged them. He regularly hauled timber to the railroad depot.

On dozens of weekends over the years, Rakes had driven Elder Hash to church meetings in nearby Patrick and Floyd Counties. A relative of the Hashes by marriage, Rakes had also helped at church workings, when the members gathered to do upgrades or repairs. He attended many church meetings as well. There was no question that Elder Hash would be there to help Rakes, even when the lawmen said he was a criminal.

He knew he was defending a man "who worked hard at an illegal operation," said Elder Goode's son, Dr. John Hash of Nashville, Tennessee, but "I think he saw two things. He saw that the whiskey business was wrong, but he saw people's lives basically depending on it. And I think he found some way to reconcile that. . . . I don't know that he ever preached a sermon condemning people who made whiskey. . . . There were things that were beyond his power to affect . . . some things he could not answer . . . and he would leave those things to the Lord."[4]

▼ ■ ■

At Rocky Mount, where the Ferrum road branched off the old Roanoke turnpike and headed west, the road worsened into a series of potholes and ruts. From there, the father and son traveled twenty-five more miles, crossing a covered one-lane bridge, and splashing through a series of mud holes before they got home. The road was treacherous. One family that drove the road regularly then recalled having to fix thirteen flat tires in the twenty-five miles from Endicott to Rocky Mount. In Endicott proper, two different steel bridges marked the center of town, where the road crossed Runnett Bag Creek twice. The large, bubbling stream ran out of Cannaday's Gap, and some believe it was named for a rennet bag used for making cheese. Runnett Bag Creek powered three different mills. Alongside the mills were two stores, a car garage, and the post office. That and the dwelling houses made up the town of Endicott.

Crossing the bridges and passing Otho James's store and post office—both contained in a single building—the road, now called Route 40 but then simply called Ferrum Road, continued on toward Shooting Creek and beyond that toward the postage-stamp town of Woolwine in Patrick County. Like most roads in the mountains, the Endicott road followed the creek, and where it wound around a bend, so did the road. People in Endicott joked that the road had been designed by a snake. It was so crooked up in those mountains that you could meet yourself coming around a bend.

There were two entrances that led across the creek to the Hash farm. Which road they used depended on the weather. If the water was low, they could drive across a rocky ford through the creek. If the water was up after a rain, they had to park vehicles alongside the Ferrum road and walk across the footbridge. But at times, even the footbridge washed out. The family regularly had trouble getting their vehicles out. On this particular day in late May, the water was down enough to allow them to drive through the creek and up the steep bank on the other side.

We know these details about particular roads, the weather, the creeks, and even about the rides to church because Elder Hash wrote all this down and kept it. He wrote notes on a calendar hanging on a wall in his house, keeping track not only of his church activities but also of death reports, illnesses, farm harvests, and the weather nearly every day, and he did this every year for fifty years, storing it all for his children. In December of each year, the Ferrum National Bank sent out a big-block calendar to their customers. Each January, Elder Hash hung the new calendar and rolled up the old one he had filled with his notes and placed it in a storage trunk. Sometimes he jotted down notes on plain white paper that he attached with a straight pin and then transferred the notes to the two-and-a-half-inch square blocks when he had time. He often wrote as much in each block as he could fit into them

FIGURE 19. Entries from a calendar kept by Elder J. G. L. Hash, which recorded significant events of his community's life for fifty years. The calendars were found by the family in a trunk years after Elder Goode died. Photograph courtesy of the Blue Ridge Institute of Ferrum College.

and at times needed the top and bottom of the calendar pages for additional lines.[5]

The following entries from February 1928 give a sampling of the kinds of comments Elder Goode wrote. His daughter-in-law Mary and son John, along with other members of the family, transcribed the old, yellowing calendars they found in the trunk. Their spelling, punctuation, and capitalization stayed true to the Goode Hash original:

> February 13: S. T. and A. W. Rakes and me went to Richmond today We got to see Govenor Byrd. Stayed at Murphys Hotel.
>
> 14: This a.m. we met Mr. Shirley in regard to a good road by here to Woolwine from Rocky Mt. Stayed with Mr & Mrs Harbour tonight.
>
> 15: Left Roanoke early reached home by 2 p.m. glad and thankful to reach home
>
> 16–18: Carried the mail
>
> 18: On truck today Worst trip ever had with truck Turning cold fast—snow squally.
>
> 19: I was almost down with cold so hoarse did not try to go to Co Line.
>
> 20–22: A little better but Cool weather
>
> 23–25: So very muddy and rough—
>
> 26: Very cold light snow squall early this a.m. I went to Pig River We had a wonderful good meeting. small crowd Took dinner with Mr. Esmon Slone.
>
> 27: Down to 20 this a.m.
>
> 28–29: Carried mail last 1 half of this month.

In the span of two weeks of calendar dates, Elder Hash recorded that he carried the mail over rough and muddy roads, in conditions so bad that he had to get Amos to drive the truck. The roads were the worst he'd ever experienced as they spun through the snow and cold. The Hashes likely got out to push on the deeply rutted, red mud-streaked snow as the truck spun its tires trying to make it up the roads to Cannaday's Gap and through the creeks to the deepest hollows, and they had to carry the mail by hand. Being out in the weather made him sick and hoarse—so much so that he could not preach at the County Line Primitive Baptist Church that weekend.

There is also a hint here about Elder Hash's lobbying efforts with the governor to get a good road up through Endicott, the road from Rocky Mount to Woolwine. His notes elsewhere indicate he went to Roanoke and Richmond with two of the Rakes family to plead the case for a state road that would support vehicle traffic year-round. Especially for someone who did not drive, he traveled more than most people in his day, and he understood the importance of good roads for the economy. The governor and the head of the Department of Transportation knew him by name. His calendar entries through the years show that by far his most important travel was to his four churches; major events such as presidential elections and wars were secondary. On February 26, 1928, for example, the elder traveled outside his usual circuit and preached at the Pigg River Primitive Baptist Church, where they had a small crowd but a "wonderful good meeting."

■ ■ ■

The younger Hash gunned the truck up the steep and slick hill of their farm road. As they topped the rise, they passed the barn on the left, a handmade structure with weathered vertical siding, with a loft and stalls for the horse and a few milk cows. Scents of hay and animals always wafted out toward passersby at that point. Descending the hill heading into the farm's center, they passed the granary on their right, where the family stored their dried corn—still on the ear—and sometimes their sacks of wheat. Past that was the garage where Amos would park the truck that night. Then up on the rise facing them was their two-story white house, surrounded by the washhouse, the spring house, and some small garden plots. Nannie Hash, Goode's hardworking partner since their marriage in 1908, had already tended her spring garden that day, washed clothes by hand, fed the livestock, and, using her family's meat and produce, either fresh or canned, had a meal simmering on the wood-burning cookstove for them when they got home.

The Hashes owned over one hundred and fifty acres, but, as this was steep farmland, only ten of those acres were on bottomland and well suited to annual cultivation. The rest was in pasture, hay, and woods. Every small field surrounding the house and barn had a simple name: the barn lot, the graveyard bottom, the graveyard orchard, and the long field. There were many patches of woods along Runnett Bag Creek and the steep banks up from it. From these woodlots, the family harvested firewood for heating and boards and posts for fencing and outbuildings. In the fields and gardens, the family grew their grain, both wheat and corn, hay, tree fruit, and all of the vegetables they needed for the whole year. They grew Irish potatoes, string beans, October beans, sweet potatoes, squash, sweet corn, cucumbers, tomatoes, and onions. They also planted turnips and mustard for fall and winter greens.

Nannie and her children spent weeks canning fruits and vegetables. They also canned beef and pork, from animals they raised and slaughtered on the farm. They hung up their salted fatback and hams in an outdoor curing shed. The Hashes had a cane mill, where they made their own molasses. They raised chickens and eggs and kept bees for producing honey for sale. Those supplies provided enough not only for their own household but also for as many as forty visitors some weekends when it was the Long Branch Church's turn to host church services. The family gave away food to relatives as well as to the needy. Elder Hash carried jellies and honey to the hosts who put up the preacher as he made his rounds. The Hashes also made baskets, brooms, quilts, and woven coverlets, as did many of their neighbors.

They made their own fences and buildings, usually with lumber from the farm or nearby. Their workhorses ate farm-raised feed, and the animals' manure went back to the soil to fertilize the crops that would feed them the following year. So, while the farm provided only a little cash income, usually from the sale of extra grain, honey, and molasses, along with the sale of a calf here and there, its bounty came from its own regeneration. In terms of self-sufficiency, the Hashes were doing well; in terms of cash income, their farm barely registered on the national agricultural census.

The Hashes were some of the fortunate ones in broader Endicott, not only because Goode had had "public work," but also because they owned fertile, limestone-based bottomland. In the bottoms, cultivation year after year didn't necessarily deplete soil if farmers rotated their crops and fertilized the soil. But on the almost perpendicular fields in the hills and hollows surrounding them, soil often washed away when big rains came, making creek water turn red-brown during the gully washers. Year after year, the lower and flatter parts of the fields gained soil from the plowed ridges above and thus produced relatively well, particularly when fertilized with horse and cow manure from the barn, while the hillsides lost inches of soil and the harvests dwindled in size. As the population grew and new sons and daughters needed land, the farmers climbed higher and steeper to clear their fields. The land shortage worsened when land barons and timber speculators moved into the region beginning in the 1880s and purchased acreage and mineral rights in huge parcels, repeating a pattern the ancestors of Appalachian farmers had seen before on another continent. With the worsening shortage, those who owned land started worrying about how hard it would be for their children to buy their own places. With eight or ten or even twelve children, common in the age before birth control, how would all of them be able to farm on the home place? Where would any of them live?

▪ ▪ ▪

The original Hashes came from Ireland and arrived first in Pennsylvania and then made their way onto their land in Endicott well before the American Civil War. The family's history says that William James Hash arrived in Endicott from Pennsylvania and first worked for Joe Champion Terry in his shop in Endicott, where he helped make harness and buggy equipment.[6] After attempting to make it as a farmer and laborer, William Hash grew frustrated with his lack of financial progress and tried to move again. There are two versions of what happened. One says that he left the family behind and headed into Virginia's western frontier to look for work and a new start. He told his wife and sons he would return when he had made a way to bring them. Another version says he simply went down to the springhouse, hung his hat on a nail, and bent down for a drink and disappeared. Both versions agree on what followed: Hash's wife and sons never saw him again. Seven years was the requisite length of time to wait before Elizabeth Hash could remarry. Her second husband was named William D. Rakes. The new family farmed and had additional children.

One of William and Elizabeth Hash's sons was named James Henry Hash. He was one of seventeen young men from Endicott who went off to the Civil War to fight for the Confederacy in the Army of Northern Virginia under the command of Gen. Robert E. Lee. Elder Goode wrote, "My father . . . was wounded ten days before General R. E. Lee surrendered to General U. S. Grant on April 9, 1865. Father was taken as a prisoner and was well cared for by the Union Soldiers. His wound was in bad shape as a ball had gone through his left thigh and gangrene had set in. The physicians in charge soon had father able to be up and out of danger."[7]

After his release, James returned to Endicott, keeping his Pennsylvania muzzle-loading rifle with him. Though officially disabled, he and his new wife, Sarah Frances "Sallie" Thompson, whom he married on January 10, 1866, bought a farm along Runnett Bag Creek and began to work it full-time. In recounting his grandparents' story, John Hash wondered why James and Sallie and their neighbors didn't simply pick up their belongings before the Civil War and leave behind what he called "a scratch type of living" and head farther west.

Every individual's story is different. Many of the Ulsterites did leave for farms to the west, including huge numbers who headed to the Ozarks. But there are many good reasons people stayed as well. As immigrants, the new settlers had already wandered for too long, and upon finding land they could purchase for the first time, some decided never to risk landlessness again. There were also real dangers in venturing into the Alleghenies when land was first available there, as William James Hash's likely disappearance shows. In the Blue Ridge, extended families lived nearby and relied on one another for work. They built churches near their homes where people worshipped together for generations in one spot. They established cemeteries on their property, and nearly every farm had a small family plot where they buried loved ones. Through burials, baptisms in creeks, weddings, singings, and dances, places took on deep meaning. On top of this, the thought of moving equipment and possessions over mountain passes was daunting, not only because it was backbreaking work, but also because it was costly. For poor people, leaving was especially hard. So sentiment and economics combined to keep people in one place.

By the 1850s, when William Hash disappeared, traffic down the Great Wagon Road began to slacken as the region filled and migratory routes by-passed the steepest mountains. With that, a million and a half people began to be cut off from major transportation routes.[8] After being a destination along a major thoroughfare, the Blue Ridge started to become a place apart, and trading and travel there became harder. Though up to the time of the Civil War, life was not any worse off in the mountains as compared to rest of the South, as famed landscape architect and designer Frederick Law Olmsted observed in 1853, afterward the region declined precipitously.[9]

Records show that the first family of settlers, the William Cannaday family, owned slaves when they arrived in Endicott in the late 1700s, and some of these enslaved peoples' descendants remained in the area for years to come and are buried in marked graves there. But Endicott and its environs was mostly a land of small white farmers.[10] In the census taken just after the Civil War, nearly all of those in the Long Branch district listed their occupation as farmer or farm laborer, including a number of women, usually widows, who owned and operated farms by themselves. A few small businesses such as a wheelwright and a harness maker were counted in the census of 1870, but mostly the people worked on their farms, going to Rocky Mount and beyond when they had something to sell: bushels of apples and chestnuts in the fall, some pigs or ducks, and always runs of liquor year-round.

No major Civil War battles were fought in the southern Blue Ridge, but Goode Hash's father returned to a more impoverished Endicott than he had left. Many Blue Ridge farms had either suffered from neglect or had been ransacked by the marauding and starving bands of war renegades and bush-whackers. In addition, James Hash had to learn to grasp the plow handle without a thumb. It had been shot off in his last skirmish. The Virginia and Carolina yeomen suffered most in the war. Sherwood Anderson wrote that at Appomattox, "It was Virginia that marched out, laid down its guns, and went home on horseback on the horses Grant let them keep."[11] Grant knew those soldiers were farmers, and without that little bit of help they may have starved. Hash had no horse to take home. At least he had his gun and his neglected farm, but that wasn't much to start a family with.

▪ ▪ ▪

James Goode Lane Hash was born on December 6, 1881, on his parents' farm on Runnett Bag Creek. "I was born the seventh of nine children," he wrote. Goode and Lane were both surnames of his ancestry. "Mother was a sweet singer and often sang good old songs for us children," was how he summed up her life in his short memoir. She was his main teacher as well. At that time, there were only a few grades of school to attend in the nearby one-room schoolhouse his parents and their neighbors had built together. A young teacher from the community taught all her pupils to read and do arithmetic as best she knew how.

Goode first learned to read by following along when people read from the Bible in church. He attended Long Branch whenever his family took him as a child, but preaching had never been part of their family tradition. Jim Goode was different, and he began to feel a pull toward the church as a young boy. He wrote the following passage about his youth: "We were all raised on a farm. I was taught to tell the truth, be sober, moral and live respectably. I was very mischievous, wild and reckless—in fact, mean and selfish. My nature was prone to sin. I loved the pleasures of this world. At times serious thoughts would come into my mind. I would try to offer some excuse for my conduct or justify myself with the thought that I am not so bad as others."[12] Then he began to feel a sense of unease, that there might be something out there that he had thus far held no part in but desperately wanted. "The first serious thought I had of death, hell, and everlasting punishment," he wrote, "came to me one morning when I was seven or eight years old. Mother sent me to the cornfield to gather something for dinner. I was full of myself singing, 'While in this vale of sorrow, I travel on in sorrow, I travel on in pain, My heart fixed on Jesus, And hope the prize to gain.'"[13] The song, always sung a cappella in his church, which didn't believe in instruments, espoused a belief long held by the Primitive Baptists that this world is sorrowful and painful, and one can only hope that God will redeem the elect from it.

The feeling intensified as Goode Hash got older. As he reached his teenage years, he wrote, "My pillow at night would be wet on account of my sins." And he asked himself, "What will you be in life?" The conviction got worse when he heard a voice say one night, "No mercy for such a wretch." Keeping this all to himself, never disturbing his sleeping parents, one night he had a seizure, as he was prone to, as his son John told it, or a vision, as Goode wrote it: "Every sin and evil thought I ever had came up before me. . . . All of a sudden, a light above the brightness of the sun came from above. . . . The burden was gone and I fell asleep with the sweetest rest in many months."[14]

This was the type of sign that the Primitive Baptists say is a hint that one is among the elect, so Goode joined the Long Branch Church in Endicott in September 1899 and was baptized. He was eighteen years old. Being the best and most prolific writer in the community, he soon was chosen as clerk of the church, a position he would hold for fifty-five years. Nine years later, he married Miss Nannie Snead, "who has proved to be a gift from the Lord," he later wrote. A few months after they were married in 1908, he was appointed rural letter carrier at the Endicott post office.

Goode worked through all kinds of weather, suffering through every manner of weather the postal service advertises, and it took its toll. Suffering from exposure after a hard day on his route, Goode awoke one night with a fever so high he thought he wouldn't last the night. Then as he lay in bed, a voice spoke to him as clear as if it had been in the room. "It was near Midnight and neither of us had had any rest. I turned to the wall when I heard a noise like a dove makes in flying. I looked up and an angel stood over me and said, 'You go preach the everlasting gospel and glorify His great and good Name.'" After several attempts to wrestle out of the calling, he relented and preached his first sermon at Long Branch several weeks later, feeling a deep sense of relief in doing so. "In a few years I was ordained by a Presbytery of Elders to the full functions of the gospel ministry. . . . I was soon called to serve several Churches: 'County Line' and 'Thomas Grove' in Floyd County; my home Church, 'Long Branch' in Franklin County; and 'Charity' in Patrick County.[15]

The four churches were located in three different counties, all in the steep mountains. Each church met on a different Sunday, so Elder Goode was able to serve each one simultaneously, needing only to travel to each once a month, with special trips to preach funerals elsewhere. In 1920, he was made clerk of the entire Smith River Association, the regional network of Primitive Baptist churches, though he never wanted to seem proud of holding any office. He wrote to his children, "I do not admire members who seek promotions." Many remember Brother Goode with affection and talk admirably of his singsong preaching, but he said often that he thought nothing of his own abilities. "In this service I have often been brought to my knees in prayer with tears to God for mercy and direct my feeble efforts," he wrote. He ended his five-page letter addressed to offspring by hoping he might "be kept at the feet of my brethren by the power of God as a servant . . . to serve them in love and not for filthy lucre's sake."[16] He handwrote these pages shortly before his death in 1959, intending to leave the pages for his children to read upon his passing. The family didn't discover the yellowed pages until some forty years later, in 1995, when they opened the trunk containing the calendars.

■ ■ ■

The Primitive Baptist faith, with roots in Calvinism, grew out of America's rural experience, a result of both neglect by organized religion and the piety of those who moved to the frontier. Having no trained clergy, they relied on local preachers who supported themselves, usually by farming. They held no affiliations, either financially or doctrinally, with churches outside the region, and the Bible was their only guidebook. Local preachers, who preached a theology of humble uncertainty regarding salvation, were their only spokespersons.

The faith fit well with the circumstances of those close-knit peoples who found themselves on society's edge in the Blue Ridge. The Primitive Baptist Calvinism grew where there was no assurance of much of anything. It was a church solidly and dependably in its place. It provided a sense of mutuality even as it preached the message of the unknown. These believers held hope in their God on high, but Goode Hash and his fellow church members never had any personal satisfaction of knowing they had it made in heaven when they died.

Goode's churches provided gathering places in homecomings and in times of loss. People brought their farm produce and meats for sharing at daylong meetings, and through these meals they recognized their dependence on one another and on their land. The long meetings provided a place for community bonding, some drinking in the woods nearby, and an excuse for the young to court. People sang together and prayed together; they ate together and stood together listening to the preaching that could go on for hours, with Preacher Goode among the best. Periodically, they ate the Lord's Supper with real wine and bread and washed one another's feet. There were no altar calls, no passing of the offering plates, no Sunday schools for children, and no talk of sending missions into the world. The faith fit well in a community where everyone was poor, where unpredictable forces of nature ruled their lives, where people hoped for rain but rued an early frost, and where only Providence, rather than health care, could keep them free of disease. Their religion, just like their food, had to be homegrown.

Those who first made it to the Virginia mountains were Protestants and often had come from the Presbyterian tradition, but many remade themselves into Baptists, though they still clung to Calvinist piety. In Charity, where one of Goode Hash's churches was located and where he served as clerk, the first congregation organized in 1778 and erected a log building with a balcony and a large fireplace.[17] In the beginning, they called it simply Union Church, without denominational labels. It was a community church in the best sense of the word and welcomed all its neighbors as members, including at least fourteen black members, enslaved people as well as freedmen.[18] Their theology was mostly of the Baptist strain, meaning they were individualized, locally governed, and free of state and hierarchical influence. They began their church by baptizing one another by immersion in nearby Smith River.

Around 1800, the Second Great Awakening swept revivalist preaching into every part of the country and deep into preacher-starved Appalachia. Through fervent camp meetings held outdoors, the new evangelism began to remake the old "hard-shell" Baptist faith by giving new converts religious assurance of heaven. New evangelists proclaimed, in opposition to Calvinists, that salvation was free to all and that "blessed assurance" of heaven could be anyone's for the asking. Revivals burned through the mountains like wildfire, consuming old somber beliefs as it passed. The optimism out of which the movement grew said much about the faith in the new nation as well.

Evangelical church membership began growing exponentially, spurred in part by new conventions, including mission societies and Sunday schools.[19] When many of these new Baptists began preaching that America was a Christian nation, they drew in many who longed for inclusion. At the same time, the new evangelization repelled traditionalists suspicious of worldly forms of organization. Marriage of church and state in any sense was anathema to the old Calvinists. The traditionalists moved toward separation, saying the new Baptists had lowered their standards so much that "even heathen, gamblers, drunkards, and Methodists could join."[20] As they clung tenaciously to the old way, the traditionalists fast became a minority.

The stalwart old Baptists met first in 1832, declaring in an address at Black Rock, Maryland, that they were opposed to new forms within the church, particularly singling out Sunday schools and missions.[21] In the following decade, they formed a separate association to differentiate themselves, using the name *Primitive Baptist* for the first time.[22] They resisted Sunday schools, deriding them as mere copies of secular models of education.[23] The one exception they made as they made their agreement at Black Rock regarded the teaching of poor children who had no education otherwise. If Sunday schools were the only way they might learn to read the Bible, then that was different.[24] They were against missions as well because the missions seemed to rely on human power and financial donations to change the status of souls. Primitives believed spreading the Gospel and salvation are completely up to God, and therefore such conventions to help out are futile and, worse, unscriptural.

Primitives thought the same thing about the temperance movement and the Anti-Saloon League that had taken root in the mid-1800s. These new alliances against alcohol, often organized through churches, employed nearly the same model of change as the mission societies, the Primitives said, and so they opposed all membership in them. John Knapp, a Primitive Baptist spokesman in the mid-1800s, was blunt: "But I will declare to you and unto all, the Bible, Tract, Sunday School, Temperance, and other Societies, are only a delusion of Satan . . . whence all the inventions of men originated, for they are directed against the reign and authority of Jesus Christ."[25] There was simply nothing in the Bible to support Christians engaging in religious societies of this sort. This resistance to the temperance movement happened to mesh well with communities that made their living from whiskey.

Some say that the Primitive Baptists had long tolerated some drinking at their all-day gatherings. Historian David Benedict, for example, claimed that early in their history, Primitive Baptists "expected the hospitality shown at Association meetings would include provision of alcohol."[26] Since drinking was a constant, imbibing outside the brush arbor at meetings was likely, too.[27] When things got out of hand, the Primitive Baptist preachers began urging moderation, but they steered away from the strong sense of self-righteousness of the antiliquor crusaders.[28] When asked whether his members should make, sell, or use alcoholic beverages, one early elder replied, "I do not myself, and I would be glad to know that none of our members did any of these things. Alcohol is a poison not found in nature, but manufactured by man."[29] It was hardly a scathing rebuke of a business he likely understood as a necessity for some.

Teetotal prohibition was never a stated Primitive Baptist goal. The Primitives have always used wine at Communion. The Hashes, for example, made some of the wine used by their churches. Rather, the problem as characterized in the Primitive Baptist literature and Scripture, is not drinking, but drinking to excess.[30] Using scattered New Testament verses on the topic, some Primitive Baptists have preached against drunkenness, and Goode Hash wrote on one of his calendars about having to expel from Long Branch a drunken member who was disrupting the church meeting. (The member was later reinstated.) Primitives like Hash refrained from preaching abstinence as enforced by the government. They found any church and state associations untenable.[31]

In contrast, some Primitive Baptist literature condemned the government's targeting of low-income moonshiners when enforcing the antiliquor laws. A Primitive Baptist writer from Georgia said that going after moonshiners who made five, ten, or fifteen gallons of liquor at a time was an "obvious attack on poor people."[32] For the Primitives at the time, poor people doing something for survival trumps self-righteousness. Poor children should not be kept from reading by a doctrine against Sunday school, for example. Poor farmers should not be kept from making money because of a religious prohibition against alcohol.[33] According to an elder named Oliphant, who wrote in the late 1880s, members should never "be ashamed of patched trousers or boots, or of wearing an old hat or bonnet. It is a grand sight to see an intelligent, modest young man or woman at work with patched clothes on, seeing after the farm or kitchen."[34] And he adds they should not hang their heads while working with their hands, as "this is an honorable and healthy way of gaining a living."[35] After all, said the elders, the farmer-preachers and other laborers closely resembled the disciples of the early church, whose members were the "poor, despised, and afflicted people, hated by the world."[36]

In the same epistle, however, Oliphant encourages young people in the faith to embrace politics. There was a subtle difference between doing something through the church and being active in politics outside it. "You will of necessity have to take an interest in the political affairs of your country. . . . Do not be governed by a low party spirit, but let your views be elevated, broad, and national."[37] These doctrines helped shape Elder Hash's views of the world and his faith. So, when Goode took some of the Rakes family with him to meet with the governor to lobby for better roads and schools and when he spoke forcefully on behalf of poor members of his community, he did so as part of the Primitive Baptist tradition. Give his community good roads and schools, he reasoned before the state's leaders, and maybe men wouldn't have to turn to liquor making. The problems might just take care of themselves.

● ● ■

Sitting in the courtroom on May 21, 1936, Goode Hash cut his eyes over at Carter Lee. Elder Hash had witnessed the commonwealth attorneys taking apart those testifying against Lee in the conspiracy trial in 1935. There was something wrong with Lee getting off while others went to prison. Something was wrong a year later with Carter Lee now sitting in the audience behind the prosecuting attorneys and speaking as a witness. How had he changed in a few short months from being the prime suspect in 1935 into a witness in the case against the jury tampering? Hash never said hurtful things about others, if he could help it. But according to those who remember him, he did have a streak of populism. One day as Jim Bryant—a local farmer widely known for his well-trained oxen—was giving the elder a ride to a church meeting, they passed by a big house near Floyd. Bryant asked, "I wonder how in the world anybody could ever accumulate enough to build a house like that?" Elder Goode replied simply, "Not honest, I guess."[38] In four words, he had summed up volumes of political analysis about the mountains.

Hash, along with the other character witnesses, was there when the defense called Carter Lee to the stand. The bailiff held the Holy Bible. Lee placed his hand on it and swore his oath. The defense counsel representing Amos Rakes questioned him first. He asked him, "Do you know Amos Rakes?"

"I do," Lee replied.

"Did Amos Rakes ever speak to you before or during the conspiracy trial about influencing the jury?"

"He did not, and I never mentioned a thing to him or anyone else."

Then Sterling Hutcheson, speaking for the prosecution, asked Lee, "Would you state whether or not you visited the home of Amos Rakes during the [1935 conspiracy] trial?"

Lee replied, "I possibly could have been there on one occasion, but I'm uncertain whether it was before or after the trial."

"What was the occasion when you were there?"

"Officer A. H. Powell and I went to Amos Rakes's home on the second Sunday of either April or May 1935, but Rakes wasn't there.

"Do you know where he was?"

"I was told he had gone to church."[39]

That was one of Goode's churches, and the mention of it made the elder perk up. Hash knew Rakes did go to church often—he went with his mother. But even if he had been home, the last thing Carter Lee wanted to say was that he spent time with a known bootlegger. He had only gone to his house with an officer. Lee was not on trial, though; Rakes was. So the prosecuting attorney asked Lee about the topic of bribery, never insinuating the witness might have been in on it.

"Wasn't anything said to you about influencing the jury?" asked Hutcheson.

Lee replied, "On one occasion Herman Shively [another of the defendants] approached me near the federal building, and asked me, 'Don't you reckon we better do something about the jury?' I warned Shively not to try to do anything like that and don't talk to me about it."

With that simple testimony, Carter Lee was allowed to step down.

After the next witness pleaded the Fifth Amendment, Amos Rakes was called by the defense.

"Where do you live?"

Amos Rakes answered, "I live in Patrick County near the Franklin County line."

"What is your occupation?"

"I'm a merchant, farmer, and lumberman."[40]

Rakes then proceeded to answer a few questions about the conspiracy trial. No, he had not been a defendant in that case. And no, he did not try to influence the jurors or furnish any money to pay them off, he said. The attorney then asked Rakes when he had first learned about the plot to bribe one of the jurors in the 1935 case.

"Hugh Rakes mentioned it to me in the corridor of the U.S. courthouse [during the 1935 conspiracy trial]. He said he could bribe the jury and make himself about $10,000. He said there were about twenty defendants, and that each could put up $1000. He said that Carter Lee was the main man the government was after and that he could put up $5000."

"Did you reply to that?"

"I told him I understood Carter was almost broke."

"Did he have a response?"

"Hugh Rakes said Carter had some kinfolks who could put up."

"What did you say?"

"I told him I didn't want to hear such talk and walked away."[41]

The lawyer went on probing about whether Amos Rakes knew about or helped raise any bribery money or put up any money for bribes on his own. Hutcheson finished with a question regarding where Rakes had been on Sunday, May 12, 1935. Rakes brought up the Primitive Baptist Church again. "My wife and I, and some of our relatives, had gone to church at Charity that day. It was Mother's Day." Back on May 12, 1935, Goode Hash had written on his calendar that he had attended a funeral of a mother on that Mother's Day at the Charity cemetery, and he added simply that the preaching service at the church had been a "good meeting." The Rakes family had attended as a group that day when the preacher delivered his sermon.

Then Hutcheson turned his attention to Amos Rakes's involvement in liquor and whether he'd paid conspirator Edgar Beckett, who had worked as a sidekick to Jeff Richards, protection for his moonshining. The defense objected; Rakes was not being tried for moonshine sales, and bringing this up would only incriminate him unnecessarily. Hutcheson argued in response that showing Rakes's involvement in the business would give him a motive for bribery. The objection was overruled, and Rakes was told to answer the question. He answered that no, sir, he had not paid a protection fee to Beckett. Then the prosecutor asked him about his sales of liquor as well as his sales of ingredients used to make liquor by others.

"You have told us you operated a store."

"Yes, sir."

"What did you sell Clifford Martin [one of the defendants]?

"Sold him anything he asked for. If I had it."

"Did that include sugar, meal, and malt?"

Not beating around the bush, he answered straight. "I had liquor dealings with Martin."

Using Rakes's phrase, the prosecutor followed, "Did you have liquor dealings with Hugh Rakes [also a bribery case defendant]?

"I sold liquor to him."[42]

From there, things turned south for Amos Rakes. He had been honest about his deep involvement in the Franklin County liquor business. Though he denied any involvement in the bribery, Hutcheson led the jury to believe that Rakes had strong reasons to pay off a jury in a case to which he had no direct connections. And he was not getting off. The character witnesses knew it. They realized they had failed to help their neighbor when the judge turned to Elder Goode, Miss Ora Harrison, and the others who had come in support of Rakes and told them they did not have to return the next day.

▼ ■ ■

As Elder Goode and his son Amos pulled the truck into the garage that evening and went inside the house, he had resigned himself to the fact that Amos Rakes was going to prison. As far as the trial went, he had done his part, even if it was but a feeble attempt against a strong team of prosecutors and a state that had settled on going after only the little men. At least he had stood up to be counted. He must have been tired from the effort, as he entered nothing on the calendar that night or the next. While the Pigg River service was going on near Ferrum that Saturday, the jury deliberated. They returned guilty verdicts for all thirteen of the defendants who had entered pleas of guilty as well as guilty verdicts for Amos Rakes and Edgar T. Marshall, the man who took the bribe and hung the jury.

Sherwood Anderson closed his article for *Liberty* magazine with an extraordinary observation about the first trial. He noted that "even some of the big shots—mountain men who had gone into the outlaw liquor business in the new big way—came out of the hills to testify for the government . . . some of them, to convict themselves." He surmised that the players in the trial, the witnesses, the jury, and even some of the defendants were mountain men who all wanted to go back to a time when the moonshine business had been smaller and perhaps more humane. To him they appeared penitent and desiring to atone for what they had done. "They seemed to want to go back to the old ways," Anderson wrote. "The big way was too cruel. It brought out too many ugly things in men."[43] At least this seemed true for some.

The judge noticed a similar contrition among the defendants of the second trial. Judge John Paul said he differed with the government's recommendation for stiffer punishments for the men and meted out much less than they had called for. Declaring the sentences "fitting" for "the degree of guilt" of each, he sentenced thirteen of those who pleaded guilty to probation only. The judge stated, as he read their sentences, "I may be wrong . . . possibly I'm making a mistake. I am going to put you all on probation."[44] Two of the defendants, one a former deputy, immediately "burst into tears and wept throughout the remainder of the proceedings."[45] But then the judge turned to the rest, including those who had pleaded innocent and a few others with guilty pleas. With them he was not so lenient; they got six months to two years. Paul sentenced Amos Rakes to eighteen months and charged him the highest fine, two thousand dollars.

Three days later, on Tuesday, Rakes, released on his own recognizance, was at home preparing to report back to serve his time, saying his goodbyes, and likely making plans with his brother for keeping their businesses running. That same day, Elder Goode and his family got into one of the older children's vehicles and headed to Roanoke to visit a sick elder in a sister church and planned to swing around the long way coming down the mountain from Floyd to make other important visits. He wrote the following on the calendar after they returned: "All the family except [his daughter] Ora went to Roanoke today Went to see Bro. Sutphin We went to Salem to see Bro. Crawford Thomas he is real poorly. We came by Floyd to see Walter Hatcher, Amos Rakes and others."[46] Walter "Peg" Hatcher and Amos Rakes, both convicted of jury tampering, both moonshiners, and both now disgraced in newspapers everywhere, were still on the list of visitors for the Hash family. They, along with those who were "real poorly" physically, needed looking after spiritually. That was the job of a pastor called to feed the Lord's sheep.

Family members say that Amos and Caley looked almost like identical twins, and likely they looked more and more alike the longer they lived and worked together over the decades. But there was one big difference between them: One was a family man with children at home; the other was not. The year and a half coming up that they were going to be separated was going to be a painful time for the entire family, particularly the children. The brothers started plotting among themselves and came up with a plan. According to some of the Rakes descendants, when Amos was to report to the federal penitentiary, his brother went in for him. Caley just told them, "I'm Amos Rakes and here to serve my time," and no one ever questioned him. With such acts of kindness, families, even the families of bootleggers, kept what Anderson called the "ugly things in men" at bay awhile longer on Shooting Creek.

Meanwhile, Carter Lee was back at his job. He sat in his office at the Rocky Mount courthouse thinking through the past several years and how well things had worked out. Sherwood Anderson was wrong about that one man it seems. Lee was one who had no plan to convict himself; he didn't believe things seemed that cruel at all, and he had no intention of going back to the old ways. He was going forward, to run for office again, to keep fighting for what he felt was right. At least that's the way he told it. More than a few others, including Elder Goode, would have begged to differ. But, of course, no one asked them.

5 Last Old Dollar Is Gone

The corn, the corn, how significant in all of American life, I thought. I thought of all the great corn fields of the Middle West, of how when I was a small boy I had often crept into them at the edge of my own Ohio town.

I used to crawl in there and lie under the corn. It was warm and close in there. On the ground, under the tall corn, pumpkins grew. There was the singing of the insects. Little insects flew about my head or crawled along the warm ground. Then also the corn fields had talked to me. Like Henry Wallace, whom I was to know later, I became for a time, a kind of corn-field mystic. —SHERWOOD ANDERSON, "I Build a House"

ELDER GOODE HASH WROTE more about corn in his calendar records than any other crop. He noted the dates he planted it in May or June and the dates when, usually about four weeks later, it had grown high enough for him to begin working it with his horse-drawn, walk-behind cultivator. He planted as much as a half-bushel of seed he had saved from the previous year's crop. The corn planter he owned looked a lot like his other farm implements: two hardwood handles and the necessary connections for horse harness. But what distinguished it was the galvanized metal canister at the base of the implement where a cast-iron wheel rotated to pick up a seed or two at a time and deposit them at perfect intervals as the operator walked behind it and his horse.

Farmers took a lot of pride in their operation of the corn planter. With the plow and disk and most other implements, one could veer off to one side or the other and few would notice, especially after a rain. But with corn planting, always in parallel rows and a crop that grew into tall plants, everyone who passed by for the ensuing three months could see how straight the rows had been laid off on the day of planting. While some joked that a farmer could get more into crooked rows, most took pains to get them straight. But it was far from easy. During planting, the farmer's job is to guide the horse, as much with verbal signals—"gee" for right and "haw" for left—as with the reins. Farmers used a lash for training but almost never used one with trained animals. With the reins tied and draped around the plowman's neck and the hands occupied with keeping the implement upright, verbal commands were all the farmers had.

Elder Goode planted corn twice: an early patch and a late patch sometimes in July. With corn taking about one hundred days to mature, the five-month growing season in his mountains afforded two plantings for insurance against drought. As corn needs rain especially when it is forming ears, two different plantings spread the risk. If a first planting hit a dry period during matura-tion, the late crop was insurance against a total loss. On occasion, with a particularly good year of rain, both crops did well. Sometimes, as in 1930, the whole year was dry.

Especially with having no irrigation or crop insurance to protect him, Goode's most frequent entries on his calendars were his weather reports. He always noted "good showers of rain" as well as the gully washers that inevitably took out his bridge. He often mentioned the foggy, rainy days he called "close, wet days." And he kept down on the calendar the days farm-hands worked for him. John and Otey Rakes, for example, helped him on many occasions in his early years of farming—at times plowing or planting corn for Mr. Goode—when he had duties, such as a funeral, that took him off the farm. If one of the Hash children did the plowing or other major chore, there was usually little mention of it. Being part of any farm family in the community meant working as much as one could to help out. Pay was usually out of the question for them, so any record keeping about family labor was unnecessary. Like every other family from Shooting Creek to Griffith Hill, the children always worked and "never knew any different." In other words, everyone worked pretty much all the time.

Unlike in the Midwest, which from the time of the Ice Age to the arrival of the Europeans had been in prairie grass, corn had been raised in small patches in the mountains for hundreds of years by the time the Europeans arrived. The Woodlands Nations imported the seed from Mesoamerica in trade for goods and began their tradition of farming with it. They called it mother. Through generations of seed selection, the women farmers—and most all of them were women—developed varieties suited for mountain climates and soils. Working alongside their children, they used small-scale slash-and-burn techniques for land clearing and fertilization and simple digging sticks for planting. When the Europeans took over these old fields,

FIGURE 20. Elder Goode Hash and his wife, Nannie, with "hickory cane" corn shocks and a basket of ears on their farm in their later years. Photographer Earl Palmer, who made this photograph in the 1950s, often had his subjects dress in traditional, sometimes outmoded, farm clothing. Courtesy of the Blue Ridge Institute of Ferrum College.

either directly or indirectly banishing the very ones who had cleared them, they, too, had only wooden tools to use. Even their horse-drawn plows were mostly made of wood with iron points. By the mid-1800s, improved metal plows became more readily available and, thanks to iron forges in the region and local blacksmiths, farmers in Endicott and elsewhere in the mountains used them extensively.

While the European grains wheat and barley had their place in mountain agriculture and distillation, corn quickly became the "mother" grain—though they never called it that—of mountain subsistence agriculture for them as well. Corn rose to that prominence both because of its prolificacy, producing as many as fifty bushels of grain per acre on new ground, and because of its versatility. The tall plant supplied both human and animal food as well as great amounts of fodder consumed by cows, horses, mules, and hogs. Through Goode Hash's lifetime, no mountain farm was without at least one field of corn, almost always grown on the best bottomland.

Corn harvest in Endicott began in September and lasted until late fall. The first step at harvest for the Hash family and their neighbors was to pull the dried ears by hand and toss them into a horse-drawn wagon or sled. After hauling the ears out of the field, the families cut the cornstalks using a hand corn-cutter, a single flat piece of sharpened iron attached to the end of a handle. These harvesters swung the blades to clip off the corn stalk at shoe-top height and then shocked the stalks teepee-style at convenient intervals to allow them to dry in the field. If pumpkins were planted under the corn, shocking up the corn revealed the orange globes. After drying the corn fodder, the family carried the stalks to the barn for use in the livestock feed. They fed cattle, horses, and mules the leaves all through the winter along with hay and ear corn, keeping the animals stout and productive. Many people turned their hogs out to feed in the harvested fields and woods, where they foraged for acorns, chestnuts, and roots. Hogs regularly received a couple ears of corn each day, both to fatten them and to keep them coming back to the farmer, who would eventually need to pen and then slaughter the animal on the first cold day. Goode mentioned hog killings on his calendar nearly every November. The Hashes and all the other Endicott farmers used nearly every part of the hogs they raised, including the brains, tongue, and heart. The Hashes gave the pigs' feet away to others, but they, and most everyone else, used almost every other part but "the squeal," as people often joked.

Gatherings known as corn shuckings were always a time to have fun with relatives and neighbors. Without help, the job of shucking each ear of corn was too huge and monotonous a job to finish in due time, so they made it into a celebration. To prepare for the big day, boys used horse-drawn sleds to haul and pile all the ears in the yard. When they gathered for the work, everyone took seats around the pile and began stripping off the dried shucks and snapping the stem and then throwing the yellow or white or sometimes multicolored ears in one pile and the shucks in another. These shucks would provide additional mule feed and, on occasion for the craftswomen in the community, the raw materials for corn-shuck dolls. People talked, sang hymns and ballads, and told jokes during shuckings. In some families, the first one to make it to the bottom of the pile found a jar of corn liquor to drink and pass around in celebration. Others hid a special red ear of corn underneath, which meant the lucky one who found it could kiss a sweetheart and maybe signal the beginning of a fiddle tune. There was little of that at the Hashes' place, but finding that last ear did signal that it was a time to feast on the food that the women, in this case Nannie Hash and her daughters and kin, had been cooking for several days. Though theirs was one of only two families in the entire community that didn't engage in some form of moonshine production or sales, Nannie's food and the family's friendship was enough to draw their neighbors. And as labor was traded, giving always meant receiving. So people worked for others because everyone needed their neighbors' help. Neighborliness also meant survival.

For the meal, there was usually farm-raised chicken and most always some pork, maybe even a shoulder or ham. Potatoes, green beans, sweet potatoes, and apples were regular additions to the table. For special occasions, there was wheat bread, almost always in the form of biscuits, served along with the regular corn bread, ground from the crop people worked in with their hands. Cucumber and beet pickles made with homemade apple cider vinegar adorned the table. Homemade blackberry, plum, strawberry, and grape jams and jellies made regular appearances as well. At the end of the meal came desserts: apple cakes with black walnuts, apple pies, pumpkin and sweet potato pies. These meals, which took maybe a half-hour to eat, represented hundreds of hours of preparation time, from planting the crops to feeding the hogs to snapping beans. The prayer before the harvest meal always prompted a recognition of bounty and of the hard work that went into making a living in the Endicott hills. Bless the ones who prepared this food and us to thy service, Goode prayed. After his amen, people began passing the foods made or grown within sight of the kitchen window, from the meats to the breads to the vegetables and fruits, and even the molasses served for the last biscuits. The only things bought were the salt, pepper, sugar, and coffee. People referred to "trading" with stores for a reason. Families took their extra eggs, butter, honey, and molasses to trade for salt and the other necessities and perhaps a stick of peppermint or a drink for the children, who had worked so hard all year.

Harvesting grains usually required the most labor of any farm activity. Along with their main crop of corn, some years Elder Hash and his family harvested over seventy bushels of wheat. Many people also grew rye, and in the mountains almost all of this grain was harvested with hand grain cradles and then shocked by hand in the fields to dry. Up through the 1930s, almost every farm in the community continued to raise at least some of its own small grain, especially as it could be planted after corn harvest in the fall.

At grain harvest, men slung the grain cradles, working together across fields. Others, often the women and children, grabbed the grain stalks from the fingers of the cradle, and stacked this into shocks, tying off a final bunch to serve as a makeshift roof, which helped shed rain from the inner shock. Sherwood Anderson wrote of the grain harvest in Troutdale. A sculptor friend was visiting, and the two walked up to a field where about six men and women worked together with their families. The two artists leaned against the fence and watched with admiration, the sculptor talking of the harvesters' graceful movements. "There is the long sweep of the cradles," Anderson wrote. "The grain cut by the scythe and caught by the cradle."

As the swing is completed, the frame of the cradles catches the bundled grain and it is laid on the ground ready for the women and children to tie into bundles. The grain cutting is something to be remembered. Often there is a group of a half-dozen men swinging across a hillside field, marching forward, the cradles swinging, the women and children following, all the men, women, and children of a neighborhood gathered, the shouting and laughing, each man trying to out-march the others.

There is a jug of moon whiskey in a fence corn at the end of the field.

It is the test of the mountaineer's manhood. Can he keep up with the others? Can he lead the others across the field? Can he keep leading them, all through a long hot summer day?[1]

Anderson then turned his attention to his sculptor friend from the city, who upon seeing the grain harvest gripped the top of the rail fence and stared at the sight, awestruck.

"Look," he cried. The mountain men were swinging across the field with sweat pouring from their faces. "Look at the rhythm of it."

"It's a dance," he cried. It was a sweltering hot day.

Then one of the harvesters, the oldest man, named Bill Graves, shouted at the onlookers. "You! You fellows," he cried to us. "I've been waiting for this."

"You city and town fellows coming in here," he shouted. "I'm going to make you come up here into this field." He stood laughing. "I want to see what you town fellows can do with this cradle."[2]

Not only did the work require straining with the cradle weighed down with grain, but the field marcher had to take a large step forward as the family behind him pulled the grain off the fingers of the tool while he readied his arms for the next swing, all done to an internal rhythm, a task repeated by the others in the next swath over. The work was a cross between a competition and a performance, all done ultimately for the purpose of eating. But the end result was temporarily set aside on this day of harvest in order to concentrate on doing the job well, which consisted of cutting off the grain stems even with the ground and at the same height over the full swath, cutting it clean and orderly, and laying it over in one direction for easy shocking. It took a whole body's coordination.

After shocking and drying the small grain, the families either used a flail to knock the grains loose from the straw or awaited the arrival of the threshing machine and its crew, a hired job that became common by the turn of the twentieth century. The threshing crews, usually farmers themselves, pulled their rigs by horse through the communities and set up the steam-driven threshers in accessible spots. The neighboring farmers hauled their wheat and rye to the machine and, by turn, fed the shocks by hand into gear-driven beaters, which knocked the grain loose from the straw and husks. The straw and chaff came out the back end of the thresher, and the wheat, sifted and mostly free of debris, was conveyed over more sifters and out a wooden spout small enough to fit into a grain sack, where neighbors worked together to bag and tie the grain. As with other machines, the thresher saved hours of hard work. But it took lots of labor to make it run, to feed the machine both coal or wood and wheat, to clean the straw, and to sack the grain. Women worked furiously to keep everyone well fed during the day and provided a large meal when the work ended. The food was considered part of the pay for the threshing crew. They took a share of the grain as well.

The U.S. Department of Agriculture (USDA) reported that in 1800 it took fifty-six labor hours to produce an acre of wheat from planting through harvest.[3] By 1930, with the most mechanized equipment available—a plow, seeder, harrow, binder, thresher, wagons, and sometimes tractors—the national average, including the breadbasket of the Midwest, had been reduced to fifteen labor hours per one hundred bushels. In 1930 in the mountains, where fields were too small to pay for machinery, little changed except for the threshing machine. Goode Hash and family continued to grow corn and wheat the way his father's generation had. Mountain yields were also less because fertilizers were unaffordable for many of the smallest farmers.

Corn took over forty labor hours in 1890 to produce one hundred bushels on two-and-a-half acres. Mechanization and fertilizer more than halved that national average for required labor in grain harvest by 1930, particularly with the addition of the tractor and the combine. As with wheat, mountain farmers like the Hashes simply could not afford this machinery with the money their farms were bringing in. Even buying machinery together with neighbors was prohibitive, as the total acreage in production in the mountain fields still failed to meet the minimum required for the machines to pay for themselves. When prices dropped during the agricultural depression of the 1920s, the situation only worsened for mountain farms as midwestern farms increased their production to try to pay off costly investments with lower crop prices.

Much of the Hash family's wheat went into their bread, which they shared on many occasions with church and kin. Their small-grain production, like that of their neighbors,' was for home and farm use, as all families tried to keep expenses down. The Hashes sold a few bushels and bartered some of the grain to the miller for grinding it. Typically, the mill charged one-eighth of the total load for the labor and use of the equipment. In exchange, the miller oversaw the pouring of the corn or wheat into the hopper, making sure not to overload the grinding wheels, and held the sacks under the chute to catch the grain. Coarsely ground corn made grits, and fine made meal. On occasion, farmers also grew buckwheat for grinding into flour. Elder Hash regularly planted buckwheat because the blossoms were good for his honeybees, and the family used the grain both for animal feed and for pancake flour. The pancakes, prepared with their own flour, eggs, and milk, made an excellent meal, especially when served with their home-cured ham or canned sausage and cooked on their wood-burning cookstove.

The three grain mills along Runnett Bag Creek were gathering places for the community and provided an indispensable service for people from miles around. Often the farmers, upon delivering their loads, were glad to sit around on the bench outside and greet others also arriving with their wagons filled with several weeks' worth of corn or wheat. When Goode Hash's friend and sometime driver, Mr. Jim Bryant, drove his team of oxen to the main mill and store in the center of town, it was always a treat for everyone. There were two different bridges near where Runnett Bag Creek passed directly behind the store and turned the mill wheel that powered the grinding wheels inside. From the bridges, a curved driveway led downhill to the mill. Bryant's oxen were the best-trained team in the county, and he liked to prove it. He got off his wagon at the first bridge, leaving his ox team standing there waiting for his voice commands. Bryant's arrival always drew a crowd. Greeting the onlookers, he went down to the mill and took a seat, which added to the drama. Then using his gee and haw, as Lane Boyd, who remembered witnessing it as a boy, told it, Bryant had the oxen "broke to where they'd back that wagon, probably I'd say it was a hundred and fifty feet down to that platform backwards down that hill. And people would gather there to watch them steers back that wagonload of corn down there." Bryant, never touching the steers, had them guide the wagon by stepping in tandem backward until the bed bumped gently against the loading platform and Bryant said, "Whoa, boys."[4]

Goode's calendar records include much about farm harvests and sales and tell the story of the family's farm income from the first days of his independent farm life in 1909 through the 1920s and '30s and beyond. During these years, Goode and Nannie did about everything they could think of beyond whiskey to make a living, though typically their farm never brought in much cash. They ate well, their children had clothing, much of it handmade, they had heat and cooking fuel harvested from their own woodlot, but cash money was hard to come by. Eggs were perhaps the most common farm product they sold, usually at fifteen cents a dozen. In September 1920, Elder Goode wrote the following: "Carried off $4.02 worth produce—Eggs 2½ doz.—butter & apples." Toward the end of the same month he added, "Sold this fall honey $10.00. Sold so far 60 bushels apples $15.00. Sold produce $33.05 today. Mr Greer sent wagon here calf, meat chickens Eggs & butter."[5] He had so much produce that a storekeeper sent a wagon to collect it, but, with apples going for twenty-five cents a bushel and honey cheap, even with his harvest the income did not break a hundred dollars for the month, and September was usually one of the top income-producing months. His income from all his farm sales, including a calf from his milk cow once a year, remained well under five hundred dollars for the year. And the Hash farm was one of the most prosperous in the neighborhood, unless, of course, one counts moonshine as farm income, which the USDA never did.

The cornfields in Endicott, the corn shuckings, and the gristmills had a major entrepreneurial use that didn't make it into farm management publications at all. Dating back to when Hash's ancestors were in Ireland, small farmers had long been taking their grain to grist mills to have it ground, soaking it in water, and condensing it into its fermented essence, which made it lighter to haul, more profitable, and an object of demand all in one process. All around the Hash farm in the 1930s, stillers carried sacks of ground corn back into their thickets—where they mixed the corn with water, malt, and increasingly with sugar—fermented it, and churned out whiskey, which they in turn carried out and had hauled off everywhere they could. It was night work usually, but it connected with their day job in the cornfields directly. The illicit distilleries dotted the landscape, with perhaps as many as two hundred in the community operating at one time and with forty-four along the Ferrum Road alone. Everyone knew those simple copper and galvanized machines turned corn into cash. The demand seemed to be there for whatever amount people could make. The only limit was their land and, of course, the law.

Goode Hash's family knew about moonshine money and realized that even their church was there in part because of profits made from it, though they never participated directly. People gave them a jar here and there, which they kept on their mantle for a little cough syrup. But refraining from making whiskey was what an elder in the church needed to do—at least that is what Goode believed. He knew that missing that income put their farm at an even greater disadvantage, especially at a time when farmers everywhere were hurting, but it was what he thought the Lord wanted for him. He wasn't going to tell others to stop making it; he just wanted to stay away from it himself. But perhaps the most important question to ask here was not why a few Endicott people refrained from moonshining, but rather why a sober, honest, and good farmer with some of the best land in his community couldn't make any money without selling whiskey. Of course, isolation was a factor, but when we look at the history of American farming over the past century and a half, the answer becomes much broader and deeper than location and terrain alone.

■ ■ ■

From the time of Goode Hash's birth in 1881 to the trial of 1935 and beyond, as the mountain farmers struggled to make any money at all, the United States experienced one farm crisis after another. Like a great threshing machine, an increasingly mechanized agriculture fueled by fluctuating export markets began chewing up and spitting out small farmers like chaff, even as it bagged and hauled off their products for profit elsewhere. During this period, huge grain fields opened in the Midwest and railroad companies finished their networks of tracks first laid during the Civil War. As technology shifted, particularly after coal- and oil-burning engines proliferated, each laborer, now using a machine, began producing more per hour and using more of the world's resources to do so. First because they could and then because they had to, farms grew in size, and, as the big got bigger, the little farmers and their simple tools were simply pushed off the land.

Those swinging the grain cradles in places like Endicott and Troutdale were some of the last to hold on, mostly because they had already learned to endure hardships and were less indebted when the hard times set in. They didn't choose to produce food for so little money, of course, but they were ready for the hard times when they came to everyone else because they'd already been in them for decades. Farmers outside the mountains were being pushed out of business and into jobs in factories in cities, but in places like Endicott where factories couldn't be reached in a day's travel, holding to places that kin had found generations before seemed the best option. "At least we have our land," they said. "And God isn't making any more land."

With the beginning of the Civil War in 1861, demand for agricultural products to supply soldiers bolstered production throughout the divided country.[6] Farmers in the Northeast and Midwest began specializing in products just for the war market, creating the first American agricultural revolution.[7] Meanwhile, Southern farmers were forced to convert their fields from raising cotton to raising food to feed its battalions, and the Confederacy forbade production of liquor from corn. Mountain farms producing mainly for their own use made little difference in the outcome of the war, but marauding bands of bushwhackers stole enough from mountain farms to keep themselves going. Few farms in the mountains remained untouched.

The year 1862—significant in Endicott because that is just after the boys left their family farms and headed to war—brought huge changes for agriculture nationwide. In addition to the boost in production for the war, 1862 also brought the Homestead Act, which opened the Midwest to new farmers, many of them from northern Europe. That same year ushered in the federal land grant for the building of the Transcontinental Railroad, a development that would soon bring major changes in agricultural transportation. The Abraham Lincoln administration knew these and other major shifts in production and transport needed regulation, so 1862 also saw the passage of the bill creating the U.S. Department of Agriculture.

When Elder Hash's grandfather returned from Robert E. Lee's army to the farm Goode later planted his grain on, the North and Midwest were already well on their way to farm modernization. By the end of the 1860s, James Oliver had received a patent for his chilled iron plow and began marketing it, and the shift away from the homemade and hand-driven in farm work had picked up steam—literally.

By the 1870s, farmers trying to participate in the farming revolution instead were caught in its whirlwind. High interest on farm loans, exorbitant freight rates, and manufacturing and processing monopolies became the most prominent rural issues of the day as power shifted from the agrarian to the financial interests in the wake of the Civil War.[8] A huge farm depression ensued, one of the worst in American history. The farms that had received credit and that had geared up to ship by railroad to begin with were the most affected. Meanwhile, the subsistence farmers in the mountains and elsewhere had to suffer only the low sales prices for their products. However, even if they had kept their land out of hock, still some were forced to leave home in search of income. As their ancestors had done before them, mountain farmers cranked out more whiskey and tried to live on the proceeds. Legal licensed distilleries, which President U. S. Grant initiated in the 1870s, became an attractive business for those with some resources to buy the permit, and many small distilleries in Shooting Creek and Runnett Bag as well as communities nearby joined in. This was one way to make whiskey pay, though producers who couldn't afford the tax, or just didn't want to pay it, continued the old way.

In 1874, the progressive farmers' organization known as the Farmers' Alliance formed in rebellion against the money changers in agriculture, starting chapters in many of the larger farming regions. Their organizing brought new economic and political recognition as farmers banded together to demand fair prices and vowed not to sell their grain unless they could make at least their cost of production. But new food-processor lobbies, arguing that cheap food was in the interest of all Americans, wielded more power in Washington. And so the big got bigger, and grain prices sank lower. Mountain families continued to raise what they ate and to barter their food for other essentials, but they could only watch helplessly as their production of a few hundred bushels of grain lost value every day. Eating it or making it into whiskey were the only sensible alternatives.

New waves of agricultural innovation came in the 1880s, including commercial fertilizers fostered by an experiment station in North Carolina, which created greater production and continued to shake out those who could not invest in the new technologies fast enough. Between 1880 and 1890, the railroad workers laid seventy-one thousand miles of new track. Plow agriculture, on land watered by windmills and fenced with barbed wire to keep out livestock, extended the plains' grain-growing areas onto formerly unplowed ground and started the range wars.[9] This heightened production dampened prices yet again, leading in 1884 to another depression and to mountains of grain piling up in the plains states, with many tons rotting as farmers waited for demand to rise.

Then the first meats and produce shipped across the country from California arrived in New York by rail in 1888. Processors encouraged by low farm prices and high urban demand were always eager to innovate, to rush shipments, and to undercut the local producers, always arguing that the consumer won out from the competition. New food integrators came into existence and grew huge by buying as cheaply as possible from farms and selling as high as possible to consumers. Middlemen capitalized, but farmers had little to show for this new concentration of farm production. The 1890s became known as the "era of great American farm surpluses."[10] Wheat prices following the Civil War and up to 1875 hovered around one dollar and five cents a bushel. By 1900, a bushel of wheat sold for only sixty-two cents.

Even with all this sifting, 38 percent of the U.S. population remained on farms in 1900, with many of the small producers clinging onto land by their fingernails as midwestern farms gobbled up more ground and the experts pushed technology and continued to recommend farmers plow up more ground. To make the same income as one did in 1875, farmers in 1900 had to produce twice as many bushels. Meanwhile, everything farmers had to buy had gone up in price, so staying even in terms of income was not actually equal after all. Not surprising, the farm population fell by several more million to 31 percent by 1910.

The second decade of the twentieth century saw three more huge developments that changed agriculture dramatically: the invention of hybrid seed corn, which meant even greater production per acre; the beginning of World War I in Europe; and the invention of the tractor, with 85,000 coming into use during World War I.[11] Horse and mule numbers declined drastically. With the United States in the war, 1917's harvest rewarded with astronomical yields those farmers who planted the new hybrids and plowed them with tractors, which, in turn, encouraged feeding grain to livestock in feedlots. Luckily for the expanding farms, international demand also skyrocketed at that time, mostly due to European farms having to forego planting because of the war and the millions of soldiers needing provisions on the battlefields. The United States was suddenly called on to be the breadbasket of the world as it had never before. Those farmers who had capitalized first—or the "early innovators" as the new cooperative extension agents first installed by agricultural universities in 1914 called them—became the focus of research and development. Meanwhile, these huge changes brought little promising news for the yeomen who had no opportunities to ride these waves of progress.

Endicott and other towns in the Blue Ridge sent dozens of boys to fight in Europe, and, as the poor usually fought on the fronts, many returned in caskets. Writers and Hollywood producers have glorified the Scots-Irish fighters during the two world wars as ferocious in combat, and likely they were, but they seemed to die as readily as anyone else. Those who were lucky enough to return able-bodied to the hills went to work with their parents in the same kind of agriculture they had left, at least until they could find some land or a job elsewhere. Their farms weren't mechanized or able to expand any farther; the hills were already denuded and planted in most communities in the Appalachians.

The old mules, oxen, or horses still provided the farm power there when World War I ended. Electricity and indoor plumbing were not even on the horizon. Professional health care was nonexistent, as the flu pandemic of 1918, which targeted healthy young adults, would highlight. Those in Endicott joined seventeen million other rural residents in caring for themselves when they confronted outbreaks of pellagra, diphtheria, measles, and hookworm, among other maladies. And neighbors were the only ones to come to the rescue when children orphaned by the war or those on farms too small to produce adequate food contracted illness or were malnourished.

The returning soldiers saw poverty in their community in a new way when they got back to Endicott. They had sacrificed in order to win that war, and now things had continued being all too much the same. Yet those who had gone away to see such horrendous sights saw value in being back home again anyway. There the people didn't laugh at the way somebody said something. They told the same kinds of jokes, and they ate the same kinds of foods. They appreciated string music and dinners on the grounds at church. It was home where families could be together, and, despite the lack of spending money, it was good to try to hold to that as long as possible, they thought. Mama and

Daddy weren't getting any younger, they said, and they were going to need help. The question on all young peoples' minds as they were trying to build their own lives heading into the 1920s, even as the storm of the next farm depression gathered just over the horizon, was whether leaving or staying was the best choice for how to help out. Neither choice was going to be easy.

The end of the war brought a decline in the European market, and farm prices collapsed again. By 1922, agricultural surpluses were the foremost rural issue. The huge jumps in technology and acreage had increased production per acre, but that hurt instead of helped the farmers, because with every increase in quantity the price dropped precipitously.[12] The Herbert Hoover administration talked of addressing the farm problem in the late 1920s, but prices continued to plummet. Farmers began driving what they called Hoover cars, old car bodies with the engines torn out that were pulled by mules. They were losing their homes and mules to foreclosure as well. By the time Franklin D. Roosevelt came into office in 1933, the farm communities across the nation had seen a decade of depression. The crash of 1929 was nothing new to them.

In the two years following 1929, six million more Americans left their farms, three-fourths of them younger than thirty-five.[13] But those in the mountains stayed, at least part-time, in greater numbers than anywhere else in the country. This was mostly because their region had no industries to go to, and the people living in the mountains often had too little education to compete for jobs in other regions, unless they were willing to work for less. But they left farms, too. Thousands of migrants from the mountains created ghettos of mountain workers and their families in "Little Appalachias" from Baltimore to Cincinnati to Chicago. Many others became migrants looking for work in other regions from Florida to California.[14]

Many stayed even when it hurt to do so. The mountain region held one-third of the nation's remaining self-reliant farms on just 3 percent of its land by 1929.[15] But with their youth returning from the war and others returning from lost jobs in the cities, their farms were shrinking due to families carving off pieces to pass along to children just starting out. The average size of a mountain farm shrank from 187 acres in 1880 to only 76 by 1930.[16]

If the 1920s were purgatory for farmers, the next four years between 1929 and 1933 were hell. Agricultural income plunged 60 percent in those years, and again the smallest farmers would be the hardest hit victims, particularly those in the South.[17] In addition, with wheat production up 50 percent, including in the sensitive western prairie, the price plunged to only forty cents a bushel, one-eighth the price a decade before. But some farmers had new machines to pay for, and machines were the new messiah, as Henry Ford had preached, so the farmers pushed their land even more, creating in the span of a few years the Dust Bowl.[18]

In the mountains where farmland was increasingly scarce, lower prices for farm products sent people searching for money off the farm even as they fought to keep their land back home. When Allegheny coal, big timber, and textiles in the Piedmont were hiring, these industries pulled skilled farmers out of the Blue Ridge into jobs where those skills meant almost nothing. They became known as "unskilled laborers" when forced to work off the farm, which belied the fact that they were some of the most multiskilled and resourceful workers the country had ever known. Leaving their ample homesteading skills at home, thousands made their way to mill towns, timber camps, and mining villages, where bosses played workers against one another, forcing down their wages, sometimes to as low as a dollar a day. "If you don't like it," one boss told a miner in far western Virginia, "there are a hundred barefoot men waiting outside who'll take your job."[19] As farm prices continued to sink and the Great Depression wore on, people were desperate for money, and the labor recruiters who scoured the mountains looking for cheap labor knew it.

Those most desperate—widows and the landless—were the first to respond to the recruiters in search of workers for the textile plants. Though they, too, offered only a few dollars a day, the recruiters filled their new factories in the South, even as the New England factories closed and moved out. As the farm depression of the 1920s wore on, Appalachian men and their families who had made their break from home headed to mill villages to live and work. As they migrated by the thousands from the mountains, the Virginia and Carolina Piedmont became the largest textile-producing region in the world, gaining 68 percent of the U.S. textile workforce.[20] The same pattern repeated in the coalfields. In both industries, families moved into houses provided by the companies and were forced to accept the conditions of the company town: paying high rent for their houses, buying only from the company store, and generally living a life on the company owner's terms. Those who had lived as small farmers before had to give up autonomy and self-reliance in exchange for a little regular income. But as there was no security in the jobs, few could ever be satisfied with the shifts they had made to industrial work. Families longed for the fields of home, and songs about communities and farms in the mountains filled the air. For that reason, Charlie Poole and the North Carolina Ramblers made their living performing tunes in mill and coal towns as well as in mountain hollows. They recorded the song "Moving Day," lamenting the move from farm to factory.[21]

As the Great Depression spread from farms to other industries, the mills and mines cut their labor forces. It was a boom-and-bust economy, and families whose income disappeared had to travel back home to try surviving with their kin on farms again. Many of those returning had not severed ties with their farms to begin with and left parents and siblings home working the land. Families moved in together again, and more people lived off the same acreage. For those who had already maintained a circuit between mines and mills and their farms—working back home for planting and harvest and every weekend they could—going back to the farm after losing their jobs was no huge change of pattern. But with so many more mouths to feed, it was a poorer way of life.

Rural poverty was rampant then, especially in the South. The *Yearbook of Agriculture* reported that in 1929, two-thirds of all farms in the South survived on less than one thousand dollars in sales. When they subtracted their expenses from their farm income, next to nothing was left, just the food they raised. A USDA report stated that "it is probable that peasants in Europe" produce more than that.[22] Most scary for those farmers in the Depression was that out-migration had ceased to be a viable option. With no place else to turn, staying and eking out a living on what the farm could produce from the soil was their only choice, at least as far as the farmers told the agricultural census takers. Any liquid spirits produced from farm products, of course, didn't make it onto the books at the government accounting offices.

Franklin D. Roosevelt came into office riding the winds of change. He promised happier days to the farmers and the city people alike, that wages and farm prices would be fair, and that he would rebuild the nation. He also let it be known that he stood for Prohibition's repeal. To implement his New Deal programs, he appointed progressives like Henry Wallace, Rex Tugwell, and Henry Morgenthau Jr., all well-trained experts in their fields and as idealistic as any Americans could be. They came in expecting real change in their first hundred days and believing their new programs would work.

Wallace, the cornfield mystic, as Sherwood Anderson and others called him, and Tugwell, his deputy at the Department of Agriculture, already knew that much of the farm problem stemmed from overproduction. Tugwell lamented the "opening of new lands in the high plains" that "had accelerated during the war," and the good years had led to "unusually large crops."[23] Some processors and large integrators had made out well, but ironically, plenty had caused hunger and poverty in America. Wallace's proposed "cure for hard times" was to return much of the profits in agriculture "back to the mass of people," as the Prophet Isaiah had preached.[24]

The New Dealers' primary plan for farms was to create the Agricultural Adjustment Act (AAA) to limit production and to raise prices closer to a parity level, a point where farmers could at least recoup their costs. Wallace, arguing that the Department of Agriculture had the "power to make contracts to reduce acreage with millions of individuals," ordered Tugwell and others to produce a draft of the program immediately after the election. After four sleepless days and nights, they produced their progressive legislation.[25] The plan was that the Ag Department, by taxing food processors, would pay farmers to take their land and livestock out of production. They projected that the reduced quantity would create higher prices. Wallace dictated that millions of acres of cotton should be plowed up immediately and that farmers should slaughter six million baby pigs to be used to help feed the poor. Killing the baby pigs was Wallace's most controversial decision. But Henry Wallace believed in this dream and that it would help all farmers alike, just as he believed farm technology would benefit all. "Undoubtedly there would be mechanized farming," he wrote. "But increasingly there is an interest in inventions designed to make it possible for the small farmer to compete on a more even basis with the large one."[26] The main problem was farming hadn't worked that way up to then, and with no controls on growth in place, such hopes were unfounded. Six million farms, mostly the large ones, voluntarily signed up for the AAA, and the cotton price doubled and farm income rose 30 percent in the AAA's first year. But the AAA's initial success would be short-lived.

The processors were outraged at having to pay most of the costs of the AAA and brought suit against the government. Then it became clear that the small farmers were in fact not participating much in the program and that the large were using the program to shore up their earnings instead. Worse, as big farmers jumped at the chance to take their poorest acres out of production and get paid for it, they in turn poured more fertilizer onto their best acres. They needed fewer laborers to work their fewer acres of land even as their production went up. Tractors replaced dozens of sharecroppers and their mules. The result was a net gain in farm production and a major loss of farm population. These displaced sharecroppers became the Joads in John Steinbeck's *Grapes of Wrath,* farm refugees searching for new fields in which to work as their shacks and fences were bulldozed to make room for larger equipment.

By the election year 1936, the AAA had succumbed to the lawsuit brought against the USDA by the "cheap food" forces, but it was clear by then that few of the smallest farms had benefited from the New Deal farm programs anyway. From then on, the government would keep farm supports but place no controls on production in the way the AAA had done. In a market dominated by large growers selling by the trainload, prices stayed low. Sharecroppers were the worst hit because they had no land, but small landowners, particularly in places such as Appalachia and the Deep South, were also squeezed. Wallace was aware of this. In one public address, he said that small farms in the mountains were producing chiefly for home use, and if the public had to rely on their own production alone, "half the people in the United States would quickly starve."[27] He failed to point out that at least mountain people were feeding themselves, which was more than many were able to do during the Depression. There were no breadlines in the Blue Ridge.

Just after Roosevelt's reelection to his second term, Wallace embarked with a small delegation on a small-farm fact-finding trip across the South, including the Mississippi Delta, the Ozarks, the Smoky Mountains, and other parts of the Blue Ridge. Most of the trip was closely covered by newspaper and magazine reporters. A few times though, Wallace sneaked away to talk alone with farm families directly, concentrating on their nutrition and health. He asked about whether their children were getting enough to eat, particularly citrus, milk, and green vegetables. When a *New York Times* reporter got wind that Wallace had made such visits, he went out to find the people Wallace encountered, informing them who they had been talking to. They couldn't believe it at first. Wallace had been so approachable, so unlike their idea of a cabinet secretary in the federal government. Yet the method of gathering facts had worked for Wallace. He returned enraged at the hunger and rural poverty in American society. A few months later, he published an article on the trip in the *New York Times Magazine.* He wrote, "City people of the United States should be thoroughly ashamed."[28] His aim was to make readers aware that U.S. farm policy had abandoned the salt of the earth.

Wallace and Tugwell's next efforts to remedy rural poverty led to the development of the Rural Resettlement program that loaned sharecroppers money to buy farms. However, the agency would meet with only moderate success and help only a fraction of the rural migrants and some black and white sharecroppers. But none of their farm aid programs reached Blue Ridge farms. When all the New Deal adjustments and resettling were done, mountain agriculture would still be on its own.

Two Depression-era USDA economists, O. E. Baker and Conrad Taeuber, addressed the small-farm crisis across the nation, particularly the problem of farm loss. To stop the rural hemorrhage, they recommended the obvious solution that the government should help by raising the standard of living in poor communities by "expanding . . . commercial agricultural production." They offered one concrete suggestion: to increase production for home consumption on the largest possible scale through building community facilities for curing, canning, and storing farm products. They then advocated a search for rural business ideas by conducting a "thorough canvass of the possibilities of stimulating rural industries, including home industries; and the development of an extended program of public works and public services in rural areas to supplement farming activities there."[29] They also promoted rural education, particularly helping children raised in rural areas to make it elsewhere. The nation, they argued, had failed "to equip the prospective migrants with the skills needed for most effective adjustment in either city or country."[30] In other words, they advocated helping people make do with better technologies for home consumption though they believed the small farmers would ultimately need to leave their farms to improve their lives. Even though the farmers would have to leave, the economists advocated that farm families have the proper education to do so with dignity. Unfortunately, Baker and Taeuber ended their article without suggesting any specific businesses that could keep people on their land or ones that might help feed the poor who could find no jobs elsewhere, a problem common to too many development schemes. The general ideas sound good on paper, but specifics are what people need.

Lewis C. Gray, coordinator of the USDA's study of Appalachian agriculture published in 1935, also gave few rural business ideas in his recommendations, but he thought the "conversion of the land to public ownership and its utilization for public forests, parks, and game preserves" the best option.[31] While preserving land from overuse may have been laudable on the one hand, the solution completely ignored what to do with the farmers themselves. They might have seasonal employment in the parks, perhaps. But where would they live? And where would their food come from? Removal was hardly a long-term solution at a time when so many others were already looking for work.

One visionary, an economic geographer named J. Russell Smith, bucked conventional thinking and advocated the development of a forest-based "mountain agriculture that will make the mountaineer prosperous and leave him his mountain."[32] He dreamed of profitable hardwood forests that would feed pigs and provide carbohydrates in the form of nuts for animals that, in turn, humans would consume. The plan would preserve soil, keep people on the land, and provide them a substantial income from sales of what they did not consume. He called his model "permanent agriculture."[33] Unfortunately, no one was on the ground to promote his ideas even as the federal government proceeded to buy up land for national forests and remove the inhabitants for parks such as the Great Smokies and the scenic highway today called the Blue Ridge Parkway and allow much of the remaining land to fall into the clutches of timber companies and mining corporations. Jobs in mines and factories as well as emigration were actual federal recommendations made public in the USDA publication addressing Appalachian social problems.[34] In light of these drastic outcomes, Sherwood Anderson's solution to have Blue Ridge farmers go back to being simpler doesn't sound so bad.

Even if he had no idea how farmers could have survived financially, at least he imagined them staying on their own land with dignity.

Perhaps Sherwood Anderson could have helped a little had he gotten his friends at the Department of Agriculture, Tugwell and Wallace, together with his friends at the Department of the Treasury. From the conversations they had with Anderson, it was clear that Secretary of the Treasury Morgenthau and his assistant Herbert Gaston already knew about the development of a particular kind of "local manufacturing" reported by Col. Thomas Bailey and his counterparts and how entrepreneurship in the mountains had indeed raised the incomes of farms across the region, even if in an illegal way. Might they have created a legal solution to the mountain farm problem, at least in part, through a local distillery bill? Could such businesses have been the mountain home-based industries Baker and Taeuber had recommended? Could the Treasury Department have made its tax revenues and the farmers have succeeded at keeping their farms at the same time? They never got to find out.

Though he didn't discuss managing small-farm-produced mountain liquor into a federal program, Rexford Tugwell did actually write of his dream of a system of "public dispensaries" of liquor that would have overseen a fair exchange between distillers and retailers. Having already been labeled "Rex the Red," however, he knew people would just see it as more "communism." Thus, instead of the government pursuing production controls as Prohibition ended, "big whiskey" took control of the market and pushed out any little producers from the legal market. Just as with corn farming, food processing, and every other kind of corporate agriculture, Tugwell lamented, "Immense fortunes resulted" for the wrong people.[35] Corn supports from the government in every facet of its production, from seed to bottle, were by 1935 going to the biggest entities needing the least help.

With the most self-sufficient farms in the 1930s of any region in the nation, and those owned by farmers with some vision and some means of surviving on their own ingenuity, the mountains might have become a model for local food production, particularly if cash crops had been marketed and production controlled with government help or at least help on making transportation routes. What if mountain agriculture had remained in the hands of local entrepreneurs? What if forest products, coupled with livestock, had found a ready market with a little government leadership? What if mountain distilleries had been made legal again, as they were in the late 1800s? Already there were many who knew how to produce and market their wares. They knew how to turn their know-how in corn raising and liquor production into profits. They had developed a way to get their corn liquor to other regions. The problem, of course, was *that* way was illegal and feds were busy combing the backwoods to eradicate it, even as millions flocked to buy store whiskey from the big producers as soon as Prohibition ended, all right in the middle of the Great Depression. Maybe we would not now be trying to invent a local food system, even in the Blue Ridge region, had such a plan succeeded.

The problem wasn't that Wallace's dream of a fair and profitable agriculture for family farmers was wrong; it was just that he couldn't turn his vision into long-range policies. He didn't direct his aid to the small farmers in particular, except to bring attention to their plight. So, no matter how hard they worked, excellent farmers like those in Endicott couldn't make it in the farm economy structured as it was. No matter how skilled they were, no matter whether their rows of corn were straight and their grain cradle swings true, there was a lot about farming they couldn't control, particularly the price of their grains. So, for all the preacher's neighbors, whiskey was their main means of turning corn into shoes, school books, or a sweet stick of candy for the children. So the thumper kegs thumped in the hollows. Stills were these farmers' tractors, and, like good farmers, they poured the fuel to them and they steamed and spit out money all through the night.

6 Entrepreneurial Spirits

In Northern cities and towns they had kind of an illusion about the mountain moon and that helped make a market. They had read books and stories about mountain moonshiners, the gun-toting, hard-eyed mountain man.
—SHERWOOD ANDERSON, *Kit Brandon*

THREE OF THE HASH CHILDREN were hoeing corn down near the creek with their parents one summer morning in 1929 when a barrage of gunshots rang out on the other side of the hill looming above them. Minutes later, two men running at full speed, one of them carrying copper still parts in his hands, ran through the Hashes' cornfield, hightailing it for cover in the woods on the other side of Runnett Bag Creek. The Hashes stood aside and braced themselves for the aftermath. But no one followed, and the two men—the Hashes' neighbors from over the mountain—got away.

As the moonshiners disappeared over the ridge, officers—they could have been federal, state, or county—found their still on the ridge above the Hash place and chopped it up with an ax and poured the liquor they found at the site out on the ground. The agents had what they were looking for and decided that pursuit on foot—their car was down at the road—was not in their best interest. How they found the still so well hidden from the road remained up for speculation . . . and suspicion.

Well before 1929, still busts had become a regular part of the business of blockading in Endicott, and people had grown accustomed to hearing the sounds of the crushing blows of axes in the hollow metal bodies, sometimes accompanied by a few gunshots here and there. Some say Shooting Creek got its name because its water shoots out of the steep mountain down toward Smith River, but just as many talk about the moonshine-related rifle shots heard up in the holler. Suffice it to say that guns discharged there regardless of the name. Charlie Poole's song about his need to take a Gatling gun and razor to visit the "best people in the world" up on Shooting Creek didn't help to dispel any such rumors either. Regardless, 1929 was a significant year nonetheless. It marked not only the year of the stock market crash—which made nary a sound in Endicott—but it also marked one decade since Prohibition began. By that ten-year anniversary, a whole new pattern of supposed eradication had got underway nationally along with countless rackets to beat it. In Franklin County in 1928, Sheriff J. P. "Pete" Hodges had been elected and had got the conspiracy not so quietly under way, and it had been up and running full bore for a year by 1929.

Despite the commotion at the Hash farm, those who have recalled life in the 1920s and '30s in Endicott say there was little shooting back from their neighbors in the mountains. The moonshiners preferred running away to fighting, and the drivers preferred swerving to keep the pursuing officers behind them to shooting back at them from their cars. The gun battles, which may have been commonplace in some places and times, were mostly mythological in Franklin County, though of course some people still like to dwell on the violent. Most of the time, the mountain whiskey makers were outnumbered or outgunned, and as ironic as it sounds, most had no intention of being criminals. The late Gladys Edwards Willis wrote in *Goin' Up Shootin' Creek,* a personal recollection of the western Franklin County community in the 1930s, that despite stereotypes to the contrary, she didn't "remember any shooting at the law or anyone else." For one thing, she said, people valued their guns too much to take them to their stills where they could lose them to confiscation. Guns would also slow them down if they had to run. She did remember people back at home shooting off warning shots to let the stillers know the law was closing in, and that was about it.[1] One of Horace Kephart's informants told him around 1913 that "they used to shoot; nowadays they run."[2] According to the U.S. Commissioner of Revenue then, whom Kephart quotes extensively, the late 1870s did see a lot more shooting from both sides, but in the twentieth century much had changed. And as running often worked, it was much preferable to a murder charge.

Because they knew the terrain, moonshine men were often successful at getting away, even if they had to leave their stills behind. For this reason, blockaders didn't drink much, if any, while working. They needed to stay alert, which gave them time to run and, if they were lucky, to grab the cap and worm, the expensive copper parts that they often had to borrow money to procure. They couldn't possibly remove and carry the larger turnip or submarine still bodies imbedded in clay and rock, especially when full of mash, but they tried to get the costliest parts, which also happened to be the easiest to remove and carry.

Mrs. Willis wrote that she and her neighbors could tell whose operations were going well: the ones whose stills were safely hidden from the law and who had not been caught lately. They were the men wearing new bib overalls and relaxing around the community store "drinking Nehi and eating salted peanuts." For a while at least, they felt "secure and successful," but "peanuts" was about right. Few around Shooting Creek were clearing much money on running shine. As we have seen, they were usually working for a big shot who skimmed profits, and they were lucky if they had enough sometimes to buy a Nehi down at the store with the proceeds they had left after the expenses and the payoffs. But even after a successful run, they weren't able to sit back for long. The same stiller might a week later have to "stand on a ridge after he had outrun the law and listen to his still being destroyed." Everyone knew, Mrs. Willis said, that raids like this meant "more poverty and being deeper in debt." A man's success was just one still bust from poverty. Stills being destroyed "sounded like distant thunder," she wrote.[3]

Though the axing surely set people back, few believed the busts would discourage the shiners from producing liquor again, including most likely the officers who did the chopping. Maybe some of the most naive lawmen believed they would win: those aggressive federal officers from elsewhere who dynamited the stills and thus destroyed the entire apparatus, including the caps and worms left behind. These officers succeeded in putting people out of business for months, and every so often they caught men in the act and put them away, sometimes for years at a time in the state penitentiary. But even those officers couldn't turn a liquor tide whose gravitational pull was poverty. They couldn't make a family stop producing liquor if it meant having the children go without basic needs, even if everyone seemed to be caught sooner or later. There was no force on earth that strong. And because there were no other jobs, particularly in 1929 and beyond, the only way out of debt from losing a still was to build another still. Though some moonshiners and bootleggers went to jail and some died doing this business, mostly from driving too fast and even from shootings, they took the risk. And what did they learn from their time in jail? And what changed inside them as a result of their time served? As one familiar with moonshine business often said, "Not a dad-blamed thing."

So as these bleary-eyed men sat inside the dark cells looking at the stained concrete floor below their feet, they knew they had committed a crime and now had a felony on their record, and that meant they couldn't serve in the military or vote, but as they thought about the children and their parents back home, most of them decided all over again that making a little money had been better than making no money at all. A man's job is to provide for his kin. The Bible says we must work by the sweat of the brow, they said. Everyone in the Blue Ridge, even the ones who couldn't read, could quote that passage from Genesis, and every one of them had lived it.

As for the operation over the hill from the Hash farm, the lawmen wielding the ax only slowed up that moonshine production, as within a week or so the family was already searching for a place to build a new rock furnace. Some of the lawmen working during Prohibition were doing their jobs seriously, and some even got a commission for each still destroyed, a bonus that helped put more pintos and cornbread on their own tables. But if they had grown up there, as most had, they also knew they might as well try to stop a creek from flowing or sap from rising in the trees come spring. They didn't have to be told the moonshiners were going to continue as long as they could. If a man got away with his cap and worm, he was well ahead of the game.

Traditionally, many of the ones hired to wield the axes were neighbors, and so they chopped with some remorse as they watched the white, foamy mash spill onto the dark forest ground. An economy orchestrated elsewhere and laws enacted far from these hills had put neighbors at odds, but their common history and their common plight told them they were not sworn enemies. So they cut into the galvanized submarine tops a few times, but not so badly that it couldn't be brazed again. They shot up into the air, and the moonshiners ran, and no one pursued. Yet another still was destroyed, and the federal government could add its demise to its total numbers, and up in Washington Mr. Wickersham and his commission and all those congressmen who overrode President Wilson's veto could believe that the "Noble Experiment" wrought by the Eighteenth Amendment was working.

Despite the great national push against illegal alcohol starting well before 1919, there was a backwoods code—one could even call it trust—between some of the local lawmen and the blockaders that new laws didn't easily break. The code was born of reality of living in a place and knowing deeper reasons why people do what they do. Deputy Luther Smith, for example, was born and raised in Endicott and hired to uphold the law. He was caught between doing his job and the guilt of taking people's money away from them for good. He chopped more than a few stills and shot at moonshiners. He told some of his kin that he even killed a man once at a still place. He said it was an accident; he had fired a low warning shot just as the man running away dropped into a hole, and the bullet caught him in the back. Smith carried that sight heavily on his conscience until the day he died. Those who remember Luther Smith say he cared for the moonshine families he was sworn to put out of business. Sometimes he called by telephone to let people know a raid was about to happen, giving people a little time to salvage what they could before he and his fellow officers arrived. His own father and father-in-law had made liquor, and he himself sold the ingredients and the cans down at the Crossroads Store. His sons continued to make it, including Roosevelt Smith, who was convicted in the conspiracy trial. Some say Luther continued to make a little on the side. This was typical, and the sheriff couldn't have found a man with a family totally cleared of the business if he'd tried.

Moonshiners understood the lawmen had their jobs to do. People say that when their relatives got caught in the act of making moonshine—when officers stepped out of the bushes, surrounded the stillers, and trained their guns on them, saying, "Get them hands up"—those boys didn't resist, not if they had nowhere to run, that is. If they couldn't get away, most cooperated, hoping that might help their cause. Mrs. Willis recounted a story of some men in her neighborhood caught in the act who said, "Well you got me, when do you want me to come in?" Some of them even cut their own stills while the deputies watched, saying, "Well, it has to be done, don't it?" When you cut your own still, as Mrs. Willis observed, "You know just where it could be patched again."[4]

The blockaders usually kept their word, too, appearing before the court when they said they would, sometimes bringing family members along, hoping their cooperation might cause the judge to "do the best he could" with their sentences. There was a certain cunning involved as the men appeared before the bench, but breaking the law had no direct connection to the shiner's trustworthiness, not traditionally anyway. Their word was good. But as the nation prepared to confront the brunt of the Great Depression, change was coming, even to Endicott.

Yet the greatest catalyst of this growing loss of faith in neighbors was not economics per se. People in the mountains had already been used to doing without and to working together to survive hardship. They had also supplemented their farm income with liquor in previous periods of government crackdown. Together, they had sent their sons off to wars, including World War I, the Great War, in which so many had lost their lives. And they had sacrificed to help the cause. And then after the war they had gone home to work. Poverty was constant through all these changes. Through all that, the community stayed tightly knit, with the preachers of the Primitive Baptist Church its mouthpiece.

The seismic shift in liquor production came the year after World War I ended: Prohibition. The feds unleashed a monster by thinking they could legislate morals and cut out a vice with a vote. With the signing of the Eighteenth Amendment into law in 1919, leaders, egged on by antiliquor brigades, deluded themselves into thinking they were doing the nation some good by outlawing an evil substance, even as they created new channels for profiteering, new avenues for running illegal liquor across state lines, and new ways for people to cheat the government, along with new envies, new usury, and new violence, turning some deep community trusts forged over generations into suspicions and resentments. Prohibition, in other words, unleashed the worst in human nature, even in little places, and helped stamp out none of the crime; the act rid the nation of nothing but legal drinking, one of the few steady sources of tax revenue the government had. The timing couldn't have been worse—or better, depending on one's perspective—to take liquor out of the taxed economy.

Just as the worst economic times ever for farmers and other rural folk intensified following World War I, the government made whiskey illegal to produce in any form. This inadvertently raised the price on the secret stuff but also made it more dangerous to produce. Dangerous because Prohibition brought huge amounts of money, some of it mob money, into the liquor business, even the local mountain liquor. Whole new schemes for selling liquor started to creep into places like Endicott. New patterns of sales and distribution exploited old customs and neighborliness, making the way for Franklin County's profit pyramid and turning the unscrupulous men at its pinnacle into rich big shots, even as they took advantage of others' desperation.

When Carter Lee took over as commonwealth attorney and a whiskey ring began forming with Sheriff Hodges's orchestration, lines between law and criminality blurred. Those who had made moonshine all their lives suddenly didn't know who their friends were and whether the lawmen they heard were coming in black cars from Ferrum were intent on arresting them or making sure their liquor got sold and to get their share. Tensions mounted for moonshiners as a shroud of secrecy settled over the Endicott community. Everything intensified when federal Prohibition agents moved in and the moonshiners got caught between the lawmen who instigated moonshine production and lawmen who would bust their stills if they could find them. So legal and moral questions surrounding drink and its manufacture went haywire.

Now the moonshiners were starting to hear from the conspiracy's treasurer, Deputy Jeff Richards, who kept track of who paid the sheriff and who in turn told the other deputies to lay off that one or to put the squeeze on another. After they started collecting, the lawmen went after only those blockaders who resisted them. So the deputies continued breaking up stills, trying to keep the outside investigators from getting suspicious, and keeping all their cooperating producers protected. At times, there were federal officers in the community doing an operation while local officers were warning their own moonshiners that the feds were coming. At other times, local deputies joined the feds in a raid, especially when the producer had not paid the conspirators, even as the same deputies entered a different home the same day in the same community to collect a payment from a producer and maybe even to take a few jars of whiskey while they were there.

All these twists on traditional trust began making people think that if their neighbors' stills were caught, theirs might be safer, or that maybe because theirs was found, it had to do with neighbors snitching. Suspicions and resentments, both justified and invented, abounded about any still bust like the one near the Hash farm. That people didn't know how it happened put them on edge. Though they thought they could trust their neighbors, and people did do a good job of warning one another, there was always a shadow of a doubt. And some chinking in the community's foundation began to crumble.

The Hash children smiled a little at one another as the men ran by, but they didn't talk. They didn't need to, either. They and everyone else all over those mountains knew that running and hiding were requirements of the blockading business. They knew that stills dotted the landscape, including places just over the hill from them. They knew that stills got raided and sometimes shooting was involved and that neighbors shouldn't go anywhere near such places even if they knew about them. They also knew of the tensions between people and that it was best just not to say anything. A knowing glance at each other was enough.

The children also knew which of their classmates came to school with an old lard bucket and only a cake of cornbread with molasses inside for lunch, the ones who seemed to wear the same clothes, clean as their mothers could wash them and dry them by the cookstove at night, day after day. They knew that during parts of the year at least most all the pupils went without shoes, so there was little class difference between them. Yet they knew which daddies worked stills successfully and which ones owned stores and how that meant some of the children had a little extra. They even knew when nearly everyone started getting some benefit from the liquor sales, whether through sales of copper, five-gallon cans, heavy car springs for hauling the drink, or sugar, the stakes were just too high for people to discuss in public.

If the Hash children knew all this and their father was a preacher, think of their peers in moonshining households. Two members of the Quinn family who wrote their memories of the Endicott community discussed how children suffered some from the burden not only of knowing but also of having to keep quiet. Sarah Hambrick and Felicia Woods wrote that children "were taught to keep their mouths shut and not spill the beans about the family business. In this way, the moonshining probably had a profound effect on school-aged children who were so easily influenced."[5] When a schoolteacher asked their father's occupation and income level for a state report, they knew the burden of lying to an authority figure rested on their shoulders. "We children were forced to grow up faster, be an adult before our time, stand up for ourselves," Hambrick and Woods wrote. "And build whatever self-esteem we could in whatever way we could."[6]

These two Quinn descendants, along with others who grew up in Endicott, now can say they were proud of their parents' hard work. But some also talk of the guilt they felt growing up, only gradually realizing moonshine was about survival and nothing to be ashamed of. The guilt was pervasive and likely plagued some adults, too. They all knew of the association of their end of the county with blockading and how many from Rocky Mount and elsewhere were scared to go into the community where they lived and how some people stared when their daddies went to town. They knew the power of stereotypes even then. This, too, was the world Prohibition had wrought for them.

Moonshine and secrecy are inseparable in American imaginations today, and if one takes a sip of homemade whiskey from a mason jar, he or she'll make sure to know who's looking first. That secrecy is nothing new, for we know that when Ulster Plantation dwellers started making poteen by the light of the moon, they did so to hide it from their rack-renting landlords and Irish lawmen and that early in its history homemade liquor manufacture and sales were clandestine. Again in America in the years during and following the Civil War and again during Prohibition of the 1920s—eras associated with resistance to the government, images of still raids, and family whiskey trag-edies in sermon and song—whiskey production and drinking were forced in the shadows again. Yet, as we have seen, moonshine cover-up has not always been the custom in America.

In the American backcountry in the mid-1700s, new landowners relaxed, knowing that rack-renting was behind them and that they no longer had to be so guarded. Even as early as the 1620s—just after Jamestown, Virginia's, settlement—such respectable residents as Capt. George Thorpe, a Cam-bridge University scholar and missionary among the Indians, showed with his distillation along the James River that religion in America and strong drink went together quite well.[7] Those associated with the very essence of American identity promoted it, as American whiskey became an early economic development scheme for the new nation. Benjamin Franklin, for example, recommended in his *Poor Richard's Almanack* the "Improve-ment of our Corn Spirits, so that they may be preferable to Rum." Knowing American grain exports were not holding up financially to the imported liquor made from sugarcane from the West Indies, Franklin tried to promote

American local liquor production. He considered turning corn to spirits an American duty.[8]

Thanks in part to these early promoters, American whiskey production soared over the ensuing decades and citizens began to prefer the taste and price of American corn and rye to anything imported. Farm-made whiskey became a source of pride shared both in conversation and in jugs with every guest. And almost no one spoke or preached against it. So no one hid it from anyone else—except to keep them from drinking it!—and there was no reason to crack down on its manufacture. American whiskey also became a great equalizer, not only giving people something to share socially, but also providing farmers with something to sell and escape debt and dependency for the first time in their lives. With no teetotaler voices yet raised, ample stocks in every home—including those of ministers—corn liquor expected at every social gathering, and no revenuers on the lookout, small-scale distilled liquor was everywhere.[9] As we have seen, French writer Marquis de Chastelleaux could find nothing else to drink as he toured America.[10]

In early Franklin County, we know how ever-present whiskey was because one of the first orders of the new court of law established there in 1786 was setting the local tavern tax rates, which included six shillings for a gallon of whiskey and eight for peach brandy. But local taxation was no anomaly, and apparently people were willing to pay extra pennies for a tavern drink. But federal taxation on whiskey *production* became another matter.

When Alexander Hamilton told Congress in 1790 he wished to levy a federal tax on whiskey, thinking it, as William Hogeland tells us, a "luxury-tax-with-concomitant-health-benefit," he missed the mark entirely.[11] When Hamilton wrote in the Federalist Papers "there is perhaps nothing so much a subject of national extravagance, as these spirits," thousands of Americans who considered whiskey no luxury at all, but essential to their households, begged to differ.[12] The tax on whiskey that resulted in 1794 was especially bitter for new landowners struggling to establish themselves, and it was regressive, costing the poorest whiskey makers the greatest percentage of their income. When the farmers on the Pennsylvania frontier decided to fight the tax and the rebellion quickly spread to other new states, the upheaval nearly broke apart the fledgling nation. It took President George

Washington, himself an owner of a distillery, and some thirteen thousand federal troops to quell the revolt.

People simply refused to go underground to make whiskey as their ancestors had done in the old country. The distillers resisted in the open instead, not just for the freedom to produce and consume their drink, but to avoid taxation in this form. The Whiskey Rebellion was a defining moment in American identity regarding individual choice. Eventually, the taxmen backed off.

It was President Thomas Jefferson, the Virginia-born planter and author of America's very definition of liberty, who agreed to lift excise taxes on whiskey in 1802, thereby ushering in a new period of American liquor-making freedom. Not until 1862 would a serious plan to collect national liquor taxes resurface. The sixty-year period in between became a golden age of untaxed liquor, allowing small producers across the nation to perfect their production of whiskey with minimal government intervention. By 1860, there were 1,138 known distilleries producing eighty-eight million gallons a year. No one knows how many thousands of small stills there were, and no one attempted to keep records about them. But pre–Civil War production, known and unknown, was ample enough to keep prices down. In 1860, the eve of the war, a gallon of whiskey cost only fourteen cents in Ohio and twenty-four cents in New York.[13] As new transportation routes opened and manufacturers began to mass produce metal and stoneware containers, whiskey transport increased, and so did competition. Though many still preferred to buy from someone they knew. One could buy rotgut easily enough in a tavern somewhere, but good whiskey from the small-batch distilleries drank better. A dual market developed, one for mass-produced whiskey and one for the stuff made by someone down the road still proud of maintaining a good reputation.

When in 1862 President Abraham Lincoln needed to fund both the Civil War and the Transcontinental Railroad, among other costs, his administration created the Office of the Commissioner of Internal Revenue. Within its first few months, it began to collect U.S. taxes on liquor and other items considered luxuries, including billiards and perfume.[14] Whiskey distillers were required to pay twenty cents per proof gallon in tax, doubling liquor prices overnight. By the war's end in 1865, taxes had increased to two dollars a gallon. In the South during the war, the price of dry corn had climbed to fifty

Confederate dollars a bushel. Jefferson Davis's administration outlawed liquor making altogether because of the dire need for food at the front.[15] Also, stills were taking good metals that could go to the war effort. Georgia Governor Joseph E. Brown pointed out that copper used in stills could "make many a battery of six-pounders, to be turned against the enemy."[16] So the largest and most visible distilleries in the South were forced to quit their production. Meanwhile in the Blue Ridge, whiskey continued to flow. Some producers turned to molasses, sweet potatoes, pumpkins, peas, and dried fruit for their mash in order to preserve corn for the war effort. Drinkers continued buying the outlawed whiskey, too, spending as much as sixty Confederate dollars a gallon in war zones. Producers in the Blue Ridge were able to keep their distilleries running in back hollows as most of the battles avoided the highest elevations and hardest places to navigate, as long as the distillers could hide it from the occasional battalion passing through or from bushwhackers looking for booty.

Near the war's end, Northern armies led by Gen. William Tecumseh Sherman marched through the South destroying the infrastructure, including railroads and manufacturing plants, and set manufacturing industries back for decades. The hundreds of small whiskey producers who had kept their small stills hidden through the war were some of the few exceptions. Farmers with stills had an immediate source of income when the war ended, but their stills would soon become a target for taxation—again.

In 1877, President Ulysses S. Grant's appointee, Commissioner of Internal Revenue Green B. Raum, began sending his agents to eradicate illicit mountain distilleries and to collect more federal tax money in the process. Focusing on the southern Appalachians in particular, he highlighted how large he believed the federal loss to be there: "In the mountain regions of West Virginia, Virginia, Kentucky, Tennessee, North Carolina, Georgia, and Alabama, and in some portions of Missouri, Arkansas and Texas, the illicit manufacture of spirits has been carried on for a number of years, and I am satisfied that the annual loss to the government from this source has been very nearly, if not quite, equal to the annual appropriation for the collection of the internal revenue tax throughout the whole country."[17]

Believing the threat to be so great that armed federal action was necessary, Raum sent his federal agents to the region in droves. In a number of mountain communities, including in Overton County, Tennessee, which the commissioner mentioned by name, the officers met armed resistance. He believed, as Horace Kephart reported, that mountain people resisted because of their opposition to the United States and that his men had been "treated . . . as though they were emissaries from some foreign country quartered upon the people for the collection of tribute."[18] To his credit, however, Kephart disagreed that the highlanders were outsiders within the American nation, arguing that mountain people were "remarkably loyal" citizens. Certainly their loyalty in times of war following this period proves this. Resistance to unfair taxes on the poor is very different from loyal citizenship.

Many eventually began producing whiskey legally under Grant's program. Especially with the commissioner's men seeking to enforce the revenue laws with guns, many distillery owners bought licenses and began to produce liquor above board. By 1878, there were 177 legal distilleries in the United States. A year later, the number had nearly tripled to 469, and the number continued to grow. As we have seen, eventually seventy-seven different distilleries in Franklin County paid their tax and began selling their legal alcohol on the open market. One among them, Royal Arch Crown Whiskey in Shooting Creek, began to advertise its "Honest Liquors," guaranteed to "be as pure and good as is made."[19] The local distilleries didn't have to look far to find employees already practiced in the art of making whiskey, and these employees, in turn, listed their occupations in the U.S. census without embarrassment. One of Goode Hash's brothers-in-law, an uncle, and his wife's father all listed jobs at what they called a "government distillery," which, they were proud to say, provided these sons of struggling mountain farms ready income.[20]

Legal distilleries, as much as they helped, were no panacea for the region, however. Though during the Reconstruction period following the Civil War the U.S. government helped some areas of the South rebuild, the southern Appalachians, which had developed iron smelters and a few other businesses before the war, were now completely off the economic development map and remained neglected for decades to come. Small distilleries were modestly profitable but represented the only manufacturing work available, except for a few early saw yards. With roads still often impassable and the region too far from larger markets for distilleries to pull them out of poverty, little hope lay in connecting to a greater economy either, at least until big timber, the mines, and the mills discovered the natural resources in the South and began eyeing this surplus labor force that resided on the East Coast.

Especially because of their out-of-the-way locations and their limited start-up funds, the legal mountain distilleries were destined to remain relatively small. The cost of transportation and lack of financing made competing with the larger distilleries near major markets impossible. While the Blue Ridge was rich in whiskey knowledge, producers couldn't build larger production plants or invest enough in marketing and advertising to compete with the bigger companies closer to cities. However, with the investment requirements high for legal distilleries and the income potential still relatively modest, hundreds of families too poor to pay for licenses and unable to get the distillery jobs, yet still interested in making a dollar off whiskey, continued to produce without a license. Most of these clandestine businesses were so small they were hard to find without local knowledge, and so most were safe from raids for awhile.

With the federal promotion of taxed liquor also came a crackdown, even on the smallest producers. Commissioner Raum singled out the southern mountain region in particular, saying it was guilty of moonshining "fraud" so extensive that it would "startle belief." He added that because "great difficulties that have been and still are encountered in many of the southern states in the enforcement of laws . . . in the mountain regions . . ., I have found it necessary to supply the [tax] collectors with breech-loading carbines."[21]

Thus, only eleven years after the Civil War ended, in one of the poorest regions in the financially devastated South where there were no manufacturing jobs to speak of, the commissioner made a product of presidents and missionaries into the contraband of criminals. It helped his cause that he could make his enemies into hillbilly desperadoes. So he wrote that moonshining was done by "unlettered men of desperate character, armed and ready to resist the officers of the law."[22] With this pronouncement, a new war against the blockaders and their businesses began. Seizures of stills ran over one thousand per year for several years, jumping to over four thousand in 1880. That same year, 7,339 people were arrested. Not surprising, in some cases the moonshiners fought back, sometimes in organized posses. Twenty-six

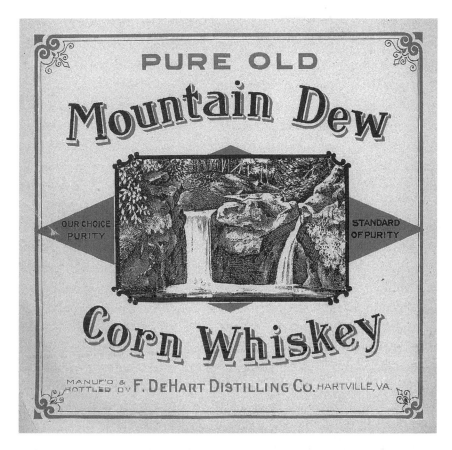

FIGURE 21. The F. DeHart Distilling Company, located near Endicott, Virginia, in Patrick County, legally produced and sold its own brands of white liquor before Prohibition. The Mountain Dew brand was one of its most popular. Author's personal collection.

revenue officers were killed in the skirmishes. No one in the government counted the moonshiner deaths or told how the battles began.

Through all of this, Commissioner Raum was mystified as to why the citizens of the region weren't supportive of his efforts or why, as Kephart reported, "public sentiment in the mountains was almost unanimously in the moonshiners' favor." Even the "leading citizens" were involved themselves "or were in active sympathy with the distillers."[23] Yet neither the commissioner nor anyone else in government, not even Kephart for that matter, connected this problem with the need for mountain development. Of course, it was too early in the history of the United States for anyone to think about using the whiskey distillers' entrepreneurial skills to help them find alternative ways of making of living or giving them small business loans to help them purchase licenses and to find legal markets. Eradication was the only strategy, and the commissioner thought the region had to be crushed with an iron fist. Armed officers moved through the mountains to stamp out distilleries, and they did so with an effectiveness that prompted Raum to declare in his report in 1881—82 that "the day of the illicit distiller is past."[24]

Starting with the premise that people in the mountains were all criminals, the strategy was bound to be unpopular and resistance a natural outcome. But the campaign was premised on a self-fulfilling prophesy. Instead of helping, the federal government's summary dismissal of the region and its crackdown alienated the population and led to increasing corruption, not less. Meanwhile, the government's vilification of the moonshiner seemed to inspire a wave of literature in the 1880s, from *McCall's Magazine* articles to novels, that characterized moonshine mountaineers as crazed and backward, romantic and rowdy. The popular imagination about moonshine was fed by federal policy, and vice versa.

Through this turn against them in the 1870s and '80s, and though shot at with carbines, arrested, and sometimes killed, the mountain moonshiners continued to operate their stills, the illicit ones now completely surreptitious, as though in Ireland on the plantations again. While the so-called government distilleries were focused on increasing their volume, broadening their marketing scope, and passing taxes on to consumers, the small producers using the old small-batch methods perfected over generations found a ready market for their cheaper and often better whiskey. The "little man" wasn't about to go away as long as there was money in whiskey, especially in the mountains, now seemingly as far as ever from the centers of commerce. Gradually, the feds' persistence paid off, though, with still seizures falling below five hundred by 1882, and the government agents seemed to back off a little. But the stillers were ready to ramp up production again when in 1894 federal taxes jumped by an additional twenty cents. But a new wave of seizures and shootings would soon occur as well.

■ ■ ■

Going back generations in the Blue Ridge's history, we find only a few precise details of how the business of moonshine ran in its early days. There are only scant records from the legal distilleries. The ones producing illicit whiskey, of course, thought it best not to say much about their businesses, especially on paper. Regardless of how slim the documentary evidence, however, by 1900 writers had already singled out Franklin County as a moonshine capital and somehow the word got out. Because of that publicity as well as local attention that came about during the folk revival of the 1970s, some fascinating stories from Franklin County do survive. Take Lincoln Gusler, for example. By the 1920s, Gusler was the best coppersmith in Franklin County. He likely learned the trade from his own kin. He ordered his copper from Jerome, Arizona, and other known smelters in the West and formed the five-foot flat sheets he received into the best stills around, including making the tubular worms, forming the still, the cap, and other essential parts without much waste. He worked in his attic where he had built a false wall. Anyone at first glance up the stairs would see four walls and a typical attic full of old clothes and furniture, along with some copper crafts, including copper musical instruments and flower pots he made by hand. Gusler, however, had devised a secret door to the other side of the attic into a windowless workshop where he stored and formed all the copper still parts, always being careful to fold and dovetail the seams and to avoid using lead solder in the joints.

Though he went public with his skills in copper and made a variety of copper crafts he sold at crafts shows in the 1970s, no one found the still workshop until after he died late in the decade. When he did pass, a whole crafting tradition died with him. The same can be said for the old ways of distilling, which even by the 1930s were already becoming too time consuming and unprofitable to continue, and new pressures were on people to cut corners in the style of their apparatuses and their ingredients.

But at one time, people say, Franklin County whiskey, because of Gusler and other craftspeople like him, was the best, particularly if one could find some of the apple and peach brandy people made only for family and friends or the pure corn whiskey made without added ingredients. That's why mountain whiskey developed a good reputation to begin with, especially when compared to gin made in bathtubs or whiskey made from reprocessed denatured alcohol common during Prohibition.

Traditional stills such as those Gusler made were the main tools of the small distiller. They were sealed copper cooking pots with a cap that fit tightly over it that funneled steam into a coil or worm that had to be submerged in water in a square wooden box called a flakestand. Whiskey makers used the stills to heat, being careful not to burn, fermented mash, often referred to as beer, until the alcohol turned to steam, which separated the clear alcohol from the spent mash. The main boiler used extensively in the nineteenth century and by the small-timers into the 1930s and beyond was most often a copper, turnip-shaped pot that moonshiners sealed within a clay-and-rock furnace. As production demands increased, people moved to larger containers they called submarines, which they also submerged within rock-and-clay furnaces, but these were for larger batches and became common after Prohibition. Most of the submarine containers for fermenting and for holding water were made from lumber milled locally and inexpensive galvanized metal, the type often seen in roofing. The galvanized versions lost some in quality as compared to the solid copper stills of the earlier generation.

To make the furnace, a moonshiner started with a clay hole into which he poured water to make his mud as needed. The red clay served as the mortar for assembling the rock structure. Anyone who has seen old chimneys from cabins still standing in the Appalachians understands how good people were at stonemasonry and knows how their chimneys stand in the hills for perhaps a century or more after the log cabins have rotted into the ground. Using the same skills for their backwoods distilleries, whiskey makers fashioned their furnaces to hold heat and smoke and to hold the weight of fifty gallons of mash. They imbedded the still within this structure, using a rye paste for clogging the seams.

The traditional corn whiskey maker started with about ten bushels of open-pollinated white corn and soaked one to two of the bushels, setting this mixture aside to sprout, either outside or in, depending on the temperature outdoors.[25] This process is called malting and requires regular tending to make sure the grain sprouts and ferments without rotting. Malt is a natural catalyst for fermentation and adds to the flavor of the whiskey.

While the bushel of grain for malt was working, the stiller took the remaining corn, still dry, to a local gristmill where the miller ground it. Gristmills were an essential part of the corn-distilling process. At the turn of the twentieth century and beyond, the three good mills in the Endicott area were trustworthy places producers could take their grain. All of the millers knew how to keep it to themselves about who came to them and why or how much they bought. Mutual dependence kept people honest.

After having his corn ground, the stiller then carried this fresh meal to his still and boiled it in small batches with water, as with making grits. After it cooked soft, this "slop" was emptied out of the still into a fermentation box or barrel equipped with a lid to keep out flies and other impurities. Then the cooked slop was mixed with some uncooked meal, stirred well, and allowed to set for a day while covered. The next day, the distiller added more water, along with a gallon of the malted grain, which by then the moonshiner had also taken to the mill to be ground. This process was repeated with the entire ten bushels of meal, which required about four fermentation boxes, usually made of solid oak.

After setting for a day covered, the mixtures in the boxes were usually working as a bubbling beer. Using a mash fork, the stiller stirred the mixture at least once a day for about four days, give or take a day depending on the temperature, to keep it working. One could tell if it was ready by looking at the "cap" on top of the mixture, or the foamy layer floating on top of the mash. While the mixture was working, the cap appeared frothy and tall; when the cap sank back into the mixture and was consumed by the fermentation process, this meant the beer was ready and had to be run that day or else it turned to vinegar, which ruined the run. This entire traditional fermentation process occurred without added sugar or yeast and was pure corn and water only.

When ready to run, the distiller poured the beer into the still and sealed the cap and arm atop and then connected the worm, all of which were sealed with a paste made of rye and water. The old-timers used tin joints and the rye paste to connect the metal parts and avoided lead altogether. This paste allowed the still to be dismantled after the run and moved to another location. When all the parts were glued in place, the still was ready to run.

The distiller started the fire slowly, building up to a boil carefully so as not to burn the mash. The wood-fired furnace trapped the flames and sent them licking up on all sides of the boiler, which then heated the mash and began making steam. When the cap caught the steam, it funneled it by way of the cap arm toward the worm, which is a spiraled copper tube that passed through the wooden flakestand filled with running cold water. The spring-water cooled the steam and turned it into clear alcohol. This is distillation.

The old method yielded on the first run several gallons of pure whiskey known as high shots. High shots were nearly 100 percent alcohol. The high shots were followed by several more gallons of "backings," which were of lesser quality. The backings were then mixed and run again with fresh beer until the mixture was exhausted. In the end, the different runs were mixed together to yield about a ninety- or one hundred-proof mix, about fifty per-cent alcohol. A good stiller could determine the alcohol content by reading the "beads," or the bubbles, that formed in the shaken mixture and floated in the clear alcohol. If the whiskey beads rested evenly on top of the liquor and showed it was close to 50 percent alcohol, it was deemed ready to put in containers and sell.

Even in the days of the highest-quality production, aged whiskey was a rar-ity. This non-aged method yielded a little less than a gallon per bushel of corn and was usually consumed pretty soon after it was made. And if the whiskey was malted well, unscorched in the cooking process, and blended carefully at the end, then an experienced drinker could tell it was good whiskey right away, even by the smell. And it went down smoothly.

Since the mash was continually heated and giving off steam, the goal was to have a steady supply of cold water always running over the coil immersed in the stand to ensure that the steam turned to liquid fast. If steam made it through the coil, it escaped as vapor, and the moonshiner lost valuable alco-hol. Thus, a cool, shaded spring that ran out of the ground at approximately fifty-five degrees year-round was ideal for the operation. The moonshiner needed only to devise a way to divert the water using a hollowed-out log and make the water run downhill toward his barrel and coil and he was set to have nature help him do the work of cooling the vapors.

A good fire was also essential, and it had to be made from only seasoned, dry wood to prevent smoke and therefore detection. Fortunately, hardwood, like cold water, was fairly easy to come by in the hills. Even when loggers began cutting much of the best timber to sell off, locals never lacked for firewood. People were used to cutting it for their cookstoves and fireplaces for heat. If they had nothing else, distillers could burn the laps and branches left from the timber harvest. Many loggers also became distillers on the side.

As the revenuers moved into the region from around 1880 on, men began carrying their cornmeal and malt on their backs to the still places, as this created only a small walking trail difficult to detect from any road. Most moonshiners also had to carry both in and out of the woods their containers—kegs, cans, and jars—to put the finished whiskey in. Walking single file and being careful not to break branches unnecessarily, the shiners kept the woods seemingly untouched. Fortunately for the moonshiners, thick hemlock and rhododendron thickets had little commercial use, and as these plants predominated along streams particularly in the steepest and dampest hollows, loggers left them intact. Places like Shooting Creek and Runnett Bag Creek, where loggers could scarcely reach with any vehicle, horse, or wagon, were ideal for hiding human-carried products. So footpaths became commercial routes of sorts, and human backs and occasionally mules or horses the transportation.

Ethyl alcohol, the kind of alcohol people want to drink, boils at 173 degrees Fahrenheit. Once ethanol begins to distill, the liquid is usually safe to drink as long as there are no leaded pipes or other impure equipment used in its manufacture. The main problem is that methyl alcohol, or methanol, known to moonshiners as the heads in the moonshining process, begins to distill at 148 degrees, so the first clear liquid dripping out of the worm is poisonous, regardless of how good the still is. Discarding these heads and keeping it out of the drinking batch were the distiller's most important tasks in order to keep drinkers alive and among the sighted. After the alcohol reaches 173 degrees, however, the distiller simply needed to keep the fire going steadily without getting too hot to burn the mash. Fortunately, there's a large margin of error between 173 and 212 degrees, when water turns to steam. If the fire got too hot and the contents boiled up into the worm where it clogged, this caused deadly explosions, so keeping tabs on the cooking process required constant monitoring as well. Even while constant, the job is slow and boring. So it was common for people to play musical instruments while watching stills, unless of course they were wary about strangers in the area. Numerous photographs of early distilleries in Endicott and elsewhere in the mountains depict people with their banjos posed around the still. People polished their tunes and picked banjos and sawed fiddles through the night as the music kept them awake and ready to toss on the water when the backings (the last of the alcohol) begin to drip through the worm. The backings smell stronger and taste rotten, so scrupulous producers always kept these latter parts of the process out of the good whiskey. The backings aren't poisonous, but people appreciated getting only the straight whiskey and a good-tasting product, even if it was the effect they were after more than anything, and it kept them coming back as satisfied customers.

■ ■ ■

By the 1890s, a whole new front in the liquor battle was beginning to open up as the temperance movement began its morality play in both the church and state. Southern Democrats, whose racist policies would give rise to the Ku Klux Klan and the infamous politicians known as Dixiecrats, rode the religious critique of big government to power, forming what Jess Carr calls a "strange alliance" with the teetotalers. By 1894, the whiskey tax, now pushed by those trying to rid the United States of liquor altogether, had jumped to one dollar and ten cents per gallon, and by 1894 still seizures were back up over a thousand and climbing. By 1898, successful raids numbered close to twenty-five hundred.[26] Seizures were what the antisaloon forces wanted. Then the same forces lobbied for and successfully passed the Webb-Kenyon Act by 1913, closing down much of the legal liquor trafficking across state lines. Antidrinking forces also began to stage demonstrations outside taverns, as teetotalers attempted to embarrass men into sobering up and tavern owners to close the doors of their old haunts once and for all.

The problem was that federal efforts to rid communities of alcohol gave urban gangsters room to develop their markets behind the scenes and allowed infamous characters such as Al Capone and John Dillinger to create their fortunes. As seizures of illegal alcohol operations climbed to near three thousand in 1914, alcohol started selling for a premium, putting money directly in the pocket of mobsters selling hooch. When liquor taxes soared to three dollars and twenty cents per gallon in 1917 as the country attempted to pay for its entry into World War I and the antiliquor brigades lobbied Washington demanding an end to liquor altogether, illegal liquor prices shot up to whatever a desperate drunk was willing to pay. Even as the Anti-Saloon League's pressures worked in the backstreets, the moonshiners in the mountains were getting word that their products were now some of the best to be found anywhere and to make more. The year 1918 saw the passage of the War Prohibition Act, which reduced the number of legal distilleries to only 236 in the entire United States, so now not only the back hollows were cranking out liquor, but people in the cities were figuring out how to make bootleg whiskey in their inner-city basements and bathtubs as well. The Mountain Rose Distillery, a few miles from Shooting Creek and one of the last remaining legal distilleries holding on in the Virginia mountains, advertised that people had better "make hay while the sun shines" and stock up by the case, because soon legal liquor would be no more.

In 1919, Congress, and finally President Woodrow Wilson, succumbed to the antidrinking brigades and passed the law prohibiting the sale of all alcohol in the United States. But even as police poured out whiskey from saloons and spread out to eradicate whiskey production, new producers poured ground corn, and now increasing amounts of sugar, into their ever-larger stills to ferment more. Prohibition made liquor both more precious and, because many jumped into the trade and pushed their stills, of lesser quality. The most law-abiding citizens stopped drinking perhaps, but for many others Prohibition just made drinking a more secretive and seductive act and made many marginal businesses suddenly profitable. Moonshining counties in Virginia readily pushed for the states to sign on to change the Constitution for more reasons than simply being part of the Bible belt.

But now with more serious laws on the books, Congress had provided G-men new ways to crack down on moonshining, and the business was suddenly riskier and more dangerous than ever. In 1920, a year after Prohibition passed, a huge number of stills—over fifty-four thousand—were destroyed, and the number of seizures continued to stay up in the tens of thousands annually for the Prohibition years as the Internal Revenue Service and then the Prohibition Bureau of the Department of Justice hired hundreds more officers and sent them to the hinterlands with arms. In 1925, their numbers had reached twenty-seven hundred officers.

And we have to remember that all of this was happening when farm prices were already plunging in the aftermath of World War I. In the rural South, particularly in the deepest sharecropping regions and in the Appalachian Mountains, the 1920s were anything but roaring. With people desperate for money, they were ready to take risks, but they were also vulnerable to easy manipulation. Picture mountain people who had left home to work in the textile mills of the Piedmont only ten or twenty years earlier, who now were losing their jobs. Recall the miners who had sought work for a few dollars a week, many of whom had recently left mountain farms, now returning home to parents' farms. Picture the government cracking down on the moonshiners, many of whom had found for a time a market selling their farm-made whiskey to bootleggers whose routes were the mill towns and the mines. Now think of thirsty people in the cities with a little money but no booze seeking a pure form of whiskey from the infamous southern mountains they had read about in magazines and places like Horace Kephart's book about noble southern highlanders. Picture bootleggers leaving cities and seeking rural whiskey makers whose liquor remained good quality, imagine them encouraging the little moonshiners to get bigger and the bigger moonshiners to seek to control the little ones, and see the pyramid schemes and sales rackets burgeoning. Then picture all of them feeling pressure from the new federal revenuers hired on to clean up the mess during Prohibition and watching their income dry up, even as they started scheming and reinventing ways of outsmarting the law. All of these groups, rich and poor, gangsters and farmers, miners and mill hands, bootleggers and speakeasy operators, wanted to use mountain liquor, or at least what people told them was mountain liquor, for gain. And then all of them got thrown in with lawmen, federal and state, all possessing varying degrees of moral uprightness, and with local law enforcers whose families also worried about them and waited on their paychecks. And all this pressure, all this corruption, was intensifying because a group of teetotalers believed they could clean up things if they could just dry up the saloons, if they could just make it too hard to get liquor. If they could just cut off the supply, they thought, all the resulting social problems would dry up, too.

Far from ending liquor problems, Prohibition created a new form of secretive and expensive want that gave rise to outlaws willing to do most anything to supply it. A whole new wave of organized crime began. With a seemingly insatiable appetite from drinkers across America and suppliers of all sorts working hard to get it to them, demand began to way outstrip what people could make back in the mountains and sent the price skyrocketing, bringing in even to the mountains all the wrong types to profiteer and even to rob from the ones whose farms had depended on whiskey for generations.

People started inventing new ways of making whiskey—not only in the backrooms and warehouses of cities, but also in the Caribbean and in the American Midwest—all calling it moonshine. The naming was a play on a stereotype, one that had started back after the Civil War, regarding lawless and wild mountain people who could make whiskey pure. Sherwood Anderson knew this story and knew it was false, and thus he wrote in *Kit Brandon* of a myth fostered in "northern cities and towns" about the people he knew made moonshine.

"They had kind of an illusion about the mountain moon and that helped make a market," he wrote.[27] They got their information from writers, who themselves got their information from God knows where. But Anderson knew that "moonshine" as it was being consumed was actually made everywhere and that people from all over the country were involved in distributing it. Anderson knew, as Elizabeth Englehardt writes, that moonshine was a "national phenomenon" born in myth and reared in greed.[28]

In communities like Endicott, people both suffered and now profited from that illusion. Though they had been made different in literature and deemed "other" to the American dream, their moonshine had cachet, and the illusions about it created an opportunity for them to sell more of their liquor. So when new buyers started coming to the county asking for more whiskey from the middlemen who bought it there, the moonshiners fired their stills up more than ever. And their neighbors saw and got into the business, too. Some among them began trying new ways to stretch their labor hours and make liquor faster. One method was to add a thumper keg, an extra barrel of mash, through which the steam in stills was run in order to increase the volume of whiskey per batch and the corn-to-alcohol ratio. This didn't change the taste so much, but when people started buying sugar by the hundred-pound sack to make sugar whiskey in order to increase output and work quicker, the taste did change dramatically. The old-timers knew instantly they didn't want to drink the new rotgut, but in the cities, especially in the speakeasies, it didn't seem to matter. People were buying and hauling away hundreds, then thousands, of five-gallon cans, millions of gallons of the stuff that people once avoided back in Franklin County. And some of the least scrupulous even learned that if they added lye or battery acid or sundry other additives they could make people think what they were getting was pure corn liquor, the old-fashioned stuff, even if it was poisonous. Prohibition was not making the liquor business go away, it was just making it bad.

In places such as Shooting Creek, producers having had such a rich history of whiskey production and accountability to their neighbors were least likely to try adulterating their liquor, but the moonshine business across the broader region quickly got to the point where so-called mountain whiskey couldn't be trusted either, unless you knew exactly where the whiskey came from. Franklin County kept its reputation intact for longer than some places, but even there people grew less interested in tradition and more in maximizing profits. Just as driving and selling liquor were growing more dangerous by the day, so was the drink itself.

New bootleggers ventured into the Blue Ridge from West Virginia to learn about suppliers and to take the drink back to the coalfields. Bootleggers in Pennsylvania and Florida and other faraway places were also making contacts; New Yorkers and Chicagoans, too. While it was good for business, all this new trafficking and greater exposure made liquor all the more a dangerous enterprise for the little people.

Yet the people in the mountains, the ones who did all the work of carrying the corn and now buying the sugar and sitting up all night with the stills, were lucky if they got a dollar or two a gallon. They took the risk, putting their land and life on the line every day, but didn't share the profits fairly. In the cities, liquor sold for up to ten or even twenty dollars a gallon.[29] But there were many middlemen, price gougers, big shots, and profiteers between mountain stills and city consumers.

Mountain trust got many small producers in trouble. One man in Endicott, for example, "sold" a load to a stranger who drove in at night in his car, and when the distiller asked for his pay the stranger cracked him over the head with a revolver. He woke up with no moonshine or money. So times changed fast, and people stopped trusting their neighbors as they once had. They began to suspect friends of accepting "snitch money" from the law. And in retaliation, livestock started to disappear, barns burned, and even a few men went missing.

Sensational stories of mountaineers feuding and shooting at each other as wanton outlaws had already proliferated through the national consciousness, and the myths of moonshine had been way overblown, but now with new buyers with big-city ideas prowling through the communities and new and often dirty money being thrown at them, some of the ones Sherwood Anderson called the "little men" started to forget about their raising. They began to think they needed their neighbors less than their liquor connections outside the community. Stress increased. Men started not to sleep very well. Fathers put more pressure on their sons, some of whom were taken out of school so they could work through the night. Mothers prayed harder even as they joined in to help hide whiskey under their kitchen floors.

Goode Hash wrote on his calendar in the 1930s of a murder, a man shot point blank, and a suicide and then another and another. His minister's job was getting more complicated, with problems growing ever deeper and now with broad connections to so many distant places. This was about a need for better policies, better roads, and better job opportunities, and that's exactly what he told the elected officials he visited in Richmond. The problem once stemmed from neglect, but now mountain distillers were getting too much attention from the wrong types. So the elder did more visiting than usual. And he preached more funerals and read the Bible to some men suffering from gunshots.

He went to his missionary neighbor, Miss Ora Harrison, and her colleague, Maude Beheler, who ran the school up the hill from his farm, the school where all his children went, and the three community leaders talked about their neighbors and how they might help them. They pondered and prayed together. One thing they knew was that these neighbors were caught in a bind. They couldn't stop making whiskey, they knew that much, but they also knew they were heading for trouble if people continued down the same paths they were on.

Just as the local scene intensified because of Prohibition and liquor prices increased, local deputies started circulating in the community with a new scheme for marketing. They showed up at stores and even at the Dugwell filling station, where people bought a shot in the backroom, offering protection from all the mess plaguing the Franklin County community. They said they could help with all the arrests and fears of reprisals and danger in high-speed chases.

The law officials had been sworn in and pledged with their hands on a Bible to uphold and protect the law. Then the sheriff called in all the deputies and told them they would need to divide up the county and start getting the moonshiners to work for them, to organize their production and sales for better profit for the law enforcers as well as the producers. The deputies started working to uphold profits from moonshine, offering protection in a different way: protection from getting caught. Sheriff Pete Hodges and then his son D. Wilson, Deputy Jeff Richards, Commonwealth Attorney Charles Carter Lee, and even the state alcohol-control man all became associated, not with laws they had sworn to uphold but with ways of avoiding arrest and making a dollar. People said the top law enforcer, Lee himself, could be seen up at the Dugwell filling station making backroom deals, even using the courthouse at times to store still parts confiscated from one place until they could be redistributed to a stiller working for the big shots.

The idea was simple. The local law officials were working with the state boys, so they knew when the raids were planned so the distillers working for them would get notice early. They could help control where the roadblocks would go. They could make anonymous phone calls and warnings that couldn't be traced. They offered this protection for a fee. They would collect the money in cash. For new people they encouraged to join them, they had still parts, caps, and worms they could make available. The demand for liquor was insatiable, they said, and they needed more production. The deputies were the promoters. They were giving out equipment, making loans, collecting. In return, the people could be fairly sure to get some of the profit.

A few people thought it such a good idea that they invested in a new car and started running such big stills that they didn't want to do their farmwork as much anymore. Some turned to selling five-gallon cans in new little stores out beside their homes, offering yeast, sugar, and even cornmeal, all for the new fast whiskey recipe, whiskey made for sale. The new buyers didn't seem to care so much about the corn anymore. This was sugar whiskey, but it was also sugar money, a sweet deal for the boys at the top. The business grew so much that it got Franklin County a special mention in the Wickersham Report, the largest investigative study of Prohibition ever commissioned.

The report, which ended up saying that Prohibition was not, after all, a lost cause, singled out Franklin County as essentially the moonshine capital of the world. Though they had suspicions when they wrote it, the authors of the report didn't even know about the conspiracy involving the major law enforcers in the county.

Yet the protection racket grew more sophisticated by the day. One person kept track of the payments. This was Thomas Jefferson "Jeff" Richards. His sidekick, nicknamed Mutt, drew his pay from the state. They worked with some of the big shots in the community and took their orders from the sheriff and likely from the grandnephew of Robert E. Lee. But not every lawman in the county participated in the scheme. It took guts, but two deputies resigned rather than participate in the conspiracy. One of them was Luther Smith. A member of Long Branch Church where Goode Hash was elder, Smith had been willing to bust stills and draw his gun on men, but when it came to the conspiracy, he told the sheriff he just didn't want anything to do with that mess and walked away. He was no saint aloof from moonshine. He sold a lot of sugar and yeast supplied by the big business known as Ferrum Mercantile, which was selling liquor supplies by the trainload. Deputy Smith had made his own phone warnings before raids, but he just didn't feel right about charging his neighbors to protect them. He'd sell to them, but he'd treat his neighbor as he'd want to be treated. He put the revolver he'd used as a deputy under the counter in his store and turned in his badge. He went back to farming, growing corn, raising his milk and beef cattle and hogs, growing hay, and running the store on the side, but always keeping a watch over his shoulder.

Everyone involved in whiskey production was growing increasingly suspicious. The protection ring added some assurance, but everyone involved knew they just as quickly could find their stills raided. The feds were involved now, and the deputies didn't control their actions, especially because some of the feds were starting to work undercover. On top of that, snitchers had now started to work with the feds, and while no one wanted to be accused of telling on their neighbors, rumors were starting to circulate in Endicott. People were more on edge than ever, and it didn't take much to set them off.

So neighbors just looked the other way, even if frightened men ran right through their cornfield. If a stranger asked about liquor, most said they didn't know a thing about that. Warning bells, car horns, and little children running through narrow woods paths alerted many of the coming revenuers. Neighbors continued to help neighbors, even if just by staying out of their business. When the phones came in the 1920s and '30s, people used them for warning. As the officers left the crossroads up toward Ferrum heading for Endicott, moonshiners received calls before the law rounded the first curve. The bad roads helped the moonshiners in times like these.

Yet tensions continued to mount. Rumors began to circulate in the community that there were snitches, even among the leaders. Luther Smith left the Primitive Baptist Church and was dis-fellowshipped by Goode Hash. It seems Smith thought the elder was guilty of turning in some of the neighbors while Smith was blamed for it. Or was it that no one was quite sure who was guilty of what, and things were getting crazy.

But the rumor that the elder was a snitch grew stronger. Despite his friendship with nearly everyone in the community and his advocacy for many who had been put on trial, at least one family stopped trusting him. So one night, while the entire Hash family was sleeping, someone crept into the barn up on the hill above the house and struck a match to their hay. Before anyone awoke to the sound of a screaming horse, the barn was engulfed in flames. There was nothing to do to save the building or its contents.

The family stood together and watched the logs, first in flame, then glowing red, then falling one by one into a blackening pile. Neighbors came and sympathized and promised to help rebuild when the family was ready with the logs and lumber. Barn raisings were the traditional way of the community, especially for someone as loved as Elder Hash. He had preached the funerals for nearly every family for miles around. He had delivered their mail. But someone thought he had started working for the law. After all, he had been going up to Richmond. One by one, the neighbors who had arrived with buckets to help went home to sleep until first light, leaving the family to return to their own beds. They gave thanks that at least they had their home.

The next morning, the children walked up to the barn. The hay and the corn were gone. They found the harness burned to a blackened crisp. The old jumper had been reduced to a few iron rings where the axles had been. Their horse had burned up in the flames; he was their most personal loss. There was nothing to salvage. But just as they turned back to the house, one of them noticed over in the middle of all the blackened mess that had been their barn a red hen setting on a pile of ashes, clucking low, making noises as if guiding a clutch of chicks. Her eggs had been in the barn before the fire. The force of instinct had pushed her back to the site again the next day. At least she had survived the fire, the children thought, but they never forgot the tragic sight of her there.

Meanwhile, somewhere someone had decided his liquor business came first and didn't care what it took to preserve it. Maybe he was feeling that he had given a snitch what he had coming to him. Maybe he was drunk when he did the deed. Perhaps sometime during the next day or week, because he had likely grown up nearby, he would feel remorse, a feeling that was bound to return every time he passed the Hash farm or the churches where Elder Goode preached or when he saw the neighbors all preparing for the barn raising. Or he could have been one of the lost ones who left no notes, one whose rifle went off somewhere out in the woods aimed at no one but himself.

7 Her Moonshine Neighbor as Herself

Oh, the snobbishness of men! There are prosperous towns and cities in some of the wide valleys, and in the towns and cities men live more easily than their neighbors in the hills. They grow proud and snobbish. Because their fields grow bigger corn, because they live in bigger houses, own automobiles and raise bigger cattle, they feel themselves superior. —SHERWOOD ANDERSON, "I Build a House"

BY THE TIME SHE TESTIFIED as a character witness for Amos Rakes at the 1936 jury-tampering trial, Ora Harrison had lived in Endicott for twenty-seven years. Always single, Miss Ora, age fifty-two, had devoted her entire adult life to teaching and relief work, serving as an Episcopal missionary and director of the St. John's-in-the-Mountains Mission for most of it. After nearly three decades of life and work in the Blue Ridge, her testimony before the judge and jury on behalf of a bootlegger came as no surprise in Endicott, yet how strange her association with him must have seemed to those outside of the community, particularly those outsiders proud, as Sherwood Anderson wrote, to feel themselves superior. But there she was, a graying, bespectacled schoolmarm from an upper-middle-class upbringing, a missionary paid by the same church they knew to be the religious home of doctors and lawyers, not just casting off any snobbishness she might've been raised with, but sitting among, even identifying with, the families of moonshiners.

She had ridden to court in the mission's car with Miss Maude Beheler, her friend and coworker who was ten years Ora's junior. Miss Maude accompanied her most everywhere she went, particularly because Ora never learned to drive. The mission's task, as Ora described it in her letters to supporters, was to serve and teach the people of the mountains and, above all, to live and minister in the community. It was the living part—staying so long in one place and in touch with neighbors—that changed Ora. She had entered Endicott with crisp ideas of right and wrong and of what needed to be changed, but the years of living among neighbors driven to break the liquor tax laws out of necessity had softened the edges of her dogma.

When Amos Rakes asked her to be a character witness for him, she agreed without hesitation and asked Miss Maude to plan to be in court with her for at least a week. When they arrived, Ora sat patiently waiting while keeping an intense focus on the proceedings. When the defense called her and the bailiff asked her to place her hand on the Holy Book to swear to tell the truth, the words she spoke to the judge and jury were out of love for a neighbor, someone she had known for years, a man who had helped her at the mission. That he was a moonshiner had little or nothing to do with his trustworthiness, she knew. She asked the court to consider Rakes as an honest community member whom she personally could vouch for. By doing so, she staked her reputation not only with Amos but with moonshine mountaineers in general.

▼ ■ ■

As a child growing up in Rocky Mount, Virginia, twenty-three miles from Endicott, no one Ora knew had ever risked going into the mountains. They were afraid of the "whiskey blockade," as they called it. They believed that an outsider could get her head blown off if she went there. Though none of her neighbors or kin had ever ventured far beyond their own improved roads to find out, most of them assumed they knew all they needed to know about the people there. Ora grew up hearing the prejudices and later wrote about it: "I heard the grown ups talking about these rough mountain people, and their cabins and their blockade or moonshine stills and even then it didn't seem to me these grown ups were much interested in them, only to want them in jail . . . for everybody seemed afraid of them and no one I knew would have dared go up into those mountains."[1]

Growing up in the 1890s, Ora walked to school from her family's home in Rocky Mount. On Monday mornings once a month, the walk provided her a special adventure. She passed by the place where people from the hills camped on her father's tobacco warehouse property. "They came on Sunday and spent Sunday night in their covered wagons in the tobacco warehouse lot," she wrote.[2] They couldn't afford lodging or meals, so they slept instead under quilts on their wagon floors and cooked outside on fires with wood they carried with them. On her way to school, Ora could smell their fatback frying and see the men in their "high boots and spurs holding frying pans over a fire," all within sight of the courthouse. She lingered as no one in her family would have dared, hearing the "rough talk" of the men. Sometimes she saw children her own age staring at her from out of the wagons, and she, with her nice dress and shoes and books, looked back and knew they had none of that. Unlike her family members, she was not afraid. She was mesmerized.

At certain points from Rocky Mount, Ora could look toward the west to the tall mountains looming on the horizon in succeeding ridges of dark purplish blue. Somehow, even as a child, she knew that was the place for her. Her people told her that area was the "worst part of the mountains then. It was the most isolated, most remote from the County Seat, and the most murders had been committed there."[3] At least that is what they told her. Yet something else stirred within her about the place. A voice spoke, born of romance and pity no doubt, but also of genuine care for others mixed with a measure of adventure. "I made up my mind then, that when I grew up, I was going to go up to those mountains and find out something about those people," she wrote.

Ora graduated from high school in Franklin County, one of the privileged few women to do so then. She attended additional months of training at the

FIGURE 22. Miss Ora Harrison (1884–1968), founder of St. John's-in-the-Mountains Episcopal Mission in Endicott, Virginia, poses (right) with weavings community members made during her tenure. She is accompanied by Miss Maude Beheler (left), who taught the weaving classes, and another teacher at the mission. The weavings were sold by mail order as a fund-raiser for St. John's. Photograph courtesy of Lonie Wagoner Rorrer.

State Normal and Industrial School for Women in Radford, Virginia. Upon graduation from Radford, she entered the teaching profession, and after a few years teaching in Rocky Mount and living at home, she applied to teach at the Sandy Level School, a one-room schoolhouse in Endicott. The school had never had a teacher from outside the community before, but when she asked about the job, the county school superintendent, H. D. Dillard, encouraged Ora to try it. He told her that few teachers were willing to take mountain positions because of the ill-equipped school buildings and difficulty boarding with poor families, but this could be a "mission" for her, he suggested.[4] He had no idea how far she would take that thought.

In October 1909, Ora Lula Harrison, age twenty-five, boarded the train in Rocky Mount and headed to Ferrum, the closest station to Endicott. At Ferrum, a twelve-year-old boy, Wid and Maude Rakes's son Willie, met her at the station. He was leading two mules. "Are you the new teacher?" he asked. When she said she was, he helped her strap her bags behind the saddle on one of the mules. Willie's family had agreed to board the new teacher but had sent only the boy to fetch her. He brought no buckboard or wagon; as likely they had neither, only the mules. Willie mounted the lead mule and handed Ora the reins to the second. The mule had been strapped with a sidesaddle, and the family sent a long black skirt to protect her clothing. As the boy waited silently, she pulled the skirt over her head and let it drape over her dress. Then she hiked up one leg to the stirrup and hopped a few times, finally pulling herself up, turning backward into the saddle as ladylike as she could muster. Ora had never ridden a mule before, let alone in this awkward fashion. When she had positioned both legs off to the mule's left side as best she could, slipping her left foot into the stirrup, the unlikely pair—a new schoolteacher and her barefoot guide less than half her age—set out on the eighteen-mile trip through Endicott and on toward Shooting Creek.

They traveled on a red-dirt road that followed the hilly terrain by farms and into the hills, where patches of trees glowed with reds, greens, and yellows in the fall light. They passed rail fences and log barns. Ora studied the houses and their outbuildings surrounded by small fields. She saw pastures with cattle and horses and cultivated land then lined with corn or its stubble, among which the corn stalks were already drying in shocks. She saw apple trees, some laden with ripening fruit. Everywhere there was beauty as well as hardship, even a girl raised in town could tell right away how much work there was to that life and how much a challenge it would be to find study time for children working there.

As they climbed into the steeper mountains, she saw that the homesteads were crowded closer together and the houses were smaller and handmade, many of them of hand-hewn logs, but others of vertical rough lumber. Smoke rose from every chimney she saw as well as from small fires under clothes-washing pots and outdoor kettles. Firewood was piled at every house. Every breath of air she took ushered in the smells of fall homesteads in the Appalachians: wood smoke from fires for lye soap, lard rendering, clothes boiling, pork frying, apple butter simmering, and hidden distilleries; the scents of workhorse sweat, chickens, hogs, cattle, their manure, and hardworking people; of drying hay and corn, brown leaves and evergreen trees, and outhouses.

Ora finally had arrived in the mountains she had dreamed of, and she was well aware she was entering alone into territory her family members said was violent and moonshine crazed. As idealistic as any young teacher could be, she ignored their warnings. Yet as her mule clopped along for hours on badly rutted roads and with the boy talking so little, she clenched the reins and began to worry. She wrote that it was an all-day trip over "rough mountain roads" into what seemed "at first an unfriendly country." As they got closer to Thompson Ridge and crossed over the hill headed down to Long Branch, the boy got braver, though not exactly friendlier. She recalled his mischief:

> The boy whistled and hummed different tunes, but had very little to say, hardly answering my questions. After a while he got tired, for he had a little fun out of the new teacher. He realized from the start that I was not accustomed to riding and that I was afraid of the mule, so he watched for his chance and when he caught me off guard he gave my mule a touch from behind with his switch, which caused him to jump suddenly; then when we would come to a level stretch in the road he would give a sudden yell, rise in his stirrups, and his mule would start off at breakneck speed, my mule following, with me suspended in air, but when I came down I always managed to land on the mule's back. Then he would remark, quite innocently, "That wore a nice trot."[5]

Staying with the Rakes family was a hardship for Ora. Their home was three miles from the school, and she was forced to walk the distance to and from the schoolhouse daily, regardless of the weather. Inside the home, there were no amenities to speak of. On top of that, old man Wid had gone deaf. He and his younger wife, Maude, had ten children living at home then, including one blind daughter who "rocked herself in a chair and sang and rocked incessantly." The oldest daughter, Lilly, who had married Luther Smith, did what she could to care for her sister and their younger siblings, but there was simply too much need to be met.

In exchange for her rent payment, the family gave Ora their sleeping loft, from where she "looked at the stars through the holes in the roof" and washed her face in icy water every winter morning. To make room for her, all of the children moved downstairs in the cabin where the parents slept. Some slept with the parents in the same bed. Others bedded down on quilt pallets near the fireplace in the kitchen. Ora's meals there were generous, but simple, crowded, and quick. The family's income, what there was of it, was from farming and moonshine. The five-dollar monthly boarding fee was a boost.

FIGURE 23. The Wid and Maude Rakes family in Endicott, Virginia, circa 1910. The young woman seated on the far left is Lilly Rakes Smith, wife of Luther Smith and great-grandmother of the author. Author's personal collection.

Ora searched in vain for another place to live, writing that the Rakes family told her there was no other option because she was new and people wouldn't trust her. Maybe they were being protective. Maybe they needed the money that much. Regardless, she stayed with the Rakes for the year, though at times she became so discouraged that "she thought she would leave and never return."[6] The accommodations and the conversation were difficult enough for a woman of her background—she had never split a stick of wood or slaughtered a chicken, and she hardly knew which end of a cow to milk—but the hardest part for her was the loneliness. Everyone knew who she was, but she had no confidant. Being Episcopalian, she found even Endicott Christianity foreign. She wrote several times of her concern that the only church there was Primitive Baptist and lamented that they didn't believe in Sunday schools. She thought that meant that people didn't care about learning at all.[7] To her credit, she stayed to find out she was wrong about both the church and the people.

Ora worked hard, and both she and her students began to change. During her first year, Ora gained the reputation as a "tight teacher" who kept order in her classroom. One of her former pupils remembered her stern expression. She "just had to look at you to get you to stop talking and pay attention, even the big boys."[8] After a few weeks, she didn't need to raise her voice at all to command her students' attention. A few months into her work, she earned the parents' respect and cooperation as well. By the end of the first year, there were so many families seeking Ora's instruction for their children that the community decided to add a second classroom onto the original building, all without government help. With that new room and additional students to aid her cause, Ora convinced the county officials to pay for an assistant teacher to help her the following year.

As her reputation and confidence grew, Ora asked about other places to live and had "no difficulty getting free board" with the Isaac T. Cannaday family just down the road from the school. They were one of the most well-to-do families in the community, though they were still small mountain farmers earning little cash. One of their descendants, Lane Boyd, said his Cannaday ancestors had originally owned thousands of acres and even held slaves in Endicott, but little remained of that original plantation by the 1930s.

Ora taught at Sandy Level and lived with the Cannaday family for four years. During that time, all the neighbors began calling her "Miss Ora" out of familiarity and respect. Community members agreed to pay her extra salary out of their own pockets. While the county paid Miss Ora for six months each year, residents raised money for an additional two months. During her tenure there, she built the Long Branch District School up from four grades to seven. She and her assistant made great headway with the resources they had, but still there was something missing for Miss Ora.

After finishing her fifth year of teaching, she informed trusted members of the community that she was considering leaving her position. Her neighbors rallied and begged her to stay, pledging to do anything they could to help her. As she considered their offer, she realized that she didn't want to leave Endicott after all, but wanted to go deeper, to do more than give the pupils a seventh grade education only to send them back home. She wanted to give the Endicott youth, particularly the promising young girls who wanted to be teachers, a different chance at life. She dreamed of teaching all the grades up through high school and to do this in a religious setting so she could introduce Sunday school as well. When some of the neighbors agreed to back her efforts, she set to work on building a mission.

Ora met with Rocky Mount's Episcopal priest, W. T. Roberts, who had helped establish a different mission called St. Peters-in-the-Mountains in Callaway, also in Franklin County, but some twenty miles away. She took his ideas for how to build a mission back to the Endicott parents. Though some of the families were too poor to spare their older children's time from farm work, most parents responded with enthusiasm, including community stalwarts Goode and Nannie Hash. With Miss Ora's guidance, community members wrote a letter to Rector Roberts requesting his help in starting a mission in Endicott and asking that Roberts recommend Miss Ora to run it. The Cannadays offered to donate land on which to build the structure. Roberts readily agreed to offer his support and sent the community's request to Bishop Lett of the Diocese of Southern Virginia, located in Roanoke. Upon receipt of the letter, the bishop interviewed Miss Ora and agreed to look for salary money for her as a diocesan employee and spearheaded efforts to raise funds for the new mission, to be named at Father Roberts's suggestion St. John's-in-the-Mountains. Lett agreed to look into the women's Episcopal fund known as the United Thank Offering (UTO) to find salary money for Ora.

Going on faith that the money was forthcoming, Ora took the job as diocesan mission worker at the beginning of the school year in the fall of 1915.[9] By January 1916, the national Board of Missions of the Episcopal Church in New York City had agreed to pay Ora a "salary of Four Hundred Dollars per annum." Quoting Father Roberts in his letter, Bishop Lett wrote an announcement about the new mission: "The Mission at Endicott is full of promise to the Church and the school is a most important adjunct to Church work in this new region of the mountains. It is quite impossible to over-estimate the value of educational work in the mountains . . . in bringing the children under Church influence."[10] Meanwhile, the community had set to work on construction of the school building. By the time Miss Ora's first salary check came in the mail from the national office, the stone exterior walls of the mission school were nearly complete. With financial contributions from both the diocese and the Rocky Mount Trinity Church, along with the community's gifts of labor, building materials, and food, the school building was finished within the year.

Father Roberts supplied the school plans, and the Endicott community members built the school to the exact specifications of St. Peters: two stories of stone and rows of large windows on all sides to let in natural light. The downstairs had three classrooms, and the upstairs was left open as a meeting room to serve as both auditorium and church sanctuary. Men who had worked with rock all their lives building chimneys and other structures joined with equally skilled woodworkers to craft the building. Jim Edwards headed the construction job, and Luther Smith worked as his helper. Those two received a small wage. The rest of the labor for what was nicknamed the Rock Church was donated by Endicott residents who worked as if to raise a barn for a neighbor. Families brought rocks out of their fields in wagons and piled them for the stonemasons. Women prepared food for meals on-site. The community, which had built every small schoolhouse their children had ever attended, knew how to work together. But this was the grandest project the community had ever undertaken. Dozens of families pitched in; even the children helped build their own school.

St. John's-in-the-Mountains would become the largest and sturdiest structure ever built in Endicott before or since. Perched on a hill about a half-mile above the Hash farm on the Ferrum Road, it commanded admiration and

FIGURE 24. Lead carpenter Jim Edwards, seated, and Luther Smith pose with their sons and their hand tools during the building of St. John's-in-the-Mountains in 1915. Author's personal collection.

offered those looking away from it a spectacular view of the surrounding mountains and farms. While few would ever consider themselves permanently Episcopalian, almost every member of the community considered it their school and the centerpiece of Endicott. Hundreds attended events there, from Christmas pageants where Ora passed out presents to every child, to musical performances, to womanless weddings, which were comedic plays in which men dressed up as the women, including the bride. Since the Primitive Baptist Church's beliefs didn't allow the use of its buildings for any purposes besides preaching, the mission became the only community center for activities outside of preaching the people had.

On the day they completed the building, a number of men climbed to the roof to mount a church bell in the belfry. They affixed the cast-iron uprights to the wood frame they had carefully measured, knotted a rope to the crank attached to the bell's yoke, and fed it through a small hole in the roof to the upstairs room. When the rope was in place, the men gave the signal that the bell was ready for testing. Miss Ora went to the big room upstairs and heaved down on the rope, turning the heavy bell upward and making the clapper hit the side with a clang. She let the rope pull back, and it rang again. She repeated the pull several more times, and the peals echoed over the ridges, telling of

FIGURE 25. St. John's-in-the-Mountains Mission, Endicott, Virginia, circa 1920. Photograph courtesy of Lonie Wagoner Rorrer.

the new mission's beginning. The people gathered that day applauded. But the boys and men off in the hollows making moonshine thought the tolling was a warning sign, like the farm bells on their own places ringing at an odd time of day. As far as they knew, bells were for signaling mealtimes or danger. Knowing it was not time to eat, more than one crew of men working stills grabbed up their copper and ran.

▪ ▪ ▪

Ora launched into her new job as missionary with legendary energy, taking on the role of communicator with the bishops and a fund-raiser to the broader public, mostly UTO representatives in the North. Like any good fund-raiser, she wrote of dire need and huge potential at Endicott. In her enthusiasm, however, she went too far and repeated common stereotypes about the community. In a letter to potential funders, she wrote that Endicott was ridden with "crime and violence and lawlessness." She criticized the Primitive Baptists for having no Sunday schools and called them superstitious people in need of religious instruction. Still, in the same pages, she said the people were "of the finest stock to be found in America," where "many of the young people when given an opportunity have proven that they can hold their own and often excel when given an equal opportunity with others."[11] Money would make the difference, she said, and the donations began arriving.

Money came for desks and for mission farm equipment. Women of the UTO in faraway states began sending checks, some of them large enough to start whole new enterprises, including an orchard and a crafts house. Ora wrote personal letters to the bishop and her donors, often writing late into the night. She invited people to spend time relaxing in the cool, green mountains and to try her mission's country-raised food. Entertaining guests was a good fund-raising strategy, though it taxed the staff and volunteers working to maintain the living quarters and kitchen. She worked at a frantic pace late into the night to manage it all, keeping her room cluttered with papers and financial books. Her haste showed in her communications. "Yours in a hurry" was the common closing to her appeals.

After the mission school opened its doors, Ora obtained permission from the diocese to use donations to buy and move a vacant two-story house from down the road to the mission property. It would be used as the teachers' residence. Amos Rakes and many others gathered to help with the big move. Elder Hash, though he walked with a cane after his accident, joined in as well. During the week leading up to the move, men cut and hewed straight logs to serve as rollers, and on the moving day as some used jacks to lift the house off the foundation, others placed the logs under the sills of the house and at regular intervals in front of it. Drivers readied their teams of harnessed horses and mules. With long, heavy ropes, they tied off their draft animals in their full harnesses and blinders to the leading side of the house. When one of the men gave the word, drivers snapped the reins lightly on their animals' rumps and spoke gently "come up," and the animals strained and the whole house, complete with chimney, began to inch forward as the logs rolled like great long wheels underneath. As each log did its job and slowly rolled out behind, men and boys lifted it and walked it around to the front and readied it for use again. The work continued for most of a day until the men brought the house to its resting place next to the school, jacked it up off the logs, underpinned the house at its corners with rocks, and set it down level. It was a feat of simple machines, animal power, and donated labor. Dozens of people and their animals had worked together so well that nothing moved out of place; even the mortar of the chimney remained unbroken. Anyone who watched had to remark on the ingenuity of it all. It was a scene that Sherwood Anderson would have loved: a work of cooperation and neighborliness that stemmed from necessity, a shared history, and skills passed down and taught to children working alongside their elders. It was a scene that, among others, inspired Miss Ora to call her neighbors the "best people in the nation." Elsewhere in her writing, she called Endicott residents "fine and intelligent people" with "multiple potentialities for development."[12] She knew that without their labor, their mutual dream of a school for all the children could never have come true.

The question Miss Ora left unanswered is how she could write with such superlatives about a people in one sentence and of their depravity in another. The violent community she wrote about was the same one that helped build her mission. Those she described as misguided, Primitive Baptists, gave their labor to build the school for their children. Of course, in Endicott there were some rough men and boys and some ready to fight faster than their neighbors, especially when they were drunk. A teenage Amos Rakes had been

FIGURE 26. Teachers' house at St. John's. Moved onto its location by members of the community, the residence served as the missionary home from 1915 to the early 1960s when the mission was closed. Photograph courtesy of Lonie Wagoner Rorrer.

part of such a group of boys. Crimes occurred there as they do everywhere. However, as those perpetrators of crimes came from close-knit families who worked together with neighbors, including many of them who worked on the mission, and all lived where everyone knew everyone's business, it's hard to imagine they were any worse than others anywhere else then or now. There was only one Endicott. It was Miss Ora who was divided.

Reading between the lines of her mission records and correspondence, the independent and curious Ora, the person who was willing to cross boundaries and defy convention and her family's wishes, always remained a part of who she was. On one level, she rejected stereotypes and stayed and committed her life to the mission despite the odds, and that alone was a major feat for anyone then. But Ora was always a creation of her time and place as well, and, in her case, when she joined the church as a missionary she inherited and became a caretaker of church history as it stood in her time, complete with its language of Christian missions. Her bishop, priest, and donors expected no less. So Ora spoke and wrote in two languages about Endicott, one born of emotion and experience and a second one passed down to her from a tradition that still included unexamined privilege and assumed superiority.

St. John's was both the brainchild of one woman and a part of the long history of the Anglican Church in Virginia dating back to the Virginia Company's landing at Jamestown in 1607. When Ora started the mission in 1915, she subjected her life and work to Episcopalian authority centered on order, prayerful reflection, and service as defined by centuries of tradition that Anglicans were convinced every New World settler needed, including those on the frontier's edge.[13] To them, the presence of other homegrown churches, particularly the Baptist, was a sign that people were being led astray from the Church of England's Prayer Book life. Meanwhile, the Baptists and other sects, coming from dissenter faiths in Europe, shunned hierarchy and believed instead in the priesthood of all believers, with each individual having direct access to God equally, wherever and whoever they were, without need of the Anglican tradition.

Conflicts arose early between Baptist and Episcopal congregations in Virginia, leading even to violent outbreaks.[14] Often their disagreements split along class lines, with the Episcopalian message appealing to the lettered and landed, and the dissenters catering to the sometimes illiterate white yeomen and sharecroppers and even enslaved blacks.[15] Episcopalians considered outlier churches with ministers called to preach within local communities and without special training threats to their authority, arguing that "historically oriented and educated ordained ministry should . . . be available throughout the nation," and some argued it should be mandated.[16] Though this sense of Anglican entitlement to religious establishment subsided with the Revolutionary War, it continued well into Miss Ora's lifetime.

On the frontier following the Revolution, Baptists and other outsider churches were mostly left to themselves, and they thrived in the Appalachians. John C. and Olive Dame Campbell, who surveyed mountain religion extensively during the early twentieth century, wrote that the rapid growth of these Baptist, Methodist, and other "dissenter churches" in early mountain settlements was due to "the fundamental democracy of their appeal, the right of every man, no matter how poor and unlettered he might be, to think for himself in matters of religion."[17] The thriving religion they found in the early 1900s had been growing for well over two centuries.

When Miss Ora became a missionary, she dutifully accepted that Episcopalians possessed Christian truth, whether she was cognizant of its historical biases or not. Her role, as she saw it, was to bring Endicott residents, regardless of the fact that many were already Christian, into the Episcopalian fold. For her, the Episcopal Church was a "teaching church," and that meant that she should lead the children of those like the Primitive Baptists out of their Endicott wilderness. Without Episcopalian instruction, they would waste away in ignorance, she thought. In fact, the problem was mostly a lack of resources and trained personnel for the schools, which Primitive Baptists in Endicott recognized as readily as she. The lack of funding for education had nothing to do with religious leanings.

The Episcopal Church did not wait on the government to do something about social problems; instead it used its resources to take education to communities where it saw a need. Their domestic missionary movement that led to Ora's job began just after the Civil War, from the beginning led by middle- and upper-class lay women.[18] The first missionaries left northern states to take education to the South during the Reconstruction period of the early 1870s.[19] They focused on the South because they believed that slavery had prevailed in some states because they had "no common school system." Ignorance, they believed, led to a chasm between "a diffused and universal education in the North and a very limited education in the South."[20] Of course, their theory didn't account for the educated racists who led the Confederacy or the educated sympathizers in the North.

The driving force for educational missions was called the Women's Auxiliary to the Board of Missions, which started in 1872 and held its first Christian Workers Conference in 1880. They sent their first woman missionary to the "white field" in the South in 1882. *The Spirit of Missions* magazine kept Episcopalians informed about this work among poor southern whites, which emphasized work with mountaineers along with "Colored Work" and "Indian Work."[21]

At the Episcopal General Convention in October 1889, the Women's Auxiliary gathered to begin a tradition known as Thank Offering Day. "In the beginning was God and the women's auxiliary!" one of the women exclaimed as the group pooled their money to reach out to the poor. Their goal was to give a major annual offering to help others through teaching as well as evangelism. They believed in ministering to the whole person—spiritually, mentally, and physically—and in helping the poor not only learn about God but also enter the American economic mainstream, just as the nation rushed toward industrialization. The missionaries, whether they realized it or not, became the harbingers of education for new workers in industry, not only teaching them through Sunday schools but also helping them acquire skills to help them leave their traditional communities to provide manpower for new urban jobs.

In Virginia, where the established Church of England had taken a beating during the Revolution, a rebirth of the Anglican church of the old and elite Virginia families was underway by 1820 and slowly spreading into the mountains. The Civil War slowed any religious advance, but after the war the Episcopal movement picked up again. By 1889, the year the UTO began, the Episcopal Diocese of Virginia had started several Virginia missions, including in the Ragged Mountains near Charlottesville.[22] Soon they had founded a number of mission churches, schools, and health centers in southern Virginia, gaining enough members to form the Diocese of Southern Virginia by 1892. In the next two decades, the diocese grew to be the third largest in the country and increased so fast that by the time Miss Ora arrived in Endicott the diocese's mission work was the most active among Episcopalians in the nation. Miss Ora's mission was but a part of a major Anglican movement in the region characterized on the diocese's Web site today as one that "brought the Social Gospel to hills and hollows, mining towns and timber camps of Southwestern Virginia."[23]

The Social Gospel was a major progressive religious response to American industrialization during the half-century following the Civil War period when new factories, banks, and railroads were beginning to create fortunes for many across the country. The new theology championed social equality, pointing out that while unprecedented American growth had created tremendous wealth, it had also opened chasms between the haves and have-nots.[24] They argued that poverty in the midst of plenty was a social sin that needed to be cleansed. Too many American people had no health care, education, and adequate housing, and Social Gospel reformers, a sizable number of them Episcopalians, argued that the church should help fight for equal access to society's benefits. Education was one of their main weapons.

St. John's came into existence at the height of the Social Gospel movement's influence, and it shows in Miss Ora's writing, as when she connected Endicott's lack of roads to its economic problems: "Much of the land is so rough and steep it is difficult to cultivate and with the bad roads and distance from market it was almost impossible for the people to sell the few things they could raise for market."[25] She also linked, in Social Gospel fashion, solving society's ills to church-sponsored education: "Whenever and wherever it can reach the people and hold them long enough to put some teaching . . . across, the people change . . . and they grow to mean something to both church and state—I have seen this demonstrated very plainly in the mountains."[26]

The quandary for the mountain missionaries espousing the Social Gospel was how to address the economy of whiskey making. Should it be represented as an individual moral problem, which was not the focus for the Social Gospel? Or, from the other end of the spectrum, could moonshining be used somehow to point to Endicott being left out economically? *Forth* magazine, a monthly periodical about Episcopal missions, chose a third option in an article about Miss Ora. The article says that moonshine was a symptom of the mountains having no laws due to societal neglect: "Enactment of public laws was difficult, and the making of illegal whiskey was rampant."[27] While it's accurate to say that moonshine production took off in part because of the lack of public attention to a region, treating moonshine as a symptom of the lack of laws makes it seem as though it was simply a social disease that came into existence because of government neglect. No Social Gospel proponent seemed to be willing to say moonshining was an economic coping strategy, a means of making money directly linked to the lack of schools, good roads, and jobs. While true, such a stance would've been too controversial for a church worker at that time.

▪ ▪ ▪

The Episcopalians weren't the only ones sending missionaries to the mountains in the early twentieth century. Two additional church bodies located schools in Endicott—the Presbyterians built a small school in the Shooting Creek community and the Methodists opened a mission school called Trinity on Runnett Bag Creek—both opening their doors shortly after Miss Ora started her work. Those schools had neither full-time missionaries nor a compound like St. John's, but their close proximity shows the kind of mainline denomination focus the mountains received at the time. To document just how extensive mission coverage was, the Russell Sage Foundation, for which

John C. Campbell had once served as secretary, commissioned a survey in 1929 of all the mountain missions and social outreach agencies in the region.[28] The study listed over one hundred fifty church-related schools in the southern Appalachians. When counting all types of outreach, including vocational training and crafts, the number rose to nearly five hundred different mission-ary institutions. These mission schools provided education where counties and the state did not and raised educational standards generally throughout the mountains.[29] Though critics say this masked government neglect and often married church support to industry's goals.

St. John's was more than a school. While one hundred twenty-five students attended at its peak enrollment, hundreds more people attended ice cream socials and other events there. Goode Hash's children were among the first to attend the school, though for theological reasons they didn't attend the Sunday-morning training and choir practice. Elder Hash befriended Miss Ora early in her stay and respected the young teacher's leadership. Goode and Nannie even named a daughter after her. Their daughter Ora Hash was one of five Hash children who became teachers.

While Miss Ora wrote, "The old Baptists still believe that what is to be will be and that other churches and Sunday Schools are the devil's work," she and Goode Hash decided on several occasions to set aside theological differences and to set their sites on mutual goals for Endicott.[30] Ora even began attending Primitive Baptist meetings periodically. Elder Hash once preached against Episcopalians when Miss Ora was present, chastising the church for believ-ing they could redeem the world. But at the close of the sermon, he leaned over the pulpit and said to his missionary friend sitting in the pew, "I didn't mean you, Miss Ora."[31]

◼ ◼ ◼

Missions in the Social Gospel tradition were the antithesis of Primitive Baptist theology. For Episcopalians, missions were meant as a human connection to persons left out of God's plan for redemption of society, which included health, education, and welfare. Primitive Baptists, in contrast, believed that human beings have no place in trying to help God redeem the world and that God, not missionaries, is in charge of the world's salvation. One elder preaching in the 1920s singled out the main rub: "Missions [teach] that the spiritual kingdom is dependent upon men . . . and not upon God's grace and the atonement of Jesus."[32] Miss Ora and other missionaries accused the Primitive Baptists of fatalism, but Goode Hash's life and work show that while he believed he personally had no power to bring about change in a spiritual setting, as might be taught in a Sunday school, he continually engaged elected officials politically and stayed involved in community issues from his first days of carrying the mail to conducting the U.S. census to traveling to Richmond to lobby the governor in later life. He was active in county politics as well. Noted Appalachian scholar Loyal Jones says Goode's kind of political work has long been common among the "hard-shell Baptists." It seems that the main difference between Primitive Baptists' and Episcopalians' views of advocacy is that the former believed that social engagement should be kept out of the church setting, though not out of a Christian's life, while Episcopalian missionaries mixed the two on Sunday as well as through the rest of the week.

While his Sunday sermons said nothing about social issues, Monday mornings Hash could be found lobbying superintendents of Franklin County schools, including Superintendent Harold Ramsey, who took office in 1927. His goal was to bring a public school to Endicott. He also advocated, along with Miss Ora, for a paved road so that a school bus might take the older students to the county high school in Rocky Mount and farmers could have a way to take produce to market. As an educator, Ramsey already knew his county needed better schooling and lamented its slow growth. Ramsey wrote a history of the school system in which he pointed out that prior to 1870 there had been no public education in Franklin County at all.

Not until the Virginia Constitutional Convention of 1869 had Virginia made provision for public schools at all. Forty years later, conditions of the schools were still deplorable, particularly for blacks. Private education was the main option in Franklin County then. In 1927 when Ramsey came into office, one- and two-room schools still dotted Franklin County, almost all of which had been built by local people and staffed by women from the communities where the schools were located. As was true of Miss Ora, all the teachers, even the outsiders, were paid paltry salaries and boarded with families. Only in the late 1930s, as the New Deal began to pump money into rural areas, did an alternative school building program begin in earnest.

Construction of the Endicott Elementary School was completed in 1936, only a few months after Ora gave her testimony for Amos Rakes.[33]

With local leadership and the arrival of federal dollars, Endicott would have found a way to educate its children without Miss Ora and the Episcopal Church. Yet everyone agrees, including the Hash family, that Miss Ora hastened the day and gave a whole generation of children, from 1914 to 1936, a chance to attend high school when they would've had no other opportunity. Goode and Nannie Hash welcomed Miss Ora's contributions for their own children even as Goode lobbied in Richmond. Education was their shared vision, and they pursued it together, though in their own traditions.

Elizabeth Hooker, a church historian in the 1930s, referred to domestic missions as one group of Christians encountering another. Before the missionaries' arrival, she said, people in the "Highlander religion" were already "keenly sensitive to the reality of spiritual things, the grandeur of human destiny, and the importance of personal choice." She complimented the Primitive Baptists in particular when she added, "Their monthly preaching services and the annual protracted meetings influence toward the resolution of inner conflicts, toward goodness, and toward peace of mind." But still she argued for new religious training away from the old faiths. While missionaries were not about to change the adults, she said, by working with children they could bring about change in the future through "molding the plastic minds of the young." Through this work, she said, "[the schools] are naturalizing the Highlanders of the future of the world . . . thus tending to lessen the spiritual isolation of the Highlands."[34] But what Hooker and the missionary movement often failed to recognize was that parents were the ones who made it possible for children to attend schools. The schools got more cooperation, even from the so-called spiritually isolated, than the missionaries sometimes admitted. Goode Hash's story and his highly educated children stand as proof, as does the St. John's construction scene.

■ ■ ■

As St. John's came into its own by 1917, new teachers began applying for jobs. Applications arrived from Massachusetts, Illinois, and later from the body of the school's own graduates. Ora hosted new volunteers and donors regularly, also from faraway states. The guests arrived by train in Ferrum, and Ora and her staff met them with horse and buggy and later with the mission's car. Ora hired local people to work in the house and garden, paying local boys a quarter a day for some field jobs and adults not that much more to do odd jobs and cook. Miss Ora bought a few milk cows and hogs and had local farmers plant an orchard and harvest hay. Local girls picked and canned garden produce and blackberries. On stormy days and during cold weather, the teachers' home served as a boarding house for students. Sally Lumsden, one of the teachers, remembered: "We had cots out where we put the children if the creeks got up or if it was too cold, rough, or stormy. The children brought their lunches, but when they stayed overnight we always had eggs, milk, meat, and cereal for breakfast. Sometimes in the winter we had buckwheat cakes."[35]

Around 1920, a nurse and doctor arrived at the mission, two single and independent women who stayed in the community for three years. They rode horses to make house calls and lived with Miss Ora. The doctor was Francis "Dr. Franc" Morrill. Dr. Franc was a godsend for many bedridden and ailing patients who had never seen a physician. She treated hundreds, perhaps thousands, while there, and she continued to stay in touch with Miss Ora the rest of her life, later bankrolling a number of different initiatives, including the sleeping porch for the children at the teachers' house. Dr. Franc also left money in her will for St. John's. Miss Ann Barlow, called Nurse Annie, was an English-trained nurse-midwife who joined the doctor. For the two years the two worked there, they were the only health providers for a thirty-mile radius, and they worked free of charge. In this way in particular, the mission made a huge difference that people remember to this day.

In its heyday, St. John's held a magnetic quality for dozens of visitors from outside the community. They were drawn there because of the good work, the tranquility of the place, Miss Ora's hospitality, and because the food was delicious. Young boarders who worked in exchange for school and a room, such as motherless Lonie Rorrer, who did much of the food preparation and a substantial number of the chores, from milking to cleanup. Guests roamed the property for exercise and fresh air, ate meals together, and left with a commitment to send donations.

With Dr. Franc's help, the mission purchased an adjacent farm. At its height, St. John's owned 177 acres stretching across the mountain and into hollows usually unexplored. One guest from England once returned from a walk in the mission's woods to report seeing a clothes-washing operation with wooden barrels. Ora laughed when she realized that the guest had come upon a moonshine still. The mission land was the site of more than one still over the years, leading to complaints from staff members that the mission owned more land than they could tend to.

▪ ▪ ▪

In 1918, St. John's hosted a famous folk-song collector from England, Sir Cecil J. Sharp. He stayed at the mission for several nights while he searched for traditional songs in the community. The visit was part of a three-year trek, from 1917 to 1919, during which he roamed the Appalachians, listening to songs and transcribing the words and music to thousands of tunes, which he said were likely from the borderlands of the British Isles. He wrote the following about the people he met: "They have an easy unaffected bearing and the unselfconscious manners of the well-bred. . . . On no single occasion did we receive anything but courteous and friendly treatment. Strangers that we met in the course of our long walks would usually bow, doff the hat, and extend the hand, saying, 'My name is _____, what is yours?' an introduction that usually led to a pleasant talk and sometimes a singing."[36] Sharp traveled with educational missionaries John Campbell, until his death in 1919, and Olive Dame Campbell on many of the excursions. Olive had previously collected ballads and tunes single-handedly and was one of the first to tell Sharp about the huge numbers of old tunes in the Blue Ridge in North Carolina and Virginia.

While in Endicott, Sharp collected twenty-seven different songs, many of them ballads with old themes from the British Isles. Sharp's goal was to capture the songs before the singers lost them to modernization. He praised the traditional lifestyle in places like Endicott, where people could sing and be "immune from that continuous grinding, mental pressure, due to an attempt to 'make a living,' from which all of us in the modern world suffer."[37] Indeed, he found his traditional songs.

But his collection from Endicott also included "The Sunny South" as sung to him by Mrs. Lucy Cannaday, with this chorus:

Take me home to the place where I first saw the light,
To the sweet sunny South take me home—
Where the mocking birds sing me to rest every night,
And why was I tempted to roam?[38]

The tune may have borrowed from earlier English ballads, but the song's theme was about a person who had left the U.S. South, likely to work in the North, and who longed to return. So, contrary to Sharp's notion that mountains were an isolated repository of dying music, Mrs. Cannaday's song's nostalgic longing for her southern home reflects not just the British Isles but human movements into and out of the mountains as well, which was happening in Endicott long before the song catcher arrived.

Sharp also seemed to imply in his essay that the mountaineer had few troubles, which during the years immediately prior to Prohibition and during the agricultural depression was far from the case. But, he admitted, "the outsider does not always see the whole of the game," particularly the "less lovely side of the picture." He said the negative side had "already been emphasized, with unnecessary insistence, by other observers."[39] In other words, most had criticized the mountaineers for causing their own problems. Instead of dwelling on such stereotypes, Sharpe's goal was to document the singers and their songs and create a positive look at a place. He wasn't oblivious to the fact that people had to scrape for a living, including making whiskey. He wrote that "there is a good deal of illicit distilling of corn spirit by 'moonshiners,' as they are called, in defiance of state excise laws." But looking for stills was not on his list, and he "personally saw nothing and heard but little. Nor did I see any consumption of alcohol in the houses I visited."[40]

Two years after Sharp completed his fieldwork, Olive Dame Campbell finished and published John C. Campbell's book entitled *The Southern Highlander and His Homeland*. The book outlines their work at their Folk School, which was modeled after Danish schools of an earlier generation, and offers advice to would-be teachers in Appalachia. The Campbells say in the book that many misconceptions existed among his fellow educators and wrote, "It behooves us, if we cannot maintain the courteous code, to leave." They also said the region is a "land about which, perhaps, more things are known that are not true than of any part of our country."[41] Regarding mountain missions in particular, the Campbells concluded that suspicions, even antagonisms, had arisen because the "foreign" church intermingled in places where churches had already existed before. "Religion," they said, "thus becomes increasingly a matter of controversy."[42]

The Southern Highlander and His Homeland was meant to serve as a set of instructions for educators and tried to set several misconceptions straight. Regarding myths about moonshiners, the authors said they made up only "a very small proportion of the whole" of the Appalachian people when one considers there are many in the region who live in cities, in small towns, on prosperous farms. Yet, they added, any teacher who goes into the mountains is likely to "encounter this moonshine sooner or later," and warned that even school administrators and parents of pupils could be involved in the mountain liquor trade.[43] They explained for the educator's benefit that blockading was no new phenomenon and that it remained in the mountains because "the conditions there have been suited to its survival."[44] They cited the Whiskey Rebellion, putting the whole of moonshining in a national context, including Prohibition, and concluded that the new antiliquor laws would lead the moonshiner to reason, "That one law applies to all and is enforced against all."[45] The Campbells were right about the highlanders learning that everyone was in danger of prosecution, but that didn't mean, however, that they shut down their stills.

A half-century after the Campbells' book came out, three scholars of Appalachia began an influential critique of missions with a passage from John and Olive Campbell's writing, and from there they launched a scathing commentary on Appalachian missionaries, especially Episcopalians in the coalfields, accusing them of colluding with coal owners and industrial exploiters. They didn't spare the Campbells either. Helen Lewis, Linda Johnson, and Sue Kobak wrote, "Mrs. Campbell, herself one of the missionaries, pointed to the 'natural' alliance of exploiters and missionaries who came together in the hills."[46] Missionaries, they wrote, saw themselves as "civilizing or opening up the mountains . . . as part of the great modernization . . . [that] made people more amenable to seeking and using outside institutional help" and "encouraged young people to leave the area."[47] Their ice cream socials and clothing giveaways were part of the scheme.

That critique applies to Miss Ora and her mission, though in reality there were no nearby extractive industries for Miss Ora to collude with. Even the

FIGURE 27. Left to right: Maude Beheler, Ora Harrison, and Dr. Franc Morrill with her visiting sister. Dr. Franc made house calls on horseback in Endicott, Virginia. After leaving the mission, she continued her support financially and through her writing. Photograph courtesy of Lonie Wagoner Rorrer.

timber barons had taken the virgin trees before she arrived. Her support of industrializing America was much less direct. Miss Ora admitted tensions existed between her church and the local community when she wrote the following: "[I]deas and codes of outsiders . . . seem to the mountain people a menace to their social order, and an effort on the part of the outsiders to break down or interfere with their customs."[48] What she didn't see was that by setting itself against local traditions, her church could side with industrial forces or she and her tradition could be at fault.

▪ ▪ ▪

The problem with criticizing missionaries for trying to remove people from the mountains, however, is coming up with answers for what to do if the people stay in their communities as they existed then. What if, through extraction and poor management, forestry products were in short supply? What if farming had already moved toward specialization enough to make local mountain production nearly irrelevant on a national scale? What if factories didn't want to locate there because of the lack of infrastructure and no flat land on which to build? Developing a strategy for sales of local value-added products directly to consumers was the last and best option. That, of course, was the logic of the whiskey trade from the first settlements onward. But if that approach was made illegal, then what options are left? Tourism might've helped, but it was unlikely that all the people of Endicott could make a living from pumping gas for travelers or making beds in their hotels as they passed through. Education without local jobs almost always means that graduates leave. This dilemma wasn't lost on Miss Ora and her colleagues.

So they struggled to think of what else people could produce locally that could help people make a living where they lived. That question brought Miss Ora her last big idea, which was also an approach championed by the Campbells' Folk School and, among others, Berea College in Kentucky. Her solution was to have the mission teach cottage industries, specifically weaving and basket making, two crafts already known in the community before her arrival.

At Ora's request in 1926, Dr. Franc Morrill gave Miss Maude a scholarship to attend a yearlong loom-weaving course at Berea College, the strongest promoter of mountain crafts at the time. She returned to start what St. John's called its industrial work program: teaching basketry and weaving to dozens of girls and women. The mission women made and the mission sold coverlets, rugs, bags, towels, scarves, and runners. The missionaries explained that the work had several goals: "Our purpose is not merely commercial. . . . To these women the weaving opens new fields. It provides a way by which older girls may partly defray the expenses at school, and the mothers and daughters can earn the money necessary for medical attention or improvements at home."[49] Advertisements were copied verbatim from flyers used by Berea.

Berea College, it turns out, began teaching crafts because of a worry about rampant commercialism in the broader society, not so much the lack of money in the mountains. Berea began, as with other missionary efforts in the South, at the close of the Civil War with the purpose of serving two groups: "recently emancipated negroes" and "the white people of eastern Kentucky and similar regions of the adjoining States."[50] In 1896, the president of the college, William Goodell Frost, who had three years earlier referred to mountain people as "our contemporary ancestors," wrote that they needed help to guard against the coming of the industrial age. Mountaineers "would be quickly spoiled and lost if they are not befriended, guided, and saved," he wrote.[51] One way to "save" the people of the mountains, he thought, was to guard them against the influences from elsewhere for as long as possible.

So the college began to teach "traditional" crafts to mountain children and adults in order to help them maintain their endangered culture, while also preparing them for the inevitable changes. Berea had what Jane Becker called a "dual vision of Appalachia" that would both preserve "select pieces of archaic culture" for the benefit of all America and teach mountain people to embrace the coming industrial age. Thus the college and missions like St. John's sent conflicting messages about commercialism in the mountains.[52] They talked of helping mountaineers trapped in poverty while at the same time maintaining the population as a "repository for the noble remnants" of pioneer America.[53] Miss Maude's industrial crafts program had adopted not only the skills taught at Berea, but Frost's philosophy as well.

This crafts approach, like ballad collecting, was an attempt to sift out what some considered the "authentic" from among the lesser, common detritus of making do. The arts-and-crafts educators celebrated the mountaineers' creativity and tradition—espousing what David Whisnant called "all that is native and fine"—even if they had to teach it, while frowning on what they considered the seedier aspects of mountain life that people already knew how to do and enjoyed. Olive Campbell, for instance, warned Cecil Sharp about whiskey making and string band music as some of the "less desirable features" of the mountains.[54]

No crafts educator would have dared think of the illicit manufacture of moon as an old art dating back hundreds of years that should be preserved. None championed moonshine as a means of preserving old pioneer ways in the face of an industrializing America or as a means that small farmers could employ to stay on their farms and resist the ill effects of modernity. But strong similarities existed between weaving a white-oak basket and crafting copper, wood, and rock into a homemade distillation apparatus that ran on local raw materials, used old recipes, and relied on skills passed down. Both were about making something from the resources at hand and preserving traditions. Of course, no missionary could talk about whiskey that way. Moonshine, as far as the literature went, was part of the problem that education was trying to overcome, even as people across America, including Episcopalians and members of every other denomination, bought whiskey from back rooms and speakeasies throughout Prohibition and beyond.

There is at least one exception to the missionary-moonshine conundrum. It turns out that Dr. Franc Morrill, after returning to Chicago, began to write about the economic life she had witnessed in the mountains, showing a depth of understanding rarely seen in missionary literature. She published an article entitled "The Southern Mountaineer," which included all the usual commonplaces about people trapped in the past while also being the nation's most "splendid people," and seemed to echo the language of her time. "The key to the entire situation is *ignorance*," she wrote, putting her most important words in italics. Then in a surprising twist, Dr. Franc turned the mirror onto the nation, not the mountains: "Not the ignorance of the mountaineer," she said, "but the *ignorance of the people of this nation*." She argued for "hard roads" and adequate school facilities as well as industries that provide a "life rich with opportunity" locally, not the jobs in the coalfields and mills. And then, though writing in 1925 at the height of Prohibition, she said, "*Instead of the revenue officer* the several states should send *agricultural agents*." She added, "Stilling is prevalent in many places for *it is the only way they can market their corn*." So she argued for better roads and markets made possible by government help, not just churches or individuals, to help develop agriculture locally:

> If there were roads and a market the mountains would yield a golden harvest. There are wonderful fruit lands which would vie with the fruitlands of the west. There are fertile bottom lands which would fill the markets of our cities. . . .
>
> The government should give this great section . . . its *rightful recognition*. No longer should the nation—its statesmen and politicians—be content to shift the burden on individuals, churches, or philanthropists. Our govern-

ment should assume its legal and moral responsibility. There should be a great construction program which would mark a new era of progress in our national life.[55]

She concluded her article by saying that the southern mountaineer was owed a "*debt long over due* and a *debt which if not redeemed* will constitute a *National Disgrace*."[56] Dr. Franc, even if she paid for Miss Maude's training, saw the roots of the mountain problems from well beyond the local community and the solutions as political rather than cultural. Federal intervention through roads, local agricultural development, and local and clean industries was the ultimate solution, she argued. In doing so, she espoused not merely a social gospel, but an Appalachian political gospel as well.

▪ ▪ ▪

On the way to court, Miss Ora had ridden the rough roads of Endicott with Miss Maude from St. John's to Roanoke and was reminded along the way of the disparities between rich and poor. They arrived at the courthouse and climbed the stairs to the second floor of the federal building, passing people milling in the post office below. As she found her seat among people from Endicott, she looked over the group and knew so many of them.

She also knew some things had begun to change since her arrival in Endicott. Now the public school was nearly complete, and within the year St. John's teachers would no longer receive pay from the school system. The mission's crafts program and the Sunday school program would soon become their main forms of outreach and, increasingly, a main source of revenue. Franklin D. Roosevelt's New Deal was finally starting to have an effect as well. The Works Progress Administration and the Civilian Conservation Corps were moving into the mountains, hiring a few local people to work on roads and campgrounds. Also, the Blue Ridge Parkway was under construction up on Cannaday's Gap in Endicott. Some said the road would bring some jobs and tourism. Yet poverty in Endicott continued, and Ora knew her job remained unfinished.

When called to the stand, Miss Ora walked through the swinging oak gateway to the front of the courtroom, placed her hand on the court's copy of the Bible, the text she taught every Sunday morning. Some of her "scholars" had told her they'd rather hear her teach the Bible than hear a priest deliver a sermon. She looked small before the bailiff, but she held her frame straight. When she had sworn the oath, she stepped up to the witness seat between the judge and jury. Community members and Franklin County officials alike trained their eyes on her. She spoke with her teacher's voice as the lawyer questioned her: Yes sir, I am neighbors with Mr. Rakes, and I know him to be an honest man. He is a man of good character, a good family man, and involved in his church and community. He has helped me in my mission at St. John's-in-the-Mountains. As she spoke, Ora glanced over at Amos and the other men sitting in suits with him, all the defendants hoping against hope they might avoid the wrath of the law. They were no strangers to her now. She knew not only Amos, she also knew his wife and children and his mama. She knew how his entire life fit together—farming, logging, roads, health care needs, and schools—and how liquor tied into it all. Bribing a juror, now, that was something else. She did not believe it about Amos. There was no motive for one thing.

Yet the court had already judged Amos Rakes and nearly convicted him before she testified. She knew such prejudice intimately; she could hear it ringing in the words her family spoke since she was a child. She could speak and write that language of judgment—of assumed violence and crime—almost without thinking. But that day she spoke as a neighbor instead.

8 Murder Trial in Franklin County

Carter Lee, the grandnephew of Robert E. Lee, was up there, facing a possible prison term, and the South was shocked. . . . He came clear. Of all the men indicted, he and two unimportant deputy sheriffs were the only ones who did come clear. —SHERWOOD ANDERSON, "City Gangs Enslave Moonshine Mountaineers"

STANDING GUARD OUTSIDE THE Franklin County courthouse is a tall statue of a Confederate soldier gazing northward, rifle at the ready. The statue commemorates the Franklin County men who fought for the Army of Northern Virginia under Gen. Robert E. Lee's command. Jubal Early, a wealthy planter and slaveholder from the Piedmont section of Franklin County, served as one of Lee's generals. Over three hundred men from the county died serving under those generals; countless others returned wounded and maimed. Though several days' march from the nearest Virginia battlefield, Franklin County suffered not only these direct losses from combat but also paid a massive price in economic setbacks that lasted for decades—well beyond the 1930s when economic depression worsened the region's plight.

After the war, as Franklin County's African American population struggled to emerge from slavery's shadows, which native son Booker T. Washington well described, the white Confederate infantrymen represented by the statue, almost all of them yeoman farmers, returned to dig their way out of an impoverished agriculture as well. They exchanged swords for plowshares but lived poorer than they had before the war started. Some in Franklin County, both poor blacks and whites, stayed in hock through the farm tenant system known as sharecropping for decades to come. With no sales outlets for their farm products, small landowners faired little better. Even as the North built massive rail systems and new manufacturing plants while fighting the war, the South lost what industry it had, including most of its agriculture, and the whole region fell into poverty. The smallest farmers fared worst.

Though the granite Confederate sentry looks well appointed and ready for action, the live soldiers heading back to their small farms or to sharecropping in 1865 were indigent and beaten down. Many brought back a horse or a secreted rifle to show for their service, but they carried no cash, and they would see little or no money coming their way from farming for a long time to come. Neither would their children. The best most of them could hope for was to feed their families. Many sharecroppers could not even say that.

By 1915, fifty years following the war, Rocky Mount had started to industrialize some. A furniture manufacturing plant called Bald Knob started buying a few board feet of local lumber, including oak and red cedar, and the sawmills and the timber cutters in Endicott and other mountain locales sold some logs as the plant hired some sixty-five workers. A few men found jobs at the new Angles Silk Mill in Rocky Mount as well. But this was hardly a boom, and even the few jobs that emerged then were dwindling by 1930 as a national decline spread to local areas.

In the first decades of the twentieth century, farmers in the most arable parts of the county, where fields were large enough to produce for off-farm sales and credit was available, began to specialize. Some dairies in the rolling hills section of the county began building their herds for increased milk sales in Roanoke and Winston-Salem, and a few others planted acres in commercial apple and peach orchards. The arrival of the N & W Railroad spur from Roanoke to Rocky Mount in 1890 encouraged sales of both milk and produce outside the county, and slowly agricultural income began to build. Henry Wallace's federal farm relief provided tobacco allotments beginning in 1934, again mostly in the eastern part of the county, and the warehouses started to fill with Franklin tobacco after record low prices in 1932. Tobacco sellers also benefited from the trains as well as warehouses that cropped up along the tracks in Rocky Mount.

But mountain agriculture—where no parcel was large enough for such specialization, no railroads or hard surfaced roads passed nearby, and there was no capital to invest anyway—saw no new growth. By 1935, most mountain farms were in worse shape than the returning Confederates had found them seventy years earlier, as ever greater numbers of offspring tried to crowd onto the same property. A few gristmills and sawmills dotted the landscape, and a few country stores sold dry goods. That was it as far as legal mountain businesses went.

The moonshine business followed much the same pattern as other industries as farmers specialized in the only way they could: by turning cheap raw corn into a transportable and profitable product. But as is true of other agribusinesses, growth in clandestine liquor wasn't just about the inventiveness of the producers alone. High-ranking men with money to invest and a propensity for risk-taking, organization, and inventiveness capitalized on what producers had started and made the business of liquor profitable for themselves. They were the moonshine bosses and middlemen. They made even more money because of the moonshine industry's lack of legal protection, which made exploiting the rank-and-file moonshiners worse than most businesses.

Pete Hodges, Peg Hatcher, Roosevelt Smith, and other top dogs of the conspiracy had found a way to exploit both local human and natural resources of the county and invented sophisticated purchasing and distribution schemes involving railroad deliveries of raw materials. Their scheme gave rise to a complex network of drivers and delivery points for sales. No lawmen stood in their way in Franklin; they were part of the plan. No unions impeded the kingpins' rise to power. So the pyramid grew, and its impact reached into every economic sector in the county. At the scheme's height, even the money Franklin County banks loaned out was associated with corn liquor profits somewhere along the line. Of the four banks in Franklin County then, the conspirators had controlling interests in every one.

Though no one ever proved it in court, many said, both under oath and elsewhere, that Charles Carter Lee, whose office was in sight of the Confederate statue in front of the courthouse, was the general who made the entire conspiracy run. Even after some of his liquor colonels testified in court that they looked to Lee for leadership and dozens of foot soldiers making and hauling liquor said he commanded it all, the prosecution still couldn't make the charges stick to Lee. Lee, who had an exceptionally high IQ, outmaneuvered the prosecutors. His pleadings as a lawyer were legendary, and this helped make him sly and effective as a defendant. Though Lee inherited his position as commonwealth attorney from his father, he was also a fast learner in his own right. His knowledge of the law was unparalleled in Rocky Mount. It sure didn't hurt him that his great uncle was the venerable Bobby Lee. Many Virginians would have rather toppled the Confederate statue in Rocky Mount than drag that famous name through the mud.

While the federal grand jury proved that the sheriff and deputies used the courthouse as a repository for confiscated stills and the back door of Lee's office became a passage for starting many new whiskey businesses, little had stuck to the man in charge of law enforcement in the county. Even after witnesses in the conspiracy trial said many times they'd seen Carter Lee himself lingering nearby as liquor and its paraphernalia were handed out, he had remained "clear" as Sherwood Anderson put it. The prosecutors thought they had him with the bribery case, but still the feds could not bring him down. After the two trials were through and other men were in jail serving time, Lee was not only free but running for office again and assured of winning.

Almost two years had passed after the close of the jury tampering when the trial for the murder of Deputy Thomas Jefferson Richards came in February 1937. It was recent enough that people all over the nation remembered well the Franklin liquor convoys the crooked law enforcers let pass through. They knew of the millions of gallons of liquor that drivers ran out of Franklin to locations all over the East. They knew how the whiskey revenue trickled up to the ones convicted in federal court and how the law enforcers had charged for every still run and every load hauled. Sherwood Anderson had published his articles and a novel in 1936 about drivers like Willie Carter Sharpe, who hauled hooch by the thousands of gallons while barreling at seventy-five miles per hour through Rocky Mount. His readers had learned how whiskey traveled through Roanoke, where others loaded it and took it farther west toward Lynchburg and from there to the big cities in the North or to Bluefield, West Virginia, the gateway to the coalfields and to the Midwest, or southward to Winston-Salem, and from there all over the textile towns. They knew that Franklin liquor had gone wherever there were a few excess dollars and dry throats. The place had earned the reputation as the moonshine capital of the world. And still Carter Lee had remained untouched.

▪ ▪ ▪

Col. Thomas Bailey might as well have been a Northern spy infiltrating General Lee's territory during the Civil War, as few warmed to him in Franklin and many suffered at his hand. Yet his investigation and written report, along with the witnesses he called, had yielded a successful federal trial, and thirty-four were now in prison because of him. He had put Carter Lee on the defensive and had come within one juror of catching him at least in a jury tampering episode. Even after Lee went free following the two trials, Bailey continued to want to bring down the commonwealth attorney, and he remained convinced that Lee was guilty.

Bailey visited the dozens of convicted conspirators in prison after the jury-tampering trial to ask about Lee. He interviewed jurors and previous witnesses as well. In one prison interview with Amos Rakes (or likely Caley serving time for Amos), Rakes said that Carter Lee had told him that without juror Edgar T. Marshall's support, "We'll be gone, sure as hell." Other damning testimonies filled Bailey's records. Yet, no matter how many witnesses fingered Marshall and regardless of the fact that he was already serving time for tampering, Bailey could never get Marshall to say who had bribed him to do so. During these posttrial investigations, Bailey and his assistant, C. S. Roth, wrote the following in a report to the U.S. attorney general:

> Some person not discovered reached juror Marshall with a proposition designed to free Lee, regardless of what happened to the other defendants; and the fact that juror Marshall held out so long, so stubbornly, and so unreasonably for the acquittal of Lee, and that he did finally succeed in acquitting him, leads to the conclusion that in all probability juror Marshall accepted the proposition.
>
> It is believed that Amos W. Rakes and Edgar T. Marshall, who were among those convicted of conspiracy to corruptly influence a juror in the Franklin County conspiracy case, and who are now confined in the Federal prison at Camp Lee, Virginia have information sufficient to convict Carter Lee . . . and others, and we shall interview them from time to time and endeavor to get them to divulge it.[1]

Bailey came so close. The other jurors he interviewed had told him they knew Marshall wouldn't budge on Lee, even as he agreed to convict all the others. He learned that Marshall held his ground, asking, "When will there be an end to this foolishness?" The rest of the jury had no choice but to compromise. Bailey knew that Lee went free because of one man, the final report was as far as he was going to go. Bailey quit pursuing Lee after that.

But no one, likely Bailey himself, ever expected he'd one day sit with Lee at the prosecutor's table in court; on opposite sides, yes, but not together! Yet in the coming Jeff Richards murder case, Bailey and Lee would sit side by side, speaking in low voices to each other, as they plotted the conviction of two West

Virginia brothers named Duling for the murder. At one time, their working together was about as likely as a Union colonel joining up with General Lee. To everyone's surprise, the two former foes would soon work together.

▪ ▪ ▪

So much money flowed in from the granny fees to the conspirators in their heyday that a lead treasurer, Deputy Jeff Richards, often working alongside a former state prohibition officer and now deputy, Edgar "Mutt" Beckett, had to invent a sophisticated collection and accounting system. They handled and banked huge amounts of money. Colonel Bailey had proved to the federal grand jury that the conspiracy had defrauded the government of over five-and-a-half million dollars. And that is only the tax value that would have been placed on the whiskey. Total liquor sales, of course, amounted to much more than that. In addition, the conspirators were raking in huge profits in protection fees that no one had ever fully added up for the courts.

Since Richards made no base salary as a deputy, his take-home pay had grown exponentially through his liquor work. He and Beckett traveled all over the county collecting, making sure the roadblock operators knew who to let through, and keeping all the principal players paid. The other deputies played their role in recruiting producers and runners and making sure all of this was kept secret from the feds. All this went through Richards. Despite his centrality to the liquor sales scheme, Richards also managed to keep up some of his official law-enforcement duties as well. The casual observer would have seen him doing his job as a deputy and probably thought he took it seriously. His compatriots knew this about him, and the trait became his undoing in the end.

Just seventeen days prior to the grand jury hearing in Harrisonburg, Virginia, Richards was transporting a prisoner, Jim Smith, an African American man who had allegedly stolen a small parcel from his white boss, to a different jail. The prisoner sat in the backseat of the cruiser. Deputy Richards was unaccompanied by any other officer that night, though many testified they had seen Richards and Edgar Beckett together at the Dugwell liquor drop-off the same night. Somehow Mutt Beckett and Jeff Richards, though they were always together, had parted ways. After leaving the Dugwell liquor stop, Richards drove up the road by Antioch Church of the Brethren, the prisoner in the backseat. No one saw—or at least no one said they saw—what happened next.

A .45 caliber pistol and a 12-gauge shotgun were the weapons used, investigators said. First another car overtook his police cruiser, and then shotgun and pistol blasts fired from the second car—there had to have been at least two assassins—ripped into Richards's back window. Experts said that the first bullets likely entered Richards's car from behind, but by the time they arrived on the scene the whole car was riddled with holes. Richards apparently ran from his car after being shot in the back, but he never had a chance to fire the gun later found in his hand. Smith, the prisoner, also ran from the car unarmed and could not defend himself. Neither made it more than fifteen feet from the car. They fell in the road, and their assassins shot them point-blank where they lay on the ground. None could have survived such a hail of bullets, especially the last ones fired. Someone wanted Richards quiet; few in the county had any doubt it related to the whiskey trial.

As the conspiracy's treasurer, Richards knew most everything there was to know about the money trail. He knew who paid whom, how much they paid, how it was delivered, how the money was laundered, where the supplies were purchased and how they came in by truck and rail, and of course he knew who gave him his orders. And Richards started talking about not going into prison alone. He was going to take others down with him if he went. People knew it was a foolish thing to go around talking about how he was going to take others with him. Even his wife knew he should not be talking about the liquor business and told him so. Maybe Richards thought talking to others was a way of protecting himself, or maybe he knew his days were numbered no matter what.

Just two weeks following the grand jury hearing, on October 12, 1934, they found Richards on the Callaway Road, back in the country near Cahas Knob—the best witness Bailey could have asked for, bleeding to death in the road. He died well before Mutt Beckett arrived to investigate the crime scene. Beckett's home was five minutes from the site of the murder. He and one other deputy arrived first. They later told the court that their first action following the discovery was to call Carter Lee. That call alone was reason for suspicion, but as with so many other clues, this one was left alone as well. Almost three years would pass by before the case was heard in a courtroom.

Most people in Franklin County were convinced Richards had been killed because he knew too much and because he had told people he was going to talk. Many who paid attention to the details thought the murder trial should have been the third of a trilogy of trials related to the conspiracy. Yet that is far from how the government handled it. In the end, federal prosecutors like Frank Tavenner Jr., who controlled the first two cases, handed over jurisdiction to the commonwealth attorney of Franklin County. That move to the Franklin County court was a stroke of amazing luck for Carter Lee. Not only had he found himself far from being a suspect in the murder by association with the conspiracy, but now, as head law enforcer in Franklin County, he would prosecute the case.

There would be no Roanoke-based federal court overseen by federal Judge John Paul. This time the trial would take place in the white-columned Franklin County Courthouse in Rocky Mount guarded out front by the Confederate statue. This was Lee territory in more ways than one. When spectators and potential jurors filed into the courtroom on May 18, 1937, for the first day, not only did they see Lee sitting at the prosecutor's table, but they also saw Col. Thomas Bailey and his assistant, C. S. Roth. Lee's arch enemies were now his allies.

Sitting at the table to their left were the defendants, Paul and Hubbard Duling, bootleggers out of West Virginia, and their court-appointed lawyers, Warren Messick, Andrew Davis, and Virgil Goode Sr. The Dulings of rural West Virginia had been regular moonshine runners from Franklin County to their home state and were major players in the distribution of illicit liquor in the coalfields. People knew them in Endicott. And they had already been fingered for a murder once before. Looking closer, spectators realized the defendants were already in cuffs.

The first case started when their older brother, a well-known whiskey driver named Frank Duling, had been killed trying to outrun officers in Franklin County two days before Christmas on December 23, 1933. He apparently had no clearance with the whiskey ring, as Franklin County officers were in hot pursuit until Duling crossed the county line. When Duling crossed the Franklin-Roanoke divide, and Richards stopped his pursuit,

Officer Clarence E. Simmons of Roanoke and others took up the chase as Duling entered his jurisdiction. The Roanoke officers began shooting, hitting one of Duling's tires. Frank Duling's car was running over eighty miles per hour when it blew the tire. He slammed on the brakes, opened his door, and jumped out, intending to barrel-roll off the road and hide in the woods, an old bootlegger's trick. But that night the ground was frozen hard, so when Duling hit the ground, nothing gave, and he broke his neck and died in the road. Simmons found Duling and called an ambulance to take him to the morgue and confiscated the whiskey load he had been hauling.

About seven months later, on July 17, 1936, Simmons was gunned down on a Roanoke back road, resulting in a murder scene all too similar to Richards's.[2] A second car approached the police cruiser and fired from behind. The weapons were said to be a shotgun and a .45 caliber pistol. Again, there were no eyewitnesses. That time, a second officer named Boone, had been riding with Simmons, asleep in the passenger seat and slumped down, and managed to steer the car into a ditch and avoid getting shot. But he saw nothing.

An investigation ensued, and the police found one witness named Tom Thomas, who said he'd seen a West Virginia car at his establishment, called Tom's Barbecue, the night of the murder. With an alleged multistate crime and little to go on, Roanoke police called in Colonel Bailey and Investigator Roth to help. Bailey asked the Roanoke County police first to round up every bootlegger in the entire county for questioning. The deputies arrested fifteen men in July 1936 and took them in to headquarters, where Bailey and Roth took statements from all of them. They also brought Thomas in for questioning. He told Bailey he'd talked with two brothers named Duling on the night of Simmons's murder. They had two women in the car with them and were eating in their car in front of the drive-in restaurant, hardly a suspicious act.

Yet it was the only lead Bailey and Roth had, so they kept Tom Thomas in custody and headed to Beckley, West Virginia, with him in the backseat. There they arrested five members of the Duling family and took them to the Beckley jail, where, sitting behind a two-way mirror, Thomas identified two as the ones who had eaten at his barbecue joint. The whole process, including travel, took only three days. There was little else Bailey could find in West Virginia, and even the evidence against the Duling brothers was slim. The two men had alibis and denied any involvement. But their connections to the moonshine business and their brother's earlier death in Roanoke were enough to arrest them for murder.

The jury was deadlocked in the government's prosecution against the Dulings for the murder of Deputy Simmons—not surprising given the flimsiness of the circumstantial evidence. Then the prosecutors, again led by Frank Tavenner Jr., called for another trial. Arguing that these brothers had clear motive—retribution—to murder the Roanoke deputy, the feds got their conviction in Roanoke in the second round. With no evidence to convict the Dulings of first-degree murder, the feds went for second-degree murder and won the case. The Dulings received twenty years, all based on a loose identification of one person who said he saw them eating with their girlfriends in Roanoke on the night of the murder.

On the day of the Dulings' conviction, July 17, 1936, the *Roanoke World News* was the first printed source to point out the similarities between the Simmons and Richards murders: "The slaying closely parallels the assassination of Deputy Sheriff T. J. "Jeff" Richards, of Franklin County, and a colored prisoner, during the early morning hours two years ago."[3] However, upon reading the article, Colonel Bailey told Sgt. G. M. Williams he remained unconvinced there was a tie-in. "Why the two-year interim?" one magazine reported he asked, referring to the 1934 slaying of Richards and his prisoner and the 1936 shooting of Simmons.[4] The answer was that both slain officers allegedly had chased Frank Duling on the same night. Both officers had been slain with the same type of weapons, though neither shotgun nor revolver had been found at the time of their first conviction. It was the best case Bailey had, though. Twenty-six months had passed since the federal grand jury hearing in Harrisonburg, after all. Bailey was likely as ready for settlement as anyone.

A month after the Dulings began serving their sentence, Tavenner wrote to his superiors asking permission to investigate the connection of the Simmons murder to the Richards case. Though Bailey and his team had found no evidence that the Dulings were connected to the grand jury investigation in 1935, Tavenner suggested the cases were "in all probability connected with the murder of Jeff Richards in the Franklin County conspiracy case."[5] The details of the murders were all too similar, he argued. The dormant police file on the murdered Franklin County deputy suddenly got hot again. When they received the go-ahead from superiors, Tavenner put Bailey and Roth to work tracking down evidence in the second murder investigation. Though he had been skeptical from the beginning, Bailey dutifully accepted his charge.

Bailey found evidence of liquor transactions between the Dulings and Franklin County liquor sellers in his second try, but he never uncovered any tie they had with any member of the conspiracy. Yet the investigators surmised there was probably one anyway, even though, of course, Richards would have never been in pursuit of someone he was in collusion with. The whole idea of the conspiracy was that those in collusion wouldn't have to run from the deputies whom they paid. Nevertheless, only months after they had entered the federal penitentiary for one crime they said they didn't do, prison authorities notified the Dulings that they would have to appear as defendants in a second murder case, this time for the Franklin County deputy.

Even though many witnesses from West Virginia told Bailey that the Dulings were at home at the time of the officer's death, he continued his pursuit. He went looking for the murder weapons as well. He found nothing in their possession, but he did locate a shotgun that had once belonged to Hubbard Duling that had been raffled off in a West Virginia turkey shoot to a certain Alex Ford. Bailey confiscated it. Though it didn't belong to Duling at the time of the shooting, a Duling had owned it once and donated it to a charitable cause. Turkey shoots were target shoots for prizes, and the money often went to support civic groups. At this particular turkey shoot, local law enforcement officers had been there to help run the event. Nonetheless, the connection to Duling no matter when he had owned it was suspicion enough to take it back to Virginia and begin test firings. The question Bailey sought to answer was whether the shells from the turkey shoot prize would match the shells found at the murder scene from 1934.

Bailey got all the evidence together he could find and wrote his report, readying it for trial. Ever the dutiful spy for the Treasury Department, he was doing as he was told. Yet there must've been at least a moment's hesitation when Bailey first heard that the trial was not like the others he had helped shepherd. No, this time the Dulings would be tried not in the Roanoke Federal Court, but in Franklin County as a state matter. Bailey must have paused when he heard that the trial's jurisdiction would be in the most corrupt place he'd ever investigated and that his evidence would in turn belong to the Franklin commonwealth attorney, the one person who'd once been on the top of his list of Franklin County conspirators. We can only guess his thoughts when he realized that he and Roth would be sitting at the prosecution's table with Carter Lee when the Dulings came to trial.

The Dulings were transported to Rocky Mount, where they appeared in suits and ties and handcuffs. Reporters snapped dozens of photographs of the men, as one Duling snarled, "Don't you have enough of them yet?" They entered Judge A. H. Hopkins's court on February 16, 1937, all the while maintaining their innocence. But they knew their having already been convicted of one murder on flimsy evidence put them at a distinct disadvantage in any further cases. They seemed angry for having so little chance of doing anything about their fate.

On the first day of the proceedings, Carter Lee and the assistant prosecutors met the defense attorneys in court for the jury selection. The court had summoned forty potential jurors; only thirty-five reported to the courtroom for selection. Of those who reported, the attorneys dismissed nineteen and asked for an additional forty persons to appear that afternoon. The lawyers chose twelve jurors and two alternates out of the mix, and the fourteen were sworn in at 2:50 P.M. on February 17. The clerk of the court read them their duties: "The defendants Hubbard and Paul Duling, having been indicted for the crime of murder, have said that they are not guilty, and have put themselves upon your country, which country you are. Your charge therefore is to determine whether the defendants are guilty of the felony aforesaid. If you find them guilty, you shall ascertain their punishment in accordance with the instructions of the court. If you find them not guilty, you shall say so and no more. Hearken to their cause."[6]

Among the twelve regular jurors selected was Elder Goode Hash of Endicott. As the lawyers questioned each of the jurors about their prior knowledge of the crimes and the people involved, no one brought up the conspiracy trial and the jury tampering as a means of selection. Carter Lee had made sure there was no legal relationship between the two. Goode Hash, already a public figure commanding respect, was an easy choice even though he'd served as a character witness for Amos Rakes. To have linked the cases in

Hash's selection would have weakened Carter Lee's position as a neutral prosecutor, so Hash remained.

After Hash and the others were chosen, Judge Hopkins appointed Endicott's Primitive Baptist preacher as jury foreman. Hash and the other eleven men took their seats in the jury box to the right of the courtroom and to the left of the judge, while the two alternates sat on the front court gallery bench awaiting work if they were needed. Lee made his opening statement, summarizing the government's case against the Dulings, who he claimed were in possession of a gun linked to the murder. "The Commonwealth will bring in an expert," he said, "to show that the shells found on the road where Richards was killed were fired by the same gun that Paul Duling later raffled off." It was a compelling thought, but the linkage was weak. The state had only found the winner of a raffle in West Virginia and through him linked the gun to the donor. But the shotgun was their main piece of evidence. No .45 pistol was ever found. Lee asked the jury to find the men guilty and to "give them the death penalty."[7] Lee wanted the Dulings dead and the case closed forever.

Defense attorney Andrew Davis began his opening statement with the argument that the Dulings had no motive to kill Richards for the death of their brother in a neighboring county and that they weren't in the county on the night of the murder anyway. Then he said the gun was actually transported to Franklin County by lawmen and that the Dulings had never used it there. He implied that even the shells allegedly found at the murder site could've been replaced with shells fired from the gun after it arrived. There were other motives for Richards's killing, after all. Then he played the conspiracy card:

> It is a "peculiar coincidence" that Jeff Richards should have been slain just a few days before he expected to go before a federal grand jury and tell what he knew about the liquor conspiracy. There "might have been" persons connected with the trial who had reasons to want Richards out of the way. The gun Mr. Lee spoke of once belonged to one of the defendants, but it was never in Franklin County until brought here by the authorities.
>
> The Dulings should not be blamed for West Virginia having imported vast quantities of Franklin County whiskey.[8]

Three hundred people packed the court that day, and hundreds more waited outside near the statue.[9] Boys skipped school to be there. Several schoolteachers took their classes to observe. Nothing quite so exciting had happened in the courthouse in years. They got what they were hoping for when they saw Lee jump from his seat upon hearing mention of the liquor conspiracy trial, at which he was suspect number one, to object to Davis's charge. But Judge Hopkins, who happened to be married to Lee's sister, sustained the objection and put out the fireworks by taking the lawyers into his chambers and out of the hearing of the courtroom.

On the second day of the Dulings' trial, February 18, 1937, Carter Lee called his onetime nemesis, and now his best witness, Col. Thomas Bailey, to the stand and asked him to state his role in the case. "I am a special investigator, Alcohol Tax Unit, Treasury Department," he replied. Lee then led Bailey through the story of how he had gone to West Virginia to acquire the shotgun allegedly used in the two murders from Alex Ford's home. Ford had won the gun at the raffle, he said. After firing test shots with it, Bailey brought both the gun and its owner to Franklin County for the trial. No one had found any gun in 1934 when Richards was murdered, of course. Now the alleged murder weapon for both tragedies was pulled out of a raffle winner's house. No one seemed to be able to answer why Paul and Hubbard Duling would put up a murder weapon for a public raffle, drawing much attention to the gun, when it would have been so much easier to simply bury it in the woods or throw it in a river if they had been trying to hide it.

FIGURE 28. The twelve jurors and two alternates selected for the Duling brothers' murder trial in 1937. Elder J. G. L. Hash (pictured eighth from left, with cane) served as jury foreman. Photograph courtesy of the Franklin County Historical Society.

Throughout the trial, the links between the murder and the conspiracy remained undeniable despite efforts to deny them. On February 23, for example, the defense counsel called former Sheriff Wilson Hodges, who had already served time as a moonshine conspirator. Attorney Messick asked Hodges whether there had been an agreement between law officers concerning the protection of manufacturers of illicit whiskey, and Hodges answered, "Yes, sir." At that point, Carter Lee shot out of his seat again, saying, "I oppose going into the conspiracy case at any length." Again at that point, Judge Hopkins called the two sides into his chambers to deliberate. They stayed behind closed doors for three hours. The late Franklin County native, attorney, and author Keister Greer, who investigated the conspiracy trail for decades, found transcripts of the chamber conversations. One of the most pointed arguments he uncovered was an exchange between Lee and Jeff Richards's wife, in which Mrs. Richards, whose first name was excluded from the record, turned to Lee and accused him of his own involvement with her husband in the conspiracy. Lee turned on her, calling her a liar.[10] Greer wrote that the conversation, "illuminates several dark recesses of the conspiracy," particularly that Lee was forced into the posture of both prosecutor and self-defense simultaneously.

While away from the jurors, Mrs. Jefferson Richards told the judge before the defense lawyers that her husband had mentioned Carter Lee in particular, and she also added that during the conspiracy trial Carter Lee had told her he would take care of her while her husband was in the penitentiary. She had said under oath then that Lee was a "Christian gentleman" and had been "tending to my business for me."[11] Yet, during the murder trial two years later, when she saw her support eroding, her tune changed.

Her brazen attack in the judge's chambers flummoxed even defense lawyer Messick, who turned to Lee and said before the judge that he never intended to bring Lee into the case.[12] Then Messick stood aside as though scared of Lee as Lee went on the attack against Mrs. Richards in the judge's chambers. Fortunately for Mrs. Richards, at least Judge Hopkins reprimanded Lee. He also fined him ten dollars. But little of what was said in the back room was allowed to enter the courtroom. The jury remained in the dark.

How strange, however, that in order to convict the Dulings, Lee had to establish his own innocence first and that he would have to run roughshod over Mrs. Richards, the widow of the murdered, to do so. "Lee should have recused himself, and left this prosecution to another," Keister Greer said.[13] On the other hand, had Lee stepped down, he would've left himself open to direct accusations and the establishment of ties between the murder and the conspiracy. His very reputation rested on proving the Dulings murdered Richards. Otherwise, he may have been brought to trial for murder himself.

While Lee, Messick, and Judge Hopkins deliberated out of the courtroom for hours, the jury was forced to wait in their seats, every minute wondering if the doors would open and the proceedings resume. Their imaginations ran, but nothing during those hours of chamber argument entered into the proceedings they had access to. The Duling brothers, with every hair greased down in place and their suits starched crisp, were forced to sit in handcuffs. Deputies fidgeted nervously, trying to act official. Impatient boys went outside, and many of the men left to smoke out front. Meanwhile in the back room, Carter Lee was defending himself, at one point shouting down Mrs. Richards, and no one but the judge and the defense attorney got to see.

With the conspiracy out of the way and the Dulings' lawyer agreeing not to bring it up again, Carter Lee's case in the courtroom centered on the shotgun, and he rammed it home. Whether the shells presented as evidence were actually found at the murder site or shot later, how the gun was tested, and who kept the gun since it had been confiscated remained in question. The defense openly suggested the whole shotgun shell test could've been rigged. At one point, the judge ordered the jury to be taken to visit the murder scene, though it was years after the shooting. Even with this grizzly reminder, there was no hard evidence left there. No blood or even tire skids marked the road. Nonetheless, Lee appeared doubt free.

Lee argued in his closing statement that this was "an absolutely airtight case." The defense of course disagreed and asked, "Does it stand to reason that Paul would have gone hunting with that gun if it had been the one that killed an officer of the law a month before? Or that he would have gone to West Virginia officers to help raffle it off?"[14] It was hardly a case that would send two men to the electric chair, as Lee requested. There was simply no answer to why there had been no evidence before, but now suddenly shells materialized that linked a two-year-old case to another. Lee argued that the Dulings had killed Richards in cold blood. Lee was good at what he did.

It was after 8:30 P.M. on the ninth day of the trial when the closing arguments ended. At that point, the judge instructed the jury on how to approach the case. They were to concentrate on the guilt or innocence of two men only. This trial was about the murder alone. Goode Hash and the eleven others filed into the jury room, sat down around the huge oak table, and began deliberations that night. Hash opened the discussion. He likely suggested a short prayer.

The next morning, the jury, looking like they "had lost considerable sleep," according to the *Roanoke Times,* but had made no headway. They were sent back into the jury room. Forty-five minutes later, Goode Hash returned and asked, "Could the jury have the transcript of all the testimony?" The judge said it would probably take all day to get it and seemed unwilling to try. Then Elder Hash replied, "We'll try to reach an agreement without it." Things had not gone well for the jury; Hash was trying a new tactic. Only twenty minutes later, Hash returned and said, "We are deadlocked." The judge sent him back to try again. Approximately an hour later, the Primitive Baptist farmer-preacher entered the courtroom again and said, "We are hopelessly deadlocked." The remaining jurors were summoned, and the judge asked one additional juror his opinion, and he also stated there was no hope of agreement. At that point, Judge Hopkins discharged the jury, thanking them for their service. Elder Goode got his cane and walked outside to meet Amos and head home. He had tried to do as the Bible instructed him: to do justice, to love mercy, and to walk humbly with his God. He was only one man, though.

The *Roanoke Times* February 27, 1937, banner headline read, "Duling Trial Ends with Jury Deadlocked." The paper reported the jury was divided roughly equally, either seven to five or six for or against, depending on whom one asked. Those who would know say Elder Hash voted for acquittal, having been convinced that the Dulings had been charged with a crime they did not commit. The preacher believed that Lee's case against the Dulings had provided insufficient evidence for the convictions sought. The Dulings were no angels, and it's possible they may have killed Roanoke Deputy Simmons, but that fact alone was not enough to convict them for murder of another several years earlier, not without more evidence than a shotgun held by a man who won it in a contest, even if someone said the shells fired were the same. Shotgun shells are easy to exchange, and Hash knew that. Surely he argued this as much as anyone could in the jury room, but he couldn't convince enough men of the Dulings' innocence.

After Goode and his contingent were replaced, the second trial ended quickly in mistrial due to biased jurors. Not enough people believed the Dulings were convincing suspects, in part because everyone in the county knew too much about the conspiracy. So then the Franklin County court subpoenaed a whole new group of forty jurors from Halifax County, a location sufficiently removed from Franklin County so few would know those in the liquor ring or about its inner workings. With jurors in place no one knew, the crowds gathering to watch the proceedings dwindled, along with the public interest in the trial. With that change, Carter Lee's arguments fared better. He also presented a new witness who said he'd heard the Dulings bragging while in jail about the look on the face of Richard's prisoner, Jim Smith, as he died. The testimony, supposedly gathered by a secret listening device never revealed in court, made the Dulings seem proud they had killed the prisoner, and the witness was convincing. Thus the third trial required only eight days. The jury deliberated a short while and returned a guilty verdict but couldn't recommend the electric chair. Instead they recommended a sentence of ninety-nine years. The judge reduced that to thirty years. Upon hearing their sentences, Hubbard Duling asked, "Your honor, may I be heard?" It was the first time either Duling brother had spoken in the courtroom. The judge granted permission, and Hubbard stood and said, "Since the court has seen fit to convict us on the charge, we wish to say to this court and everyone else in the hearing of my voice that we are absolutely innocent of the charge. That is all."[15] The handcuffed brothers were led out of the room by uniformed deputies, placed in the backseat of a squad car, and driven away to continue their time, now with added years, in the Virginia State Penitentiary. The crowd gathered outside the courthouse watched the police car top the hill and disappear.

The last of the courtroom conspiracy references ended with that sentence. Carter Lee never again had to argue on the record for his innocence. He died in 1958 with a clean slate of service. He was only fifty-two when he succumbed to illness. He had been only twenty-nine years old in 1935, thirty-two at the Duling murder trial.

Two men uninvolved in any of the trials, Hallie Bowles and Sherman

Wimmer, confessed to the murders of Richards and Smith six years after the murder trial. Both seemed to have carried guilt about the murders as the Dulings sat in prison. After living with his anguish, Hallie Bowles committed suicide in 1942, eight years after the killings, and left two signed notes on his person addressed to Carter Lee. Both notes said he killed Jeff Richards and Jim Smith and that the Dulings had nothing to do with it. Bowles's widow issued an affidavit following the suicide that confirmed her husband's claim. She had known of Bowles's guilt for years, she said. Wimmer, who was serving a sentence in the state penitentiary for an unrelated crime at the time of Bowles's death, never confessed on record, but his wife signed an affidavit while he was serving time saying that she knew Wimmer was Bowles's accomplice. These small-time criminals likely did not work alone.

The Dulings served ten years for Richards's murder and were paroled, Paul in 1948, Hubbard in 1949. They returned to West Virginia to live the rest of their lives.[16] They always maintained their innocence.

Keister Greer studied the conspiracy trial with intense focus, compiling extensive records about the conspiracy. Though he never found some of the missing trial transcripts, even after putting ads in area papers and traveling the nation looking in archives, he was responsible for uncovering many of the documents heretofore lost to the public and that helped make this account possible. In the end, he remained convinced that the Dulings were innocent. In the process of his research, he thought a great deal about the business of moonshine and why people got into producing liquor to begin with. He concluded that the "federal government itself was not without responsibility for the conditions that spawned the production of illicit spirits." He also linked moonshine making to poverty. As he put it in an interview with me, it is "nature to stave off starvation."[17]

Of course, for those at the top of the conspiracy pyramid, starvation had nothing to do with their involvement. Making a profit by taking payments from a lot of people, manipulating the circumstances of production, and charging people at every turn were their central goals. They were hungry for profit. They sought to make money regardless of who got hurt in the process. Some of the conspirators were never caught and lived to see their careers flourish long after Colonel Bailey had completed his investigations and reported back to Washington, DC. Some of the convicted conspirators

FIGURE 29. Multiple generations of the Ingram family pose in front of their turnip still in 1929. Photograph courtesy of the Blue Ridge Institute of Ferrum College.

got out of prison after a couple of years and went right back into the moonshine business. Some returned to good farmland and sound bank accounts left in someone else's name.

No one has ever been able to eradicate moonshine from Franklin County. Long after Bailey went home, the men and boys and sometimes women in the backwoods were still distilling whiskey. Bootleggers continued to sell the product as well. And the profits continued to roll in to middlemen, though fewer than they once were. Along with that, a few store owners kept making a little off cans and ingredients like malt and yeast. Sugar sales remained good as well. But the vast majority of producers made just enough to keep them going for the next batch, just making a little to tide them over. Too many of them, like those whose names are carved into the base of the granite Confederate, continued to be underpaid foot soldiers sacrificing their all for someone else's plan.

Epilogue

It is again, as I have found in so many other levels of American life, a matter of just people. Mean ones, generous, tricky, fierce, gentle—they are there. —SHERWOOD ANDERSON, "Jug of Moon"

ENDICOTT AND FRANKLIN COUNTY forever changed when the United States entered World War II in 1941. By 1945, 2,309 people from the county—nearly 10 percent of the population—had served in the military. Mountain communities in Franklin and elsewhere gave more than their share. The town of Henry, just down the tracks from Ferrum, for example, sent 18 percent of its population to war.[1] They went because Uncle Sam was calling, because they wanted to beat Hitler, and after Pearl Harbor, the Japanese, and because soldiering was a paying job.

A few farm boys and men in the county who could show that they were "necessary to and regularly engaged in an agricultural occupation," as Congress mandated, qualified for a farm deferment. The draft boards were looking for farmers who could help produce war rations, and this pressure as much as anything helped increase U.S. farm output. However, few mountain men could argue to their draft boards that they were feeding more than their own families; if a boy was only helping raise corn and hogs with his parents for home use, he was usually sent to the military.

The good news for those drafted was that the pay of a private in the Army far exceeded typical mountain farm incomes. According to *Barron's Magazine,* even a buck private earned the equivalent of thirty-six hundred dollars a year.[2] Mountain farms were lucky to clear five hundred dollars annually—above board, at least. Unfortunately, it was the below-board part that tripped up some who wanted to serve.

The draft board members in Rocky Mount had to turn many of Franklin County's finest away when the Richmond Selective Service Office, following national orders, ruled in late 1940 that the county's otherwise qualified men who had been convicted of making and hauling liquor would be classified 4-F: unfit for military service for physical, mental, or moral standards. Richmond sent word to Rocky Mount that even if blockaders showed up as volunteers, they should be rejected. Rocky Mount board members fought back, joining with other draft boards throughout southwestern Virginia to protest the ruling, arguing that many moonshine convictions were unrelated to fitness for service but were a matter of financial hardship. After months of local officials lobbying Washington, Gen. George C. Marshall, the U.S. Army chief of staff, amended the Selective Service's decision. He ruled that if a man had only one conviction for a liquor-related offense and was no longer on probation, he could serve his country. This allowed the Franklin County board to turn twenty-five 4-F rejects into 1-A recruits overnight.[3] Soon they would begin dying for their country.

The county lost fifty-five of its sons to the war; several hundred more returned wounded. For the returnees, even the healthy ones, there was a long slog of hard work, rationing, and worry awaiting them at home, even as the national economic outlook began to change. And the change began to affect even the hidden places. By the middle of the war in 1943, the massive unemployment of the late 1930s had turned into widespread hiring, even leading to shortages of workers, including farmworkers. With a temporary shortage of white men to fill jobs, blacks and women found work in industries that made war products. Newport News, Virginia's, shipyards were a common destination for women from Endicott and Ferrum. Radford, Virginia's, munitions plant also hired mountain people who had never worked off the farm. Even so, few jobs were generated in the Blue Ridge. To find work off the farm, many people were forced to leave the mountains. Some were even picked up and bused out daily by companies such as Dan River Mills in Danville. People remember boarding before daylight and returning after dark during the war. The busing kept up into the postwar years as well.

As laborers became scarce in agriculture and even the moonshining boys left home, farms either grew larger and specialized as they figured out how to increase their output per hour, or else they shrank in importance and became just means of supplementing factory incomes for family members in the military or those who had manufacturing jobs who were sending money home. The ones who stayed in business as full-time farmers had to buy up their neighbors' land in order to make farming pay. Those who had saved up money from their liquor making and hauling in Franklin County bought pieces of land in the flatter sections and increased their farm size this way. This was one way that moonshine continued to factor into the mountain economy well after the war.

Even as manufacturing and other off-farm options arose, moonshine never went away. People continued to make it and haul it, and the product supported a number of Franklin County families well into the 1980s and even today. Periodically, the national media rediscovers mountain liquor, and the "moonshine capital" hype about Franklin County revives. But World War II marks the time many Franklin County people gave up moonshining. After that, youths were able to find jobs elsewhere and eventually were able to commute on better roads to Roanoke and beyond or, if they were lucky to have the money to buy land, to settle on their larger farms and raise cattle and other products for sale.

This is my family's story. My grandfather had a sizable farm for the area, and all his children left home to work in other jobs. But even with his hundred and fifty acres, Grandpa still needed sidelines, as did all his neighbors. As he had done before, my grandfather continued driving to make part of his living, though he hauled legal products. On his two-ton farm truck, he hauled fertilizers, cattle, his and other people's animals, logs, lumber, hay, fence posts, Christmas trees and holly, and gravel—all to make an extra dollar or two. Nothing made me happier as a child than to sit in the cab of the black Chevy with a handmade wooden bed fitted for log or cattle hauling, depending on the day, and ride with him and help, taking in the smells of oily gloves, rope, sweat, and vinyl intermingling in the air blowing in from open windows, while now and then helping operate the big gear shift and split-axle overdrive. He'd say "Now" when the clutch was depressed, and I, sitting right in front of the knobs in the days before seatbelts, shoved the lever into place with both hands.

Hauling and driving was all fun for me as a child. It took me forty-some years of riding, then driving him, to learn that he hauled whiskey to Roanoke and on into West Virginia, and how he did it at times while being shot at. I also learned late that when he first got his first flatbed truck, he cooked up a business of hauling brewer's yeast out of Milwaukee, Wisconsin. He brought back tons of the yeast to Ferrum and sold it by the hundredweight to men who had figured out how to hasten their whiskey production using the beer ingredient. Yeast, like sugar, became a common additive when people sought every way to speed up and increase their distilling. With yeast, there was no need to wait for corn to malt in order to use that as the catalyst for fermentation. There was no law against selling yeast; sugar was the same way. Though everyone knew the big loads of the whiskey-making ingredients coming into the county were what tipped off agents first. So people were discreet, so much so that their own grandchildren grew up without a clue.

My grandfather and grandmother bought their farm from my grandmother's father, Luther Smith, the farmer and former deputy who had purchased the extra land a few years before that. Both he and Lilly Rakes, my great-grandmother who was the daughter of Wid and Maude Rakes, with whom Miss Ora had stayed upon her arrival in Endicott, had come from having nothing, so having any land at all was a huge accomplishment. When my grandparents bought the place, it had an old house out back that became Grandpa's storeroom for goods to sell to the blockaders. During the conspiracy trial, more then one witness mentioned Clifford Thompson and his father-in-law, Luther Smith, as the largest suppliers of whiskey ingredients anywhere around. Tony Ferguson's statement about my Grandpa Smith at the trial says it all: "I tell you who bought more sugar than anybody up there, Luther Smith; he had a little store, he bought more than anybody as I know of; he would send his boy there and get it, in a truck and I would load it for him; he bought more sugar."[4]

Selling ingredients for whiskey was profitable enough to help several of my relatives purchase farms. As former Franklin County Supervisor Hubert Quinn explained, they weren't alone. He said nearly every farm through the rolling land in Ferrum and on toward the farms near Rocky Mount was purchased with moonshine money in one form or another.[5] My grandfather, whose family needed him to work and who couldn't attend school beyond the seventh grade, was just one among many who took this route to independence. His people used the term *smart* to mean both intelligent and hard working. He was both.

Hauling moonshine was how Clifford Thompson left his father's hollow and got away from working for an abusive father. Ultimately, that break was how my grandparents had the means to raise healthy children—my father and his siblings—in their new brick house, pay their bills, and participate in their community as good citizens. As roads improved, my grandfather hauled goods and worked on the farm every other spare minute. Given his good foothold on land to begin with, he made it and left it all paid for. But he always needed to work off the farm. For over a decade during my childhood, he hauled the *Roanoke Times* in his farm pickup, depositing rolled-up newspapers in over six hundred plastic paper boxes all over Franklin County and beyond. He left home at 11:00 P.M. and returned after sunup, only to turn around after a short nap to cut hay and bale it during the summer daylight hours or to feed his cattle and scrape the road during the winter. He delivered the paper by the same road Willie Carter Sharpe flew by in her coupe. He passed Tom's Barbecue by night, where folks still gathered to visit in the parking lot, the place that saw its share of runners going by. He traveled the mountain roads in the wee hours. I rode with him on many nights, and all was tranquil then.

Farming beef cattle, my grandparents' main source of farm income, meant raising hay on the best land and grazing cattle on the slopes and sometimes in the woods. My grandparents always raised a garden and had hogs and chickens, too, and so a majority of their food was homegrown. It was the extra hauling, however, that brought in the money for clothes and most anything store-bought. Hauling, along with the logging, was what raised the money to buy a new Impala several times. Grandpa had tried a small dairy operation in the 1940s and even tended an orchard for a while. There were no tobacco allotments in that section of the county. In the parlance of our time, theirs was a small, diversified farm—local agriculture maintained by an owner-operator. People don't usually think of the sidelines as essential parts of that kind of farming, but that's the way it worked his whole life.

When Grandpa needed adult men to help him on the farm for a day or two, he usually headed back into Endicott. There were a few families there then who had never left their home places. A few people had stayed back to care for aging parents and had become the caretakers of their old farms. The helpers he hired were much poorer than most people in the county and always seemed ready to work. They had no phones, so the best way to get them was to drive up their old dirt roads to find them at home. One man we found was named Freddie Midkiff. He had always walked wherever he went, and sometimes we just stopped and picked him up along the road. People say he walked all the way to Martinsville to work when he was young—thirty miles each way. Sometimes he got a ride; sometimes he didn't. Those people were poor, but they were not lazy.

As nearly all the farms had grown into woods, Grandpa bought and sold timber "up in the mountain" in Endicott, always cutting only the largest and leaving the younger trees to grow. He hired three men from up in the hollows to help him load the logs. Grandpa also took his big truck to the Snead Brothers garage in Endicott for servicing; they were the best mechanics around for farm equipment. Their old wood-sided shed, painted with used crankcase oil, was beside Runnett Bag Creek in what used to be the center of Endicott. There was an old voting precinct nearby, though the store and post office that once sat beside it were long torn down. Except for the Sneads, all the businesses were gone. Not even the ruins of the gristmills were there anymore. Driving up to Endicott, we passed the Long Branch Primitive Baptist Church, which is kept up to this day, and went by St. John's, which had become just a shell of the old rock church it once was but has recently been refurbished as a residence. Shooting Creek was our regular route.

The roads that Goode Hash and Miss Ora lobbied for and that the government provided made a huge difference for the haulers like Grandpa and the rest of us who traveled them. Route 40 was the same road that used to carry people out of those communities into the Dan River Mills in Danville or to the J. P. Stevens or DuPont in Martinsville or even to Roanoke to work on the N & W Railroad yards. Of course now we know that the textile jobs, the coal mines, and most any other American manufacturing jobs, regardless of pay, were far from the permanent salvation to any American problem that people thought when they first came.

Already by the 1960s, only a few farmers around Ferrum saw a way to have their children take up the yoke after them. My father was one of the ones who left for a job elsewhere. Our family moved one hundred miles away from Ferrum, but we all went back to the farm every chance we got, and for as long as I can remember I'd run to climb into grandpa's truck and go with him wherever he went, trying to glean every kernel of knowledge from him I could at every chance. Even as a child I could see his and my grandmother's lifestyle was already a rarity. Most of my friends in the manufacturing town where we moved had no such treasure to draw on.

When I was eighteen in 1979, I went to live with my grandparents full-time and attended college at the same place my grandmother and great-aunts had gone to mission high school. It was called Ferrum Training School when my grandmother drove her father's Model T from the Smith farm every day to attend school there. By the time my father came along, it was called Ferrum Junior College, still owned and operated by the United Methodist Church. When I went for my freshman year of college, the "Junior" had been dropped and a four-year degree had been added.

During the year I lived in Ferrum full-time, I got to know Goode and Nannie Hash's daughter, who was an elementary school teacher in Ferrum. Ruth Hash Jones took me to her parents' farm and introduced me to her sister, Virginia Franc Hash, who had been named for the good doctor at St. John's. I also got to know Old Man Lincoln Gusler, as Grandpa referred to his neighbor, and saw his copper crafting up close. And I learned to play the fiddle tunes that my grandparents had once danced to in house dances in Endicott. They remembered Charlie Poole and even the Foggy Mountain Boys, featuring Lester Flatt and Earl Scruggs, passing through. Bill and Charlie Monroe played for the grand opening of the Endicott Elementary School. When my grandmother and I heard Lester Flatt again the year I lived with them, it was a highlight for both of us.

By the late 1970s, Ferrum College had become a landmark on the folk revival landscape, and the college's Blue Ridge Institute had started a folklife festival of its own. The Institute's staff invited women who had studied with Maude Beheler at St. John's, most notably Myrtle Trail Scott, to demonstrate their weaving. Few talked about how Miss Maude had learned the craft first through Berea College's influence. It all seemed like a traditional mountain craft by then, and the prices people paid for the bedspreads and rugs had increased a hundredfold. Endicott weavers who had kept at it were finally making some money. There were also the men at the festival who showed their dogs and guns, ran steam-powered sawmills, and, those like Vernice Martin, who distilled water through their old copper stills, firing them up on the campus and letting them chug away in broad daylight as the curious newcomers and those reminiscing gathered around to watch.

After a short run through the exhibits and the food tents, my grandfather dragged me straight to the music tent, where fiddlers sawed away on old tunes with a sound that made him want to dance every one. We got out on the plywood dance floor together and flatfooted to tune after tune—an eighteen-year-old with jeans, boots, flannel shirt, long hair, and beard and his grandfather in his narrow-brimmed black straw hat, polyester pants, and button-down shirt, and shiny loafers, just cutting the rug together.

During my year living with my grandparents, I learned about a professional photographer's work with Goode and Nannie Hash. Earl Palmer had portrayed them as quintessential mountain farmers fit for folksy calendars. The church clothes in which they appeared in most family photographs had been replaced with an old straw hat and bib overalls for Goode and a bonnet and long dress for Nannie. They were posed making molasses, brooms, and baskets, which they could make well, at one time out of necessity. Some of Palmer's photographs made it into Standard Oil's national magazine that was meant to entice people to get out onto the new American highways, burn gas, and drive to see such sights as a mountain family making their own baskets. Driving became a pastime.

One highway built for recreation, a product of the New Deal, is the Blue Ridge Parkway, the national scenic highway that runs across Cannaday's Gap in Endicott. The project, built by the Civilian Conservation Corps (CCC), employed hundreds of young men, though no one from Endicott remembers anyone from the community getting a job on the Parkway. They do remember the CCC boys building the Smart View overlook to allow passersby to view down into the Endicott community and its surroundings. By 1950, people were thronging to the mountains to see the scenery through their windshields. Few from beyond the area had any idea that what they were passing was more than pretty mountains.

As the first drivers passed by on the Parkway, the community of Endicott was already beginning its diaspora. Miss Ora and Miss Maude were preparing to retire, and the mission was starting to close down. Farms and homes had been abandoned, as the buildings and even the owners stood for photographers to record as remnants of America's past. Few passersby would remember the Blue Ridge as a place of work and livelihood. Most visitors would stand in awe of the mountains' majesty and not miss the people now gone.

The old ones remembered a different Blue Ridge, and I began asking them about the details while at Ferrum College. As part of this research, I remember first learning about the moonshine conspiracy back in 1979, and someone gently told me then that my family had been involved. I didn't believe it at first. I had known my great-grandparents Luther and Lilly Smith when I was a child, and I remembered snippets of scenes of them: once when we all stood out in the driveway while some of the family shot a .22 rifle at some bottles down by the barn. But no one back then had breathed a whisper about blockading and law enforcement.

When I was eighteen and moving in with them to live, I thought my grandparents had found the economic equilibrium, the community, and the sense of home that I believed the rest of America was sorely missing. Only slowly did I learn that people far away still made decisions about agriculture and profits and their lives and that good policy making is needed to make local farming work. Ultimately, it became clear that moonshine was a strategy for survival and a way to circumvent the profiteers sucking the life out of independent agriculture. For a while, moonshine entrepreneurs had saved their farms with it and lived with dignity, but then profiteers moved into the moonshine scene as well. Small distilleries and their support industries could've worked if policies had made them legal and the profiteers had been curtailed.

Now I know that Grandpa risked his life to buy his land. He was shot at because people were trying to stop him from what some called illicit money. I also now know that the lawmen running after him were possibly part of the problem. Those deputies who fired at his car may have been some of the ones who eventually served time. One of them could have been Thomas Jefferson Richards. Those details are lost. But we do know that Clifford Thompson kept driving and his tires did not blow. He got married, moved onto a good farm and paid for it, and raised a family in Franklin County who were well fed and clothed. I was born a generation later, and Grandpa and I would grow close over the years, and in the last month of his life we would drive up Shooting Creek together to Floyd, go out on a dance floor at the general store, and flatfoot to a tune that a band member said was simply called "Corn," as far as the singer knew. It was about the kind of corn people drink—the kind of spirits that just men made and lived from.

Notes

Chapter 1. Conspiracy Trial in the Moonshine Capital of the World

1. "Investigator Bailey," editorial, *Roanoke World News,* July 3, 1935.
2. Sunday, "Famous 'Booze' Sermon."
3. Hohner, "Prohibition and Virginia Politics," 8–11, 42–49, 55–64, 120–26.
4. Report by Col. Thomas Bailey to the Alcohol Tax Unit, quoted in Greer, *The Great Moonshine Conspiracy of 1935,* 24.
5. Ibid.
6. Ibid., 29.
7. Ibid., 47.
8. Salmon and Salmon, *Franklin County,* 396.
9. J. L. G., *Roanoke Evening News,* January 29, 1904, p. 2, col. 4, quoted in Salmon and Salmon, *Franklin County,* 397.
10. *Report on the Enforcement of the Prohibition Laws of the United States,* 71 Cong. 3 Sess. H.D. 722, Summary, 33, quoted in Salmon and Salmon, *Franklin County,* 515, fn. 57.
11. Wickersham Commission, *Report on the Enforcement of the Prohibition Laws.*
12. Ibid.
13. Dezendorf, *Wickersham Commission Report,*1075.
14. Sinclair, *Prohibition,*182–84, cited in Salmon and Salmon, *Franklin County,* 515, fn. 58.
15. Greer, *The Great Moonshine Conspiracy,* 836.
16. "Franklin County Deputy and Prisoner Found Murdered," *Roanoke Times and World News,* May 18, 1935, p. 1.
17. Ibid.
18. Anderson, "City Gangs Enslave Moonshine Mountaineers," 12.

Chapter 2. Wettest Section in the U.S.A.

1. Hoover, "Memorandum for Assistant Attorney General Keenan," in Greer, *The Great Moonshine Conspiracy,* 59.
2. Wingfield, "The Liquor Conspiracy Case," 194–204.
3. Arnold et al., *Preliminary Report.*
4. Interview with Diamond and Lane Boyd, June 25, 2003.
5. Greer, *The Great Moonshine Conspiracy,* 51.
6. Ibid., 65.
7. Ibid., 66.

8. Ibid., 69.

9. Ibid., 114–15.

10. Ibid., 316.

11. "Defense Again Attacks Veracity of Witnesses," *Roanoke Times and Evening News,* May 31, 1935, pp. 1, 11.

12. "Witness States He Divided Fees with S. O. White: Jury Also Told of Federal Officer's Transfer to Charleston, W. Va.: Negro Admits He Drank Evidence," *Roanoke Times and World News,* June 22, 1935, p. 1.

13. "Trio of Lawyers Assail U.S. Witnesses: Claim Case Built upon a Foundation of Hate and Malice," *Roanoke Times and World News,* June 28, 1935, p. 1.

14. Anderson, "I Build a House," in Taylor and Modlin, *Southern Odyssey,* 39; see also Anderson, *Memoirs.*

15. Anderson, "I Build a House," in Taylor and Modlin, *Southern Odyssey,* 39.

16. Ibid., 41.

17. Ibid.

18. Anderson, "Virginia," in Taylor and Modlin, *Southern Odyssey,* 81.

19. Greear, "Sherwood Anderson as a Mountain Family Knew Him," 8.

20. Ibid.

21. Anderson, "I Build a House," in Taylor and Modlin, *Southern Odyssey,* 54.

22. Ibid., 51.

23. Rideout, *Sherwood Anderson,* 288.

24. Ibid.

25. "Treasury Headed by Morgenthau Jr.," *New York Times,* November 16, 1933, p. 1; Taylor and Modlin, *Southern Odyssey,* 217–18.

26. Anderson, "Letter to Karl Anderson," June 20, 1935, in Modlin, *Sherwood Anderson,* 184.

27. Rideout, *Sherwood Anderson,* 236.

28. Taylor and Modlin, *Southern Odyssey,* 221.

29. "Woman Pilot of Whiskey Cars Is Placed on Stand," *Roanoke Times and Evening News,* May 24, 1935, p. 1.

30. Rideout, *Sherwood Anderson,* 287.

31. Anderson, "Give Rex Tugwell a Chance," 5, 21.

32. Anderson, *Kit Brandon,* 118–19.

33. Anderson, "Why I Live Where I Live," in Taylor and Modlin, *Southern Odyssey,* 401.

34. Howard Mumford Jones, "*Kit Brandon:* Review," *The Saturday Review of Literature,* 1936, quoted in Greer, *The Great Moonshine Conspiracy,* 852.

35. Anderson, "A Sentimental Journey," in Taylor and Modlin, *Southern Odyssey,* 74.

36. Anderson, *Kit Brandon,* 29.

37. Taylor and Modlin, *Southern Odyssey,* 40.

38. Anderson, *Kit Brandon,* 28.

39. Ibid., 115, emphasis added.

40. Ibid.

41. Ibid.

42. "Arguments Open in Franklin Co. Conspiracy Case: Ring Operating in Defiance of Government Tavenner Declares," *Roanoke Times and World News,* June 27, 1935, p. 1; Greer, *The Great Moonshine Conspiracy,* 564.

43. "Arguments Open in Franklin Co. Conspiracy Case: Ring Operating in Defiance of Government Tavenner Declares," *Roanoke Times and World News,* June 27, 1935, p. 1; Greer, *The Great Moonshine Conspiracy,* 566–72.

44. "Trio of Defense Lawyers Assail U.S. Witnesses: Claim Case Built upon a Foundation of Hatred and Malice," *Roanoke Times and World News,* June 26, 1935, p. 1; see also Greer, *The Great Moonshine Conspiracy,* 581.

45. "Hutcheson Will Make Final Plea," *Roanoke Times and World News,* June 28, 1935, p. 1; Greer, *The Great Moonshine Conspiracy,* 582.

46. "Text to Judge Paul's Charge to Jury in Conspiracy Case," *Roanoke Times and World News,* June 26, 1935, p. 10f.

47. Greer, *The Great Moonshine Conspiracy,* 596; "Terms Total 18 Years and Fines $39,500; U.S. Moves to Collect Tax," *Roanoke Times and World News,* July 2, 1935, p. 1.

48. Taylor and Modlin, *Southern Odyssey,* 219.

49. Letter from Sterling Hutcheson to Attorney General of Richmond, Virginia, July 22, 1935, in Greer, *The Great Moonshine Conspiracy,* 619–25.

50. Taylor and Modlin, *Southern Odyssey,* 219.

Chapter 3. Appalachian Spring

1. Anderson, "Virginia," 66, 74, 77–83, in Taylor and Modlin, *Southern Odyssey,* 119.

2. Anderson, *Kit Brandon,* 119.

3. Ibid., 120.

4. Ibid., 119.

5. Ibid., 124.

6. See Wingfield, *Pioneer Families;* Greer, *Genesis of a Virginia Frontier.*

7. Nixon, "DNA Tests," B1.

8. Campbell, *The Southern Highlander,* 51.

9. See, for example, Hackett-Fischer, *Albion's Seed.*

10. Fraser, *The Steel Bonnets,* 65, quoted in Hackett-Fischer, *Albion's Seed,* 629.

11. Many scholars of Appalachia have criticized Hackett-Fischer for characterizing those who settled in the Appalachians as too distinct and unified a group, too pure to reflect the reality of the diversity of people who settled there; see the entire issue of *Appalachian Journal* 19 (Winter 1992) dedicated to the Appalachian Studies Association's discussion of Hackett-Fisher's *Albion's Seed* and his response.

12. Bailyn, *The Peopling of British North America,* 20.

13. Ibid.

14. Dunaway, *The Scotch-Irish,* 14.

15. Bardon, *A Shorter Illustrated History of Ulster,* 71.

16. Kephart, *Our Southern Highlanders,* 152; Roosevelt, *The Winning of the West,* 91; Miller, *Emigrants and Exiles.*

17. Cunningham, *Apples on the Flood,* xxiv.

18. Leyburn, *The Scotch-Irish*, 15.

19. Ibid., 4–5.

20. Ibid., 23–24.

21. For a sampling, see Philip, *The Penguin Book of Scottish Folktales*.

22. Holt, *Alcohol*, 34; see also West, *Drinking with Calvin and Luther*.

23. McCrum, Cran, and MacNeil, *The Story of English*, 152.

24. Leyburn, *The Scotch-Irish*, 7.

25. Bardon, *A Shorter Illustrated History of Ulster*, 71.

26. Jackson, *A Social History of the Scotch-Irish*, ix.

27. Bardon, *A Shorter Illustrated History of Ulster*, 72.

28. Robinson, *Plantation of Ulster*, 178.

29. Leyburn, *The Scotch-Irish*, 111.

30. Ibid., 34.

31. McCrum, Cran, and McNeil, *The Story of English*, 152.

32. Leyburn, *The Scotch-Irish*, 116.

33. Robinson, *Plantation of Ulster*, 178.

34. Blethen and Wood, *From Ulster to Carolina*, 17.

35. Dunaway, *The Scotch-Irish*, 30–31.

36. Blethen and Wood, *From Ulster to Carolina*, 18.

37. Bardon, *A Shorter Illustrated History of Ulster*, 74.

38. Robinson, *Plantation of Ulster*, 187.

39. Leyburn, *The Scotch-Irish*, 167–73.

40. Dickson, *Ulster Immigration*, 9.

41. Miller, *Emigrants and Exiles*, 155.

42. Connell, "Illicit Distillation," 1.

43. Ibid., 29.

44. Ibid., 50.

45. Hogeland, *The Whiskey Rebellion*, 64.

46. Connell, "Illicit Distillation," 23–24.

47. Ibid., 50.

48. Ibid., 6.

49. Leyburn, *The Scotch-Irish*, 167–73.

50. McCrum, Cran, and MacNeil, *The Story of English*, 152.

51. Ibid., 156.

52. See Weber, *Protestant Ethic*.

53. Dickson, *Ulster Immigration*, 27–28.

54. Ibid.

55. Smith, *Colonists in Bondage*, 325.

56. Dickson, *Ulster Immigration*, 91.

57. Bailyn, *The Peopling of British North America*, 85–86.

58. Miller, *Emigrants and Exiles*, 155.

59. Salstrom, "Newer Appalachia," 94.

60. Dickson, *Ulster Immigration*, 224–25.

61. Bailyn, *The Peopling of British North America*, 55.

62. Leyburn, *The Scotch-Irish*, 213.

63. Ibid., 257–58.

64. Blethen and Wood, *From Ulster to Carolina*, 29.

65. Webb, *Born Fighting*, 17.

66. Wray, *Not Quite White*, 17.

67. Leyburn, *The Scotch-Irish*, 237.

68. *The Reverend William Beckett's Notices and Letters concerning incidents in Lewes Town, 1727-1742*, MS Historical Society of Pennsylvania, 21, quoted in Dunaway, *The Scotch-Irish*, 8.

69. Penn Manuscripts, Official Correspondence, 1683–1727, II, p. 145, quoted in Dunaway, *The Scotch-Irish*, 8.

70. Dunaway, *The Scotch-Irish*, 166.

71. For more information on German settlers to the Virginia backcountry, see Thompson, *The Old German Baptist Brethren*.

72. Quoted in Blethen and Wood, *From Ulster to Carolina*, 38.

73. Cunningham, *Apples on the Flood*, xxii.

74. Ibid., xxiii.

75. Leyburn, *The Scotch-Irish*, 257–58.

76. On discrimination against eighteenth-century German immigrants, see Thompson, *The Old German Baptist Brethren*, 11–17.

77. On the Irish and their humanity in America, see Ignatiev, *How the Irish Became White*.

78. Hackett-Fischer, *Albion's Seed*, 729.

79. Hogeland, *The Whiskey Rebellion*, 66.

80. Ibid., 67.

81. Dabney, *Mountain Spirits*, 1:51.

82. Blethen and Wood, *From Ulster to Carolina*, 33.

83. Dunaway, *The Scotch-Irish*, 197; see also Albert, *History of Westmoreland County*, 171, cited in Dunaway, *The Scotch-Irish*, 197.

84. Williams, *Appalachia*, 118–19.

85. Ibid.

86. Hogeland, *The Whiskey Rebellion*, 67.

87. Anderson, *Kit Brandon*, 118.

88. Salmon and Salmon, *Franklin County*, 24–27; Thompson, *The Old German Baptist Brethren*, 18–19.

89. Drake, *History of Appalachia*, 33.

90. Ibid.

91. Roosevelt, *The Winning of the West*, 105.

92. Ibid., 110–20.

93. Ibid., 133.

94. Blethen and Wood, *From Ulster to Carolina*, 60.

95. Carr, *The Second Oldest Profession*, 11–12.

96. Theobald, "When Whiskey Was the King of Drink."

97. Anderson, *Kit Brandon*, 120–21.

Chapter 4. Elder Goode

1. Greer, *The Great Moonshine Conspiracy*, 601–2; see also Greer Papers.

2. Greer, *The Great Moonshine Conspiracy*, 732.

3. Interview with Dr. John H. Hash, December 13, 2005, Vanderbilt University, Nashville, Tennessee.

4. Ibid.

5. Hash, *Calendar Record*.

6. Sutphin, *The Hash Family*, 163–64.

7. Hash, "Experience and Call to the Ministry," in *Calendar Record*, 412.

8. Albanese, *America's Religions*, 327–28.

9. Cunningham, *Apples on the Flood*, 100.

10. Epperly, *A Collection of Cannaday Family Records*, 5.

11. Anderson, *Memoirs*, 397.

12. Hash, "Experience and Call to the Ministry," in *Calendar Record*, 412.

13. Ibid.

14. Ibid., 413.

15. Ibid., 413–16.

16. Ibid., 413–17.

17. Ware, "Charity Primitive Baptist," 1, 9.

18. Saunders, "A Brief History of the Charity Primitive Baptist Church," 2.

19. Ibid., 14.

20. Taylor, *The Formation of the Primitive Baptist Movement*, 50, 65.

21. Lambert, *Rise of the Anti-Mission Baptists*, 369.

22. Taylor, *The Formation of the Primitive Baptist Movement*, 12.

23. Ibid., 36; in the Black Rock address, the Primitive Baptists issued the following statement regarding Sunday schools: "But whilst we thus stand opposed to the plan and use of these Sunday Schools and the S.S. Union, in every point, we wish to be distinctly understood that we consider Sunday Schools for the purpose of teaching poor children to read, whereby they may be enabled to read the Scriptures for themselves, in neighborhoods where there is occasion for them, and when properly conducted, without that ostentation so commonly connected with them, to be useful and benevolent institutions, worthy of the patronage of all the friends of civil liberty."

24. Primitive Baptists, "The Black Rock Address," 4.

25. Quoted in Taylor, *The Formation of the Primitive Baptist Movement*, 41.

26. Benedict, *Fifty Years among the Baptists*, quoted in Taylor, *The Formation of the Primitive Baptist Movement*, 86.

27. See Isaac, "Religion and Authority," 36.

28. Taylor, *The Formation of the Primitive Baptist Movement*, 86.

29. Hassell, "Questions and Answers."

30. Primitive Baptists, "Frequently Asked Questions," 4.

31. Taylor, *The Formation of the Primitive Baptist Movement*, 86.

32. Ibid.

33. Berry, *The Kehukee Declaration*, 26–27, quoted in Jones, "Old Time Baptists," 124; see also Lambert, *Rise of the Anti-Mission Baptists*, 369.

34. Oliphant, "Advice to Children."

35. Ibid.

36. Taylor, *The Formation of the Primitive Baptist Movement*, 71.

37. Oliphant, "Advice to Children."

38. Interview with Lane Boyd, June 25, 2003, Endicott, Virginia.

39. Greer, *The Great Moonshine Conspiracy*, 690.

40. Ibid., 691.

41. Ibid., 692.

42. Ibid., 694.

43. Taylor and Modlin, *Southern Odyssey*, 223; see also Carr, *The Second Oldest Profession*, 119.

44. Greer, *The Great Moonshine Conspiracy*, 728.

45. "Jury Tampering Case Placed in Hands of Jury," *Roanoke Times*, May 23, 1936, pp. 1, 11; quoted in Greer, *The Great Moonshine Conspiracy*, 728.

46. Hash, *Calendar Record*, 116.

Chapter 5. Last Old Dollar Is Gone

1. Anderson, *Memoirs*, 392.

2. Ibid., 393.

3. For these and the following agricultural statistics, see Smith, *Chronological Landmarks*.

4. Lane Boyd, interview with the author, June 25, 2003, Endicott, Virginia.

5. Hash, *Calendar Record*, 31.

6. Wirth, *The Development of America*, 500.

7. See Gabriel, *Toilers of Land and Sea*.

8. See House, "Proposals of Government Aid."

9. See Webb, *The Great Plains*.

10. Wirth, *The Development of America*, 502.

11. Kennedy, *Freedom from Fear*, 17; for additional tractor usage numbers, see "History of Tractors," *Cornways*, http://www.cornways.de/hi_tractor.html (accessed September 2, 2010).

12. Alexander, "Overcrowded Farms," 870–86.

13. Baker, "Farm Youth," 207–9.

14. See Maris, "Farm Tenancy."

15. Salstrom, *Appalachia's Path to Dependency*, 101.

16. Hall et al., *Like a Family*, 9.

17. Kennedy, *Freedom from Fear*, 18, 141.

18. Egan, *Worst Hard Time*, 74–77; see also Ford, "Machinery: The New Messiah."

19. Thompson, "The Pittston Strike," 6.

20. Hall et al., *Like a Family*, 10, 33.

21. Rorrer, *Rambling Blues*, 34–35.

22. U.S. Department of Agriculture, *Yearbook of Agriculture 1934*, 833.

23. Tugwell, *Roosevelt's Revolution*, 51.

24. Culver and Hyde, *American Dreamer*, 99.

25. Ibid., 116.

26. Wallace, "The Future of the American Farmer," quoted in Tugwell, *Roosevelt's Revolution*, 56.

27. Culver and Hyde, *American Dreamer*, 160.

28. Ibid., 170.

29. Baker and Taeuber, "The Rural People," 845.

30. Ibid., 846.

31. Gray and Clayton, "Introduction," 6, quoted in Salstrom, *Appalachia's Path to Dependency*, 127–28.

32. Smith, *Farming Appalachia*, quoted in Salstrom, *Appalachia's Path to Dependency*, 107.

33. Smith, *Tree Crops*, 18–19.

34. Ronald Eller, *Miners, Millhands, and Mountaineers*, 226 n. 8, also quoted in Salstrom, *Appalachia's Path to Dependency*, 133.

35. Tugwell, *Roosevelt's Revolution*, 303–4.

Chapter 6. Entrepreneurial Spirits

1. Willis, *Goin' Up Shootin' Creek*, 138.

2. Kephart, *Our Southern Highlanders*, 179.

3. Willis, *Goin' Up Shootin' Creek*, 140.

4. Ibid., 138.

5. Hambrick and Woods, *The Quinn Clan*, 456.

6. Ibid.

7. Carr, *The Second Oldest Profession*, 11–12.

8. Gately, *Drink*, 189–90.

9. Leyburn, *The Scotch-Irish*, 264.

10. Hackett-Fischer, *Albion's Seed*, 729.

11. Hogeland, *The Whiskey Rebellion*, 67.

12. Freeman, *Alexander Hamilton*, 213.

13. Carr, *The Second Oldest Profession*, 23.

14. U.S. Treasury, "Fact Sheet OPC-77."

15. Carr, *The Second Oldest Profession*, 24.

16. Dabney, *Mountain Spirits*, 1:74–75.

17. Kephart, *Our Southern Highlanders*, 180.

18. Ibid., 184.

19. Salmon and Salmon, *Franklin County*, 396–97.

20. Sutphin, *The Hash Family*, 163–64.

21. Carr, *The Second Oldest Profession*, 31–33.

22. Kephart, *Our Southern Highlanders*, 167.

23. Ibid., 183.

24. Ibid., 186.

25. For more information on whiskey making, see Dabney, *Mountain Spirits,* vols. 1 and 2, and Wigginton, "Moonshining as a Fine Art."

26. Carr, *The Second Oldest Profession,* 70.

27. Anderson, *Kit Brandon,* 218.

28. Englehardt, "Writing That Old Moonshine Lit," 65.

29. Kephart, *Our Southern Highlanders,* 190.

Chapter 7. Her Moonshine Neighbor as Herself

1. Harrison, "St. John's-in-the-Mountains."

2. Ibid.

3. Ibid.

4. Newman, "Survey—St. John's in the Mountains."

5. Harrison, "St. John's-in-the-Mountains," quoted in Maxey, *Miss Ora and Miss Etta,* 6.

6. Newman, "Survey—St John's in the Mountains," 1.

7. Ibid.

8. Interview with Diamond and Lanc Boyd, June 25, 2003, Endicott, Virginia.

9. Armistead, "Mission in Mountains," 9.

10. Board of Missions, "Request for Appointment."

11. Harrison, "St. John's-in-the-Mountains."

12. Miss Ora Harrison, "St. John's," 1940, p. 1, Box 61, File 18, Virginia Tech Special Collections.

13. Sugeno, "The Establishmentarian Ideal," 287.

14. See Isaac, "Religion and Authority," 3–36.

15. Butler, Wacker, and Balmer, *Religion in American Life,* 132.

16. Sugeno, "The Establishmentarian Ideal," 288–89.

17. Campbell, *The Southern Highlander,* 159.

18. Fletcher, "Through Heart and Hearth," 153.

19. Masters, *The Call of the South.*

20. Hooker, *Religion in the Highlands,* 198–99.

21. Young, *Thankfulness Unites,* 8.

22. Hooker, *Religion in the Highlands,* 199.

23. Brown, "A Historical Sketch of the Diocese of Southwestern Virginia," 3.

24. Hopkins, *The Rise of the Social Gospel,* 3.

25. Harrison, "St. John's-in-the-Mountains," 1.

26. Ibid.

27. Armistead, "Mission in Mountains," 9.

28. Hooker, *Religion in the Highlands,* 243.

29. Ibid., 203.

30. Harrison, "St. John's-in-the-Mountains," 1.

31. Mabel N. Marmion, "Anecdotes," unpublished manuscript (1982), 2, quoted in Maxey, *Miss Ora and Miss Etta,* 27.

32. Cash, "Why Primitive Baptists Stand Alone."

33. Ramsey, *Franklin County Schools*, 3–21.

34. Hooker, *Religion in the Highlands*, 292.

35. Maxey, *Miss Ora and Miss Etta*, 28.

36. Sharp, *English Folk Songs from the Southern Appalachians*, xxiii.

37. Ibid.

38. Ibid.

39. Ibid., xxv.

40. Ibid., xxiv.

41. Campbell, *The Southern Highlander*, xx–xxi.

42. Ibid., 191.

43. Ibid., 104–5.

44. Ibid., 107.

45. Ibid., 110.

46. Lewis, Johnson, and Kobak, "The Missionary Movement in the Southern Mountains," 1.

47. Ibid., 11, 19.

48. Harrison, "St. John's-in-the-Mountains," 3.

49. Harrison, "Industrial Department," 1.

50. Peck, *Berea's First 125 Years*, 63.

51. Ibid., 72–73.

52. Becker, *Selling Tradition*, 42–43.

53. Ibid., 59.

54. Olive Dame Campbell, quoted in Becker, *Selling Tradition*, 58.

55. Morrill, "The Southern Mountaineer," 15–16.

56. Ibid.

Chapter 8. Murder Trial in Franklin County

1. Bailey and Roth, "Final Report."

2. "C. E. Simmons, Roanoke County Deputy Sheriff, Shot to Death in Auto," *Roanoke Times*, July 18, 1936, pp. 1, 4.

3. Ibid.

4. Sgt. G. M. Williams, "Moonshine Murder," *True Detective Mysteries*, 1937, quoted in Greer, *The Great Moonshine Conspiracy*, 742.

5. Letter from Prosecutor Frank S. Tavenner to Special Assistant to the Attorney General Parrish, October 17, 1936, T. Keister Greer Collection, Ferrum College, Stanley Library Special Collections, Ferrum, Va.

6. Greer, *The Great Moonshine Conspiracy*, 750.

7. Ibid., 751.

8. Ibid.

9. M. Carl Andrews, "Dulings Trial Gets Under Way," *Roanoke World News*, February 17, 1937, pp. 1, 4.

10. Greer, *The Great Moonshine Conspiracy*, 777.

11. Ibid., 749.
12. Ibid., 780.
13. Ibid., 797.
14. Ibid., 814.
15. Ibid., 842.
16. Ibid., 844–48.
17. Interview with T. Keister Greer, October 25, 2003, Rocky Mount, Virginia.

Epilogue

1. Salmon and Salmon, *Franklin County,* 447.
2. Tillitt, "Army-Navy Pay Tops Most Civilians."
3. Salmon and Salmon, *Franklin County,* 431.
4. Greer, *The Great Moonshine Conspiracy,* 142.
5. Interview with Olivia Quinn, December 29, 2003, Ferrum, Virginia.

Works Cited

Albanese, Cathy L. *America's Religions and Religion*. Belmont, Calif.: Wadsworth, 1999.

Albert, G. D. *History of Westmoreland County, Pennsylvania*. Philadelphia: L. H. Everts, 1882.

Alexander, W. W. "Overcrowded Farms." In *Yearbook of Agriculture 1940*, 870–86. Washington, DC: USDA, 1940.

Anderson, Sherwood. "City Gangs Enslave Moonshine Mountaineers." *Liberty* 12, November 2, 1935, 12–13.

Anderson, Sherwood. "Give Rex Tugwell a Chance." *Today*, June 8, 1935, 5, 21.

Anderson, Sherwood. *Kit Brandon: A Portrait*. New York: Charles Scribner's Sons, 1936.

Anderson, Sherwood. *Memoirs*. New York: Harcourt, Brace, 1942.

Anderson, Sherwood. "Virginia." *Vanity Fair* 32 (August 1929): 66, 74.

Armistead, Mary Bland. "Mission in Mountains Is Ora Harrison's Creation." *Forth Magazine*, January 1953, 9–10.

Arnold, A. K., Thomas Bailey, M. H. Caffey, and A. E. Joyce. *Preliminary Report of July 31, 1934 to Acting Deputy Commissioner, Alcohol Tax Unit, United States vs. Charles Carter Lee, Report*. Washington, DC: National Archives Box 25—80—48, Department of Justice, 1934.

Bailey, Thomas, and C. S. Roth. "Final Report to the U.S. Attorney General, Special Investigator Thomas Bailey and Investigator C. S. Roth, May 1936." T. Keister Greer Collection. Ferrum College, Stanley Library Special Collections, Ferrum, Va.

Bailyn, Bernard. *The Peopling of British North America*. New York: Alfred A. Knopf, 1986.

Baker, O. E. "Farm Youth, Lacking City Opportunities, Face Difficult Adjustment." *Yearbook of Agriculture 1934*, 207–9. Washington, DC: USDA, U.S. Government Printing Office, 1934.

Baker, O. E., and Conrad Taeuber. "The Rural People." In *Farmers in a Changing World: The Yearbook of Agriculture 1940*, 827–47. Washington, DC: U.S. Government Printing Office, 1940.

Bardon, Jonathan. *A Shorter Illustrated History of Ulster*. Belfast, Northern Ireland: Blackstaff Press, 1996.

Becker, Jane S. *Selling Tradition: Appalachia and the Construction of an American Folk, 1930–1940*. Chapel Hill: University of North Carolina Press, 1998.

Benedict, David. *Fifty Years among the Baptists*. New York: Sheldon, 1860. Reprint, Little Rock: Seminary Publications, 1977.

Berry, W. J., ed. *The Kehukee Declaration and the Black Rock Address with Other*

Writings Relative to the Baptist Separation between 1825–1840. Elon College, N.C.: Primitive Publications, n.d.

Blethen, H. Tyler, and Curtis W. Wood Jr. *From Ulster to Carolina: The Migration of the Scotch-Irish to Southwestern North Carolina*. Raleigh: North Carolina Department of Cultural Resources, Division of Archives and History, 1998.

Board of Missions. "Request for Appointment of Miss Ora Harrison as Teacher at Endicott." February 1916 (R.210.16) C of A 127. New York: Archives of the Episcopal Church.

Bondurant, Matt. *Wettest County in the World: A Novel Based on a True Story*. New York: Scribner, 2008.

Brown, Katherine L. "A Historical Sketch of the Diocese of Southwestern Virginia." Episcopal Diocese of Southwestern Virginia, http://www.dioswva.org/digital_faith/dfcfiles/31 (accessed August 23, 2010).

Butler, Jon, Grant Wacker, and Randall Balmer. *Religion in American Life: A Short History*. New York: Oxford University Press, 2003.

Campbell, John C. *The Southern Highlander and His Homeland*. Lexington: University of Kentucky Press, 1969. Originally published by Olive Dame Campbell by the Russell Sage Foundation, 1921.

Carr, Jess. *The Second Oldest Profession: An Informal History of Moonshining in America*. Englewood Cliffs, N.J.: Prentice-Hall, 1972.

Cash, Elder Walter. "Why Primitive Baptists Stand Alone: A Sermon Delivered at the One Hundredth Annual Meeting of the Salem Association of the Primitive Baptists, Boone County, Missouri, September 2, 3, and 4, 1927." *Bible Truth Forum*, http://www.bibletruthforum.com/cords2/art210a.htm (accessed September 4, 2010).

Connell, K. H. "Illicit Distillation." In *Irish Peasant Society: Four Historical Essays*, 1–50. Oxford: Clarendon Press, 1968.

Culver, John C., and John Hyde. *American Dreamer: The Life and Times of Henry A. Wallace*. New York: W.W. Norton, 2000.

Cunningham, Rodger. *Apples on the Flood: The Southern Mountain Experience*. Knoxville: University of Tennessee Press, 1987.

Dabney, Joseph Earl. *Mountain Spirits*, vols. 1 and 2. Asheville, N.C.: Bright Mountain Books, 1974, 1980.

Dezendorf, Frederick C. *Wickersham Commission Report on Law Observance and Enforcement*. Washington, DC: U.S. Department of the Treasury, 1931.

Dickson, R. J. *Ulster Immigration to Colonial America, 1718–1775*. Belfast, Northern Ireland: Ulster Historical Foundation, 1988.

Drake, Richard B. *History of Appalachia*. Lexington: University of Kentucky Press, 2001.

Dunaway, Wayland F. *The Scotch-Irish of Colonial Pennsylvania*. Baltimore: Genealogical Publishing, 1979.

Egan, Timothy. *Worst Hard Time*. Boston: Houghton Mifflin, 2006.

Eller, Ronald. *Miners, Millhands, and Mountaineers: Industrialization of the Appalachian South 1880–1930*. Knoxville: University of Tennessee Press, 1982.

Englehardt, Elizabeth. "Writing That Old Moonshine Lit: Gender, Power, and Nation in Unexpected Places." *Journal of Appalachian Studies* 13, nos. 1 and 2 (Spring and Fall 2007): 49–74.

Epperly, Loyd. *A Collection of Cannaday Family Records and Pictures.* Madison, Va.: Loyd Epperly, 1998.

Fletcher, Wendy. "Through Heart and Hearth: Redefining Womanhood as a Missiological Work." In *Deeper Joy: Lay Women in the 20th Century Episcopal Church,* edited by Frederica Harris Thompsett and Sheryl A. Kujawa-Holbrook, 151–62. New York: Episcopal Church Publishing, 2005.

Ford, Henry. "Machinery: The New Messiah." *Forum,* March 1928, 359–64.

Fraser, George M. *The Steel Bonnets.* New York: Knopf, 1972.

Freeman, Joanne, ed. *Alexander Hamilton, Writings.* New York: Library of America, 2001.

Gabriel, Ralph H. *Toilers of Land and Sea.* New Haven, Conn.: Yale University Press, 1926.

Gately, Ian. *Drink: A Cultural History of Alcohol.* New York: Gotham Books, 2008.

Gray, L. C., and C. F. Clayton. "Introduction." In *U.S. Department of Agriculture, Economic and Social Problems and Conditions of the Southern Appalachians,* USDA Miscellaneous Publication no. 205. Washington, DC: U.S. Government Printing Office, 1935.

Greear, Caroline. "Sherwood Anderson as a Mountain Family Knew Him." *The Winesburg Eagle* 14, no. 2 (Summer 1989): 1–12.

Greer, T. Keister. *Genesis of a Virginia Frontier: The Origins of Franklin County, 1740–1785.* Rocky Mount, Va.: History House, 2005.

Greer, T. Keister. *The Great Moonshine Conspiracy of 1935.* Rocky Mount, Va.: History House, 2003.

Greer, T. Keister. Papers, Stanley Library Special Collections, Ferrum College, Ferrum, Va.

Hackett-Fischer, David. *Albion's Seed: Four British Folkways in America.* New York: Oxford University Press, 1989.

Hall, Jacquelyn Dowd, James Leloudis, Robert Korstad, Mary Murphy, Lu Ann Jones, and Christopher B. Daly. *Like a Family: The Making of a Southern Cotton Mill World.* Chapel Hill: University of North Carolina Press, 1987.

Hambrick, Sarah Quinn, and Felicia Hambrick Woods. *The Quinn Clan.* Franklin, N.C.: Genealogy Publishing Service, 1993.

Harrison, Ora. "Industrial Department, St John's in-the-Mountains." Box 39, 1928 Archives of the Southwestern Virginia Diocese of the Episcopal Church, Blacksburg, Virginia Tech Special Collections.

Harrison, Ora. "St. John's-in-the-Mountains, Endicott, Virginia." Box 61, file 18, 1939, Southwestern Diocese of the Episcopal Church Archives, Blacksburg, Virginia Tech Special Collections.

Hash, James Goode Lane. *Calendar Record of Events of James Goode Lane Hash.* Edited by John H. Hash and Mary B. Hash. Nashville, Tenn.: Printing, Etc., 1997.

Hassell, Sylvester. "Questions and Answers." From *Gospel Messenger* and *Advocate and Messenger,* compiled by R. H. Pittman, 1935. *The Primitive Baptist Web Station,* http://www.pb.org/pbdocs/pittman.html (accessed September 1, 2010).

Hogeland, William. *The Whiskey Rebellion: George Washington, Alexander Hamilton and the Frontier Rebels Who Challenged America's Newfound Sovereignty*. New York: Scribner, 2006.

Hohner, Robert A. "Prohibition and Virginia Politics, 1901–1916." PhD diss., University of Virginia, 1965.

Holt, Mack P., ed. *Alcohol: A Social and Cultural History*. Oxford: Berg, 2006.

Hooker, Elizabeth R. *Religion in the Highlands: Native Churches and Missionary Enterprises in the Southern Appalachian Area*. New York: Home Missions Council, 1933.

Hoover, John Edgar. "Memorandum for Assistant Attorney General Keenan." Federal Bureau of Investigation, U.S. Department of Justice, Washington, DC, April 18, 1935 (Criminal Division file 23—20—48).

Hopkins, Charles Howard. *The Rise of the Social Gospel in American Protestantism, 1865–1915*. New Haven, Conn.: Yale University Press, 1940.

House, Albert V. Jr. "Proposals of Government Aid to Agricultural Settlement during the Depression of 1873–1879." *Agricultural History* 12 (January 1938): 46–66.

Ignatiev, Noel. *How the Irish Became White*. New York: Routledge, 1996.

Isaac, Rhys. "Religion and Authority: Problems of the Anglican Establishment in Virginia in the Era of the Great Awakening and the Parsons' Cause." *The William and Mary Quarterly* 3rd ser., 30, no. 1 (January 1973): 3–36.

Jackson, Carlton. *A Social History of the Scotch-Irish*. Lanham, Md.: Madison Books, 1992.

Jones, Loyal. "Old Time Baptists and Mainline Christianity." In *An Appalachian Symposium*, edited by J. W. Williamson. Boone, N.C.: Appalachian State University Press, 1977.

Kennedy, David M. *Freedom from Fear: The American People in Depression and War, 1929–1945*. New York: Oxford University Press, 2005.

Kephart, Horace. *Our Southern Highlanders: A Narrative of Adventure in the Southern Appalachians and a Study of the Life among the Mountaineers*. New York: Macmillan, 1922.

Lambert, Bryan Cecil. *Rise of the Anti-Mission Baptists: Sources and Leaders, 1800–1840*. New York: Arno Press, 1980.

Lewis, Helen Matthews, Linda Johnson, and Sue Kobak. "The Missionary Movement in the Southern Mountains: A Case Study of the Episcopal Church in Southwest Virginia." Paper presented to the Society for Religion in Higher Education, Maryville, Tenn., August 1979.

Leyburn, James. *The Scotch-Irish: A Social History*. Chapel Hill: University of North Carolina Press, 1962.

Maris, Paul V. "Farm Tenancy." In *Yearbook of Agriculture 1940*, 887–906. Washington, DC: USDA, 1940.

Masters, Victor Irvine. *The Call of the South*. Atlanta: Publicity Department of the Home Mission Board of the Southern Baptist Convention, 1918.

Maxey, Esther Fox. *Miss Ora and Miss Etta: Folk History of the Women at the Episcopal Mission Schools*. Rocky Mount, Va.: Esther Fox Maxey, 1984.

McCrum, Robert, William Cran, and Robert MacNeil. *The Story of English.* London: Viking, 1986.

Miller, Kerby A. *Emigrants and Exiles: Ireland and the Irish Exodus to North America.* New York: Oxford University Press, 1985.

Modlin, Charles E., ed. *Sherwood Anderson: Selected Letters.* Knoxville: University of Tennessee Press, 1984.

Morrill, E. Franc. "The Southern Mountaineer." *The Royal Neighbor* 28, no. 9 (September 1925): 15–16.

Newman, Deaconness. "Survey—St. John's in the Mountains—Ferrum, VA." N.d. Box 61, file 18, Archives of the Southwestern Virginia Diocese of the Episcopal Church, Blacksburg, Virginia Tech Special Collections.

Nixon, Ron. "DNA Tests Find Branches But Few Roots." *New York Times,* Nov. 25, 2007, B1.

Okrent, Daniel. *Last Call: The Rise and Fall of Prohibition.* New York: Scribner, 2010.

Oliphant, James H. "Advice to Children." In *Principles and Practices of the Regular Baptists* (1883). Landmark Independent Baptist Church, http://libcfl.com/articles/advice.htm (accessed September 1, 2010).

Peck, Elisabeth S. *Berea's First 125 Years: 1855–1980.* Lexington: University of Kentucky Press, 1982.

Philip, Neil. *The Penguin Book of Scottish Folktales.* New York: Penguin Books, 1995.

Primitive Baptists. "The Black Rock Address." *The Primitive Baptist Web Station,* http://www.pb.org/pbdocs/blakrock.html (accessed September 1, 2010).

Primitive Baptists. "Frequently Asked Questions." *The Primitive Baptist Web Station,* http://www.pb.org/pbfaq.html (accessed September 1, 2010).

Ramsey, Harold. *Franklin County Schools: A Century of Progress.* Rocky Mount, Va.: County School Board of Franklin County, 1975.

Rideout, Walter B. *Sherwood Anderson: A Writer in America,* vol. 2. Madison: University of Wisconsin, 2006.

Robinson, Philip S. *Plantation of Ulster: British Settlement in an Irish Landscape, 1600–1670.* Dublin, Ireland: Gill and Macmillan, 1984.

Roosevelt, Theodore. *The Winning of the West.* Lincoln: University of Nebraska Press, 1889, 1995.

Rorrer, Kinney. *Rambling Blues: The Life and Songs of Charlie Poole.* Danville, Va.: McCain, 1982.

Salmon, John S., and Emily J. Salmon. *Franklin County: A Bicentennial History, 1786–1986.* Rocky Mount, Va.: Franklin County Bicentennial Commission, 1993.

Salstrom, Paul. *Appalachia's Path to Dependency: Rethinking a Region's Economic History, 1730–1940.* Lexington: University of Kentucky Press, 1994.

Salstrom, Paul. "Newer Appalachia as One of Appalachia's Last Frontiers." In *Appalachia in the Making: The Mountain South in the Nineteenth Century,* edited by Mary Beth Pudup, Dwight B. Billings, and Altina L. Waller, 76–102. Chapel Hill: University of North Carolina Press, 1995.

Saunders, Elder Randall. "A Brief History of the Charity Primitive Baptist Church."

Paper distributed at the Primitive Baptist Smith River Association meeting, June 1991. Copy in author's possession.

Sharp, Cecil J. *English Folk Songs from the Southern Appalachians.* London: Oxford University Press, 1932.

Sinclair, Andrew. *Prohibition: The Era of Excess.* Boston: Little, Brown, 1962.

Smith, Abbot Emerson. *Colonists in Bondage: White Servitude and Convict Labor in America, 1607–1776.* Chapel Hill: University of North Carolina Press, 1947.

Smith, J. Russell. *Farming Appalachia.* Reprinted from *American Monthly Review of Reviews* 53 (1916).

Smith, J. Russell. *Tree Crops: A Permanent Agriculture.* New York: Devin-Adair, 1950.

Smith, Maryanna S., ed. *Chronological Landmarks in American Agriculture.* Agricultural Information Bulletin No. 425. Washington, DC: USDA, 1980.

Sugeno, Frank E. "The Establishmentarian Ideal and the Mission of the Episcopal Church." *Historical Magazine of the Protestant Episcopal Church* 53, no. 4 (December 1984): 285–92.

Sunday, Billy. "Famous 'Booze' Sermon." BillySunday.org, http://billysunday.org/sermons/booze.html (accessed August 23, 2010).

Sutphin, Linda. *The Hash Family: Treasured Recipes and Family History.* Colleyville, Tex.: Linda Florence Sutphin, 1993.

Taylor, Jeffrey Wayne. *The Formation of the Primitive Baptist Movement.* Kitchener, Ont.: Pandora Press, 2004.

Taylor, Welford Dunaway, and Charles E. Modlin, eds. *Southern Odyssey: Selected Writings by Sherwood Anderson.* Athens: University of Georgia Press, 1997.

Theobald, Mary Miley. "When Whiskey Was the King of Drink." *Colonial Williamsburg Journal,* Summer 2008, http://www.history.org/Foundation/journal/Summer08/whiskey.cfm (accessed August 31, 2010).

Thompson, Charles D. "The Pittston Strike." *Southern Changes: The Journal of the Southern Regional Council* 11, no. 6 (1989): 1, 3–6.

Thompson, Charles D. Jr. *The Old German Baptist Brethren: Faith, Farming, and Change in the Virginia Blue Ridge.* Urbana: University of Illinois Press, 2006.

Tillitt, Malvern Hall. "Army-Navy Pay Tops Most Civilians': Unmarried Private's Income Equivalent to $3,600 Salary." *Barron's National Business and Financial Weekly,* April 24, 1944. Available at American Merchant Marine at War Web site, http://www.usmm.org/barrons.html (accessed August 26, 2010).

Tugwell, Rexford G. *Roosevelt's Revolution: The First Year—A Personal Perspective.* New York: Macmillan, 1977.

U.S. Department of Agriculture. *Yearbook of Agriculture 1934.* Washington, DC: USDA, 1934.

U.S. Treasury. "Fact Sheet OPC-77: History of the Tax System in the United States." Available at http://www.ustreas.gov/opc/opc0077.html (accessed October 20, 2010).

Wallace, Henry. "The Future of the American Farmer." *The New Republic,* November 8, 1939, 48–52.

Ware, Virginia E. "Charity Primitive Baptist Organized Before Patrick County Was Formed." *The Enterprise* (Stuart, Va.), August 4, 1976, 1, 9.

Washington, Booker T. *Up from Slavery: An Autobiography.* New York: Doubleday, Page, 1919.

Watman, Max. *Chasing the White Dog: An Amateur Outlaw's Adventures in Moonshine.* New York: Simon and Schuster, 2010.

Webb, Jim. *Born Fighting: How the Scots-Irish Shaped America.* New York: Broadway Books, 2004.

Webb, Walter P. *The Great Plains.* Boston: Ginn, 1931.

Weber, Max. *Protestant Ethic and the Spirit of Capitalism and Other Writings on the Rise of the West.* Translated by Stephen Kalberg. New York: Oxford University Press, 2009.

West, Jim. *Drinking with Calvin and Luther.* Lincoln, Calif.: Oakdown, 2003.

Whisnant, David. *All That Is Native and Fine: The Politics of Culture in an American Region.* Chapel Hill: University of North Carolina Press, 1983.

Wickersham Commission. *Report on the Enforcement of the Prohibition Laws of the United States.* Report recommendations, January 7, 1931, http://www.druglibrary .org/Schaffer/library/studies/wick/wick10.html (accessed August 23, 2010).

Wigginton, Eliot, ed. "Moonshining as a Fine Art." In *The Foxfire Book,* 301–45. Garden City, N.Y.: Anchor Books, 1972.

Williams, John Alexander. *Appalachia: A History.* Chapel Hill: University of North Carolina Press, 2002.

Willis, Gladys Edwards. *Goin' Up Shootin' Creek.* Rocky Mount, Va.: History, Etc., n.d.

Wingfield, Marshall. "The Liquor Conspiracy Case." In *An Old Virginia Court,* 194–204. Memphis: West Tennessee Historical Society, 1948.

Wingfield, Marshall. *Pioneer Families of Franklin County, Virginia.* Berryville, Va.: Chesapeake Book, 1964.

Wirth, Fremont P. *The Development of America.* Boston: American Book, 1936, 1948.

Wray, Matt. *Not Quite White: White Trash and the Boundaries of Whiteness.* Durham, N.C.: Duke University Press, 2006.

Young, Frances M. *Thankfulness Unites: A History of the United Thank Offering, 1889–1979.* New York: United Thank Offering, 1979.

Interviews by Charles D. Thompson Jr.
Transcriptions by Frances A. Copeland.

Elizabeth S. Beale (widow of Rector Beale, Trinity Episcopal Church), Rocky Mount, Va., July 24, 2003.

Sylvia Doris Bowling, Endicott, Va., June 26, 2003.

Diamond and Lane Boyd, Endicott, Va., June 25, 2003.

Diamond and Lane Boyd, Endicott, Va., December 30, 2003.

Roy DeHart, Woolwine, Va., June 2002.

T. Keister Greer, Rocky Mount, Va., October 25, 2003.

Dr. John H. Hash, Vanderbilt University, Nashville, Tenn., December 13, 2005.

Arbutis Ingram, Roanoke, Va., March 2, 2004.

Alfred James, Roanoke, Va., March 2, 2004.

Ruth Hash Jones, Rocky Mount, Va., December 24, 2000.

Bruce D. Martin Sr., Bristol, Va., December 16, 2000.

Vernice Martin, Rocky Mount, Va., July 24, 2003.

Bill and Ann McCarthy, Endicott, Va., July 1, 2003.

Hubert and Olivia Quinn, Ferrum, Va., December 29, 2003.

Olivia Quinn, Ferrum, Va., June 26, 2003.

Carlton Rakes and Glennie R. Roop, Martinsville, Va., June 19, 2007.

Janice M. Rakes, Ferrum, Va., August 21, 2007.

Vivian Rakes, Ferrum, Va., August 21, 2007.

Lonie Wagoner Bryant Rorrer, Stuart, Va., July 17 and 21, 2003.

Myrtle Trail Scott, Rocky Mount, Va., July 24, 2003.

Willie Martin Scott, Ferrum, Va., July 24, 2003.

Noel and Jean Spencer, with Lane Boyd, Endicott, Va., October 25, 2003.

Ora Hash Thomas, with Elaine Belcher (daughter), Stuart, Va., April 23, 2004.

Dr. Camille Wells, Virginia Foundation for the Humanities, Charlottesville, Va., March 25, 2009.

Macie Woods, Ferrum, Va., December 29, 2003.

Index

236; tavern tax and, 154; temperance movement effect on, 10–11, 15–16; Wickersham Commission on, 16–18, 29; World War II participation from, 229–30. *See also* liquor ring
Frost, William Goodell, 204

Gaston, Herbert E., 46, 143
general stores: barter practices at, 125–26; as equipment suppliers, 42; as hub of social discourse, 1–2; as moonshine ingredients suppliers, xiv–xv, xxviii–xxx, 2–3, 42
German settlers, 61, 76–78, 82
"Give Rex Tugwell a Chance" (Anderson), 49
Goin' Up Shottin' Creek (Willis), xix, 146–47, 149
Goode, Virgil, Sr., 216
government: Agricultural Adjustment Act (AAA), 139–41; Alcohol Tax Unit (Dept. of the Treasury), 7–8, 18; anti-liquor legislation, 166–67; Bureau of Prohibition, 7; Department of Agriculture (USDA), 132, 142; early liquor taxation, 154; economic policy affecting mountain families, xxv–xxvii; frontier public services, 23–24, 49–50, 81, 135–36, 196–97; national parks and forests, 142; "permanent agriculture" New Deal approach, 142–43; World War II military draft, 229–30. *See also* law enforcement; taxation
grain farming: grain cultivation, 126–29, 131–32; grain mill operations, 128–29, 162–64; labor costs of grain farming, 128; mechanized farming and, 133–34; mill workers as moonshine customers, xxv
granny fees, 37, 42, 214
Grant, Ulysses S., 15, 133, 156–57
Graves, Bill, 127
Gray, Lewis C., 142

Great Depression: agricultural income and, 136–38; effect on national consciousness, 25–26; effects in Franklin County, 33–34, 63–64; farm-to-job migration, 25–26, 63–64; moonshine importance during, xxiv; New Deal recovery initiatives, 33–34, 46–47, 50, 138–41, 236; unemployment rate, 7–8, 63–64; urban migration, 135–36. *See also* economy; New Deal recovery initiatives
Great Wagon Road, 60, 76, 81, 83, 106
Greear, Caroline, 44–46
Greer, T. Keister, xxii, 223–24, 228
Guilliams, Charles, 87
Guilliams, Lee, 41
Gusler, Lincoln, 161–62, 235

Hackett-Fischer, David, 240n11
Hambrick, Sarah Quinn, 152–53
Hamilton, Alexander, 80–81, 154
handicrafts, 203–4, 206
Harrison, Ora: biographical sketch, 93, 178–79; as conspiracy trial witness, 93, 117, 177–78, 206–7; as Episcopalian, 177, 183–85, 190–94; as Franklin County missionary/teacher, 178–96; Goode Hash relationship with, 171; as outsider, 6; photograph, *179, 202*; retirement, 236; St. John's-in-the-Mountains and, xxi, 183–89, 198–99; as teacher, 183–84. *See also* St. John's-in-the-Mountains Episcopal Mission
Hash, Abram, *95*
Hash, Amos, 94, *95*, 96, 97
Hash, Elizabeth (wife of William James Hash; wife of William D. Rakes), 105
Hash, James Goode Lane: barn burning of, 174–75; biography and personal life, 91–97, *95*, 103–9; calendar notes of, xx, 100–103, *101*, 116, 130; on corn planting, 121–22; as Duling juror, 220–21, *222*, 225–26; as Endicott visitor, 6; farm operation of, 121–31,

198–99; missionary-based schools, 191–97; Ora Harrison as missionary, 93, 178–96; Primitive Baptist view of, 111–12; as providers of outside services, 5; settlers' original religious beliefs and, xxiv. *See also* religion

Monroe, Bill, 235

Monroe, Charlie, 235

Monroe, James, 78

moonshine: as agricultural commodity, xxiv, 6, 49–50, 58, 130–31, 143; broad-based moonshine sales market, xxv–xxvi, *xxix*, 6, 43, 78–79, 84, 95, 170, 211–12; communal farm labor and, 124–26; Confederate liquor prohibition and, 15, 132, 155–56; drinking habits of moonshiners, 5, 146–47; Franklin County moonshine production volume, 8–9; high quality reputation of, 161–62; moonshiner support for Prohibition, 167; "moonshine" term, xv, 70, 168–69; post-Prohibition importance of, 7; as source of national pride, 153–54; as traditional craft, 203, 235. *See also* legal alcohol; liquor ring; production; running; *particular ingredients*

Moore, John, 85

Moran, Bugs, 11

Morgenthau, Henry, Jr., 46–47, 138–39, 143

Morrill, Francis "Dr. Franc," 198–99, *202*, 205–6

Mountain Rose Distillery, 167

music: bluegrass/country performances in Endicott, 235; bootlegging references in, xv; Cecil Sharp at Endicott, 199–200, 204; at corn shuckings, 125–26; Crooked Road Music Trail, xv–xvii; down home nostalgia imagery, 58, 138, 200; Floyd General Store Jamboree, xv; folk revival, 235–36; moonshine production and, 165–66; musicians as outsider-visitors, 6; Primitive Baptist music, 107; "Shoot-ing Creek" song, xv, *xvi*, 145; string band music, 204

national parks and forests, 142

Native Americans: corn cultivation by, 22, 122–23; indigenous land claims, 75, 81; Ulsterite prejudice against, 77–78

Nelson, Baby Face, 43

Ness, Eliot, 7

New Deal recovery initiatives: Anderson trial writings and, 46–47; anticommunism resistance to, 143; approach to agricultural development, 139–41; education programs, 196–97; impact in Franklin County, 33–34, 50, 236; success of, 206–7; tobacco allotments, 210. *See also* Great Depression

Nicholson, David, 87, 90

Oliver, James, 132

Olmstead, Frederick Law, 106

oral history, 62

organized crime: Prohibition alcohol kingpins, 11; Prohibition as impetus for, 166; urban liquor buyers and, 43. *See also* liquor ring

Palmer, Earl, *123*, 236

Parsons, T. X., 88

Paul, John, 29–30, 34–35, 41–42, 53–54, 87, 117–18, 216

Penn, Thomas, 75

Penn, William, 71

"permanent agriculture" New Deal approach, 142–43

Philadelphia, 73, 78, 95

place names, xv, 145

Poole, Charlie, xv, *xvi*, 138, 145, 235

potatoes, 22, 104

poteen, 69–70, 79, 153

Powell, A. H., 115

Presbyterian Church, 62–63, 66–67, 68, 71, 77, 109, 194

Prillaman, Nick, 42

Primitive Baptist Church: Goode Hash as preacher, 90–91, 94–96, 102–3, 107–9; Long Branch Primitive Baptist Church, 234; Ora Harrison and, 183, 187–88; Primitive Baptist music, 107; theological principles of, 109–11, 183, 187–88, 195–96, 243n23

production (of moonshine): overview, 161–64; aging, 163; boiler explosions, 2; class status and, 152; corn as ingredient, xxvii–xxviii, 21–23, 79, 83, 84; equipment sources, 42, 79; Franklin County moonshine production volume, 8–9; general store as ingredients distributor, xiv–xv, xxviii–xxx, 2–3, 42; moonshine stills, *xxvi, 22, 35, 74, 161, 228*; noiseless transport cans, 57; poisonous additives, 169–70; raw ingredients sources, xxvii–xxviii; recovery from raids, 148–50; thumper kegs, 169; use of local ingredients, xxv, xxvi–xxviii, 79; yeast as ingredient, 231–32. *See also* moonshine

Prohibition: affect on alcohol production, 149–50; historical overview, 7–8, 166–67; local resistance to, 148–50; moonshiner support for, 167; organized crime and, 11; overturning of, 7, 17–18; state and local ordinances, 9–11; Wickersham Commission on, 16–18, 29. *See also* temperance movement

Puritans, 75

Quinn, Hubert, 232
Quinn, Joel, *35*

rack-renting (Scotland), 65–66, 67–68, 153

railroads, 210

Rakes, Amos: biographical sketch, 92–93, 96–99, 102; jury bribery charges against, 87–90, 97–98, 115–17, 213; Ora Harrison as character witness for, 177–78, 207; photograph, *91, 98*; sentencing of, 118–19; as teachers house construction worker, 188

Rakes, Caleb (Caley), 89, *91*, 98–99, *98*, 118–19

Rakes, Charles, 32

Rakes, Hugh, 116–17

Rakes, John, 122

Rakes, Lilly. *See* Smith, Lilly Rakes

Rakes, Maude, 180, *182*, 232

Rakes, Otey, 122

Rakes, Sparrell C., *xxvi*

Rakes, S. T., 102

Rakes, Wid (author's great, great grandfather), 180, *182*, 232

Rakes, William D., 105, 180

Rakes's distillery (Shooting Creek), 15–16

Ramsey, Harold, 196

Raum, Green B., 15, 156–60

religion: Anglican/Episcopal Church, 177, 183–85, 191–95, 201; Calvinism, 66–67, 98, 109–11; community churches, 109–11; evangelism, 111–12; Hash as circuit preacher, 91–92, 93–96; Methodist Church, 111–12, 194, 235; outsider frontier churches, 191–92; Presbyterian Church, 62–63, 66–67, 68, 71, 77, 109, 194; Protestant/Catholic tolerance for liquor, 66–67, 98, 109, 112–13; Social Gospel movement, 193–95; Ulster Protestantism, 71. *See also* missionaries; Primitive Baptist Church; St. John's-in-the-Mountains Episcopal Mission; temperance movement

Richards, Mrs. Jefferson, 223–24

Richards, Thomas Jefferson "Jeff": as conspiracy trial defendant, 32; as Duling pursuer, 216–17; as liquor ring accountant, 37–38, 116, 151, 172–73, 214–15; murder of, 18–19, 57, 212, 215–16, 218–19, 221–22, 226–27; relationship with local farmers, 3–4

Roanoke (Virginia), xxv, 4, 6, 48

Roberts, W. T., 184
Robert the Bruce, 67
Rock Church. *See* St. John's-in-the-
   Mountains Episcopal Mission
Rocky Mount (Virginia): alienation
   from mountain areas, 8, 93, 153, 178;
   as farm market, 107; industrial development in, 210; moonshine tourism
   in, xv; Rakes's saloon, 15–16
Roosevelt, Franklin D., 17–18, 21, 25,
   33–34, 46–47, 50, 138–41
Roosevelt, Theodore, 65, 77, 83
Rorrer, Lonie, 198
Roth, C. S., 85, 213, 216
Royal Arch Crown Whiskey, 157
Runnett Bag (Virginia), xv, 16, 23–24,
   145, 165
running: Clifford Thompson as runner,
   xvii–xviii, 237; early Blue Ridge export markets, 84; high-speed driving
   tactics, 96–97; noiseless transport
   cans, 57; outsider pickups, 6; women
   as runners, 48–51
Rural Electrification Administration,
   50
Rural Resettlement program, 141
Russell Sage Foundation, 194–95

Saunders, Bud, 41
Scotch whiskey, 66–67
Scots-Irish (Scotch-Irish), 62–63,
   64–65, 75, 76–78, 135. *See also* Ulster-
   ite settlers
Scott, Myrtle Trail, 235
Scruggs, Earl, 235
sharecroppers, 25–26, 140–41
Sharp, Cecil J., 199–200, 204
Sharpe, Willie Carter, 48–51, 97, 212
Sherman, William Tecumseh, 156
Shively, Claude, 87
Shively, Herman, 41, 87, 115
Shively, Luther, 22
Shooting Creek (Virginia): Charlie
   Poole song, xv, *xvi*, 145; lack of pub-
   lic services, 23–24; Mountain Rose

Distillery, 167; Peterson farm, *xiv*;
   place name origin, 145; R. F. Rakes's
   distillery, 15–16; Royal Arch Crown
   Whiskey, 157; terrain favorable to
   moonshine production, 165; Willie
   Sharpe as runner for, 48–51
Simmons, Clarence E., 216–18, 225
Slusher, Claude, 87
Smith, Jim, 215, 226
Smith, J. Russell, 142
Smith, Lilly Rakes (author's great-
   grandmother), 182, *182*, 232, 236–37
Smith, Luther (author's paternal great-
   grandfather): family connections of,
   182, *182*, 236–37; farm purchased by,
   xviii, 231–33; general store operated
   by, xxviii–xxx; as ingredient supplier,
   232–33; as law officer, 4, *30*, 149; photograph, *xxiii*; resignation of, xxii,
   173; as Rock Church construction
   worker, 185, *186*
Smith, Roosevelt (author's great uncle),
   xxii, 20, 41, 87, 149, 210–11
Snuffy Smith, 8, 12, 50–51
Social Gospel movement, 193–95
Soil Conservation Service, 21
speakeasies, xxv, 11
Spotswood, Alexander, 81
Steinbeck, John, 25–26, 140
stereotypes: Anderson efforts at cor-
   recting, 46–47, 50–51, 169; Cecil
   Sharp view of, 200; in conspiracy
   trial reporting, 40–42; Franc Morrill
   on, 205–6; Franklin County moonshine stories, 8–9, 60; of German
   settlers, 76–77; John Campbell view
   of, 200–201; "lubbers" stereotype, 74;
   moonshiner stereotype, xxv, 50–51,
   168–69, 200–201, 204; nineteenth
   century moonshiner literature, 158–
   59; Ora Harrison views of Franklin
   County, 188–94; in posed photographs, 236; Scotch-Irish stereotype,
   76–78; urban gang stereotype, 43
St. John's-in-the-Mountains Episcopal

Charles D. Thompson Jr., a native son of Franklin County, Virginia, is the curriculum and education director at the Center for Documentary Studies at Duke University. His other books include *German Baptist Brethren: Faith, Farming, and Change in the Virginia Blue Ridge.*

THE UNIVERSITY OF ILLINOIS PRESS
IS A FOUNDING MEMBER OF THE
ASSOCIATION OF AMERICAN UNIVERSITY PRESSES.

Composed in 10.25/13.25 Adobe Minion Pro
at the University of Illinois Press
Manufactured by Sheridan Books, Inc.

University of Illinois Press
1325 South Oak Street
Champaign, IL 61820-6903
www.press.uillinois.edu

5/23/11